MEGATHREATS

MEGATHREATS

TEN DANGEROUS TRENDS
THAT IMPERIL OUR FUTURE,
AND HOW TO SURVIVE THEM

NOURIEL ROUBINI

Little, Brown and Company

New York Boston London

To my parents, Djalil and Rachel, and
my siblings Niki, Davide, and Sabrina

———————————

Little, Brown and Company
Hachette Book Group
1290 Avenue of the Americas, New York, NY 10104
littlebrown.com

First Edition: October 2022

Little, Brown and Company is a division of Hachette Book Group, Inc. The Little, Brown name and logo are trademarks of Hachette Book Group, Inc.

The publisher is not responsible for websites (or their content) that are not owned by the publisher.

The Hachette Speakers Bureau provides a wide range of authors for speaking events. To find out more, go to hachettespeakersbureau.com or call (866) 376-6591.

ISBN 9780316284059

LCCN 2022942584

Printing 1, 2022

LSC-C

Printed in the United States of America

CONTENTS

Contents

MEGATHREATS

MEGATHREATS

Prologue

Every day we face all kinds of risk. Some risks are relatively minor. We can err and still go on as before. If I invest $100 in a common stock, I can afford to lose some or all of that money. But if risks can cause serious and lasting harm, we call them threats. Buying a beach house on the edge of a cliff overlooking the ocean raises the stakes to threat level. Climate change, storms, and erosion at the base of the cliff imperil a much larger investment—and possibly my life, if I am so foolish as to watch the cliff erode right up to my foundation.

Individual decisions at least give us a say in our own fate. Choices get more complicated when they involve collective or societal risks, the domain of policy makers. Should a country go to war? Should a government bail out an industry? Should policy makers impose a high carbon tax to slow global climate change? For decisions like these, individual citizens have very limited input, but huge consequences can befall each and all of us. Look no further than the 2008 Global Financial Crisis or a bumbling pandemic response—as in COVID-19—to see how flawed policies drain bank accounts and imperil the livelihoods and lives of millions. Collective responses are much harder than individual ones. It can be hard even to get a decision made when policy makers disagree and squabble with one another, nationally or at the international level.

As an economist, I observe risk and its consequences. In 2006 I saw stratospheric prices for houses, dangerous levels of mortgage debt, and overbuilding. New houses went begging for buyers. I warned that a historic bubble would soon burst and precipitate a global recession and financial crisis. Saying so in public venues won me no friends. Mocking critics called me Dr. Doom. They dismissed my urgent calls for caution. When events unraveled as I foresaw, culminating in the Global Financial Crisis, housing prices crashed across the United States (and other countries with housing bubbles), with worldwide reverberations for financial institutions and economies.

Risks and threats lurk everywhere. But some are slow moving, and some are far more dangerous than others. Some of the most dangerous are also the slowest moving, which makes it especially hard to generate a collective response. In this book, I want to draw attention to the biggest threats we face on our planet, whether they are slow moving or not, whether they will hit us very soon or a bit later. I call them "megathreats," which I define as severe problems that could cause vast damage and misery and cannot be solved quickly or easily.

I do not use *megathreat* to refer specifically to warfare, though wars do cause immense misery, as the recent and brutal Russian invasion of Ukraine has shown. Wars have happened for as long as history has been written, if not longer; some are local, some are global; some happen quickly; some drag on for many years. But warfare is not a new challenge, and evading war is not my expertise, even if I will consider also the geopolitical megathreats that could lead to war among great powers and cause severe human, economic, and financial impact. Instead, the megathreats that concern me more are broad economic, financial, political, geopolitical, trade, technological, health, and climate-based challenges. Some, like the geo-political ones, can lead to cold and eventually destructive hot wars. I wrote this book because I believe we are facing ten of them, of such immense scale and urgency that we need to look ahead with clear vision and do what we can to prevent them from destroying us.

Memories fade, especially where economic discomfort is concerned. Apart from a handful of interruptions since World War II, the world has seen a long stretch of rising wealth, prosperity, peace, and productivity. For the past seventy-five years, we have enjoyed relative stability. Recessions have been, with a few exceptions, brief. Innovations have improved our quality of life. We have not experienced outright war among great powers. Each generation, in most nations, has been able to improve standards of living compared to their parents' and grandparents' generations.

Unfortunately, this long stretch of relative prosperity is not likely to continue much longer. We are facing a regime change from a period of relative stability to an era of severe instability, conflict, and chaos. We are facing megathreats unlike anything we have faced before—and they are interconnected.

We totter now on a precipice, the ground shaking beneath us. Yet most of us still imagine that the future will resemble the past. That's a whopping mistake. New warning signs look clear and compelling. Economic, financial, technological, trade, political, geopolitical, health, and environmental risks have morphed into something much bigger. Welcome to the era of megathreats: they will alter the world we thought we knew.

We must learn to live on high alert. Economic and geopolitical certainties we once took for granted—from job security, to a sustainable and healthy planet, where most infectious diseases were conquered, and to peace among rival great powers—are disappearing. The postwar decades of economic growth and rising prosperity, interrupted only briefly by stagflation and short-lived recessions, are at serious risk of giving way to economic and financial crises unlike anything we've seen since the Great Depression. Those crises will be made worse by climate change, demographic collapse, nationalist policies that curtail trade and migration, global competition between China (and its revisionist allies such as Russia, Iran, and North Korea) and the United States and its allies, and a technological revolution that will displace more jobs in less time than any that has come before.

This book explores the ten key megathreats bearing down on us. Assembling them in one place reveals how they overlap and reinforce one another. There are links between debt accumulation and debt traps, easy money and financial crises, artificial intelligence (AI) and workplace automation, deglobalization, geopolitical clashes among great powers, inflation and stagflation, currency meltdowns, income inequality and populism, global pandemics and climate change. Each hampers our ability to address the others. A single threat sounds distressing. Ten megathreats happening at once is far, far worse.

After examining each threat in its own chapter, I will consider our collective prospects for surviving them. Spoiler alert: without amazing luck, almost unprecedented economic growth, and unlikely global cooperation, this won't end well. We are in way too deep.

We are the authors of our own fate. Many of the megathreats in this book arose from actions that looked at one time like solutions to particular problems: misguided financial deregulation and unconventional macroeconomic policies, carbon-emitting industrialization, the offshoring of manufacturing jobs, the development of artificial intelligence, and empowering China to compete globally, among others.

To combat the megathreats discussed in these pages, we must discard cherished assumptions. We cannot assume that automating certain jobs will lead to new and better jobs elsewhere, as it often has in the past. We cannot assume that lowering tax rates, liberalizing trade, and reducing regulations will unleash economic energy that will benefit everyone. Our very survival may hinge on subordinating individual freedoms to the common good, national and global. Failure to restore sustainable and inclusive growth could plunge us back into the tribal dark ages, when competing interests spurred endless national and global conflicts, to no one's benefit.

While this book takes a medium-term view of the megathreats that imperil our future over the next two decades, these threats were clearly starting to manifest themselves already in 2022: the return of stagflation risks in advanced economies as inflation was rising sharply and the risk of recession increasing. The financial fragility and the risk of default of many highly indebted sovereigns and private sector actors as central banks were increasing interest rates to fight inflation. The bear market in global stock markets and the crash of numerous asset bubbles including the crypto ones, now that the era of cheap money was starting to reverse. The peristent talk and practice of deglobalization and fragmentation of the global economy; the Russian invasion of Ukraine and the risk that this conflict could expand geographically and in unconventional ways; the drum-beats of talk of a new Cold War between the US (and its Western allies) and China (and its effective allies Russia, Iran, and North Korea), and the rising tensions between the US and China on Taiwan; the massive droughts and heat waves from India and Pakistan to Sub-Saharan Africa and to the West of the United States, as global climate change is becoming more severe; the Chinese growth slowdown and the risk of a hard landing given its misguided Zero Covid tolerance policy; a global pandemic that was not yet controlled in many poorer nations and likely to mutate further in new variants; the risk of energy insecurity, of hunger, and even famines given the spike in food, energy, and other commodity prices. These were all ominous signs of a much worse and dangerous future and megathreats in the decade ahead. Indeed, by the spring of 2022, Kristalina Georgieva — the head of the ever-watchful International Monetary Fund — and two of her colleagues stated with alarm that the world economy is on the verge of "perhaps its biggest test since the Second World War" and that "we face a potential *confluence of calamities*."[1]

I would rather sound bullish on our future prospects, reporting that stocks will rise, earnings will grow, incomes and jobs will increase, nations will flourish as peace and democracy expand globally, that sustainable and inclusive growth will emerge, and global agreements will set rules that are fair for and accepted by everyone. I wish I could predict that. But I cannot. Change is coming, like it or not. The megathreats we face will reshape our world. If you want to survive, do not be taken by surprise.

PART I

DEBT, DEMOGRAPHICS, AND DANGEROUS POLICIES

Chapter 1

The Mother of All Debt Crises

I have lived through, studied, and tried to solve debt crises over four decades, both as an academic and at pivotal times as a policy maker in the US government. Some crises were confined to a single region. Others swept the globe. Some left few traces. Others devastated entire economic sectors and upended millions of lives. No one should pretend to have all the answers to such a complex problem as managing economic policy, but I've learned this much: experience is a poor teacher. We keep making the same stubborn mistakes. Time and again, enthusiasm and easy money policies inflate bubbles; time and again, they burst. The Looney Tunes Road Runner could sniff out dynamite in gift wrapping. Why can't we? Whether packaging or human nature is to blame, the worst debt crisis of my lifetime lies right ahead of us, as if we have forgotten every single one of its predecessors.

One country that should reckon with the lessons of the past is Argentina. In 2020, the Argentine government defaulted on its debt for the fourth time since 1980 and the ninth time in its history. In August 2020 the country's finance ministry announced an agreement with weary creditors. They extended maturities on the debt and slashed interest payments with hours to go before South America's third-largest economy was prepared to terminate negotiations.

Hope springs eternal in countries that try to avert financial catastrophe. "May we never again enter this labyrinth [of indebtedness], please,"

Argentine president Alberto Fernandez declared at the time. Promising that Argentine debt will shrink by half over the next decade, the president signaled that the government would do what it takes to keep a beleaguered economy viable. He thanked regional governors and members of congress who were at his side; he thanked Pope Francis and the leaders of Mexico, Germany, France, Spain, and Italy. As the *Financial Times* reported, he stated, "None of this was easy, but if there's something Argentines know how to do, it is to pick ourselves up when we fall."[1]

It was the kind of true-grit statement that political leaders love to make in the face of adversity. But Argentina — and the world — is far from passing the current crisis. The country continues to labor under about $300 billion in public debt, nearly equal to its entire economic output in 2020. And inflation was ravaging the country during and after the COVID-19 crisis with the inflation rate for 2022 expected to be over 50 percent.

Increasingly, the entire world resembles Argentina. Public debt owed by governments, on top of private debt owed by corporations, financial institutions, and households, was soaring out of control *before* the gigantic tab for the COVID-19 pandemic response came due. In the United States, the $1.9 trillion COVID-19 relief package passed in 2021, plus two huge stimulus measures passed during the Trump presidency, added $4.5 trillion to its public debt since 2019. That "would represent the boldest act of macroeconomic stabilization policy in US history," former treasury secretary Lawrence Summers warned in early 2021 in a *Washington Post* op-ed, where he correctly expressed concerns that such a large, excessive stimulus would overheat the economy and cause high inflation.[2] And then the Biden administration promptly planned another $3 to $4 trillion of infrastructure and social spending that would be only partly financed by higher taxes. Luckily only a portion of such a large-scale additional spending was passed.

Responses to COVID-19 wrenched loose any semblance of debt restraint, regardless of which party or coalition was in power. Europe is barely coping. "Those [European] debts are surging to levels not seen since World War II," the *New York Times* reported in February 2021.[3] In many European countries, debt is growing so fast that it is vastly outpacing the size of national economies.

Based on data from the Institute of International Finance, global debt—private and public—by the end of 2021 was well over 350 percent of global GDP, and it has been climbing fast for decades (from 220 percent of GDP in 1999) and spiking after the COVID-19 crisis.[4] The ratio has never before come close to this level in advanced economies or emerging markets. US debt is right on pace with the global average. Current US private and public debt-to-GDP ratio is much higher than the peak debt during the Great Depression, and more than twice the level when the United States emerged from World War II and entered a period of robust growth.

This steep trend prompted a blunt warning by the Institute of International Finance, which tracks global debt. "If the global debt pile continues to grow at the average pace of the last 15 years, our back-of-the-envelope estimates suggest that global debt could exceed $360 trillion by 2030—over $85 trillion higher than current levels."[5] That would bump the global debt ratio to more than *four* times global output, a level that would smother economic growth under the massive costs of debt service.

A habitable, progressive world requires levels of debt that countries can repay without stifling growth. A government has a healthy level of debt when it can run it up in recessions (to spur growth and end the recession) and pay it back in recoveries. A government has an unhealthy level of debt when it has no realistic chance of paying it back. When that happens and a debt crisis hits, countries, regions, and even the entire world may face recessions that throw economies into reverse. When the debt bills come due, governments have no good options. The kinds of harsh remedies available—devaluing currencies and cutting off the social safety net, for example—often lead to all manner of unintended consequences, including market crashes, authoritarian populism, and even the quiet sale of missile and nuclear technologies to the highest rogue bidders.[6]

"The pace of global debt accumulation has been unprecedented since

2016," the Institute of International Finance warned in a November 2020 *Weekly Insight* report entitled "More Debt, More Trouble." In other words, this crisis was already coming. The pandemic only accelerated it.[7]

Although debt ratios are higher in advanced economies, emerging markets get into trouble much faster. Argentina is not even a highly indebted country overall, by emerging market standards. Its private debt is only about one-third of GDP, which is comparatively healthy. But as the record shows, debt denominated in foreign currency crippled its ability to service and repay international loans. Argentina had pegged its peso to the US dollar, and when its economy went south in 2001 while the US economy remained strong, its currency crashed. That put inordinate pressure on its ability to repay its loans in foreign currency. And a new debt crisis is now looming. In advanced economies, meanwhile, the levels of debt are extraordinary, already at 420 percent of GDP and rising. The coming tsunami will not spare China, where credit-fueled economic growth has built a Himalayan mountain of debt, about 330 percent of GDP.

True, we have survived financial bubbles and economic dislocations for decades and centuries. As I stated, I have witnessed multiple debt crises over the past forty years, and in each case the country or region has eventually recovered. But readers who suppose that crises come and go — with scarring at worst—are mistaken this time. We have crossed into new territory. With global income growth flagging, countries, corporations, banks, and households owe more than they can repay in most foreseeable scenarios. Debt that was manageable when interest rates were zero or negative will become unsustainable as central banks now have to sharply raise their policy rates to fight inflation. This time, we are racing toward an inflection point that will alter life for lenders and borrowers whether public or private, prudent or profligate. The Mother of All Debt Crises may take place sometime during the current or next decade.

The current dilemma evokes déjà vu. Back in the spring of 2006, the US real estate sector went on a binge. Homes were selling like hotcakes to any borrower whose breath could fog a mirror. Never mind if their assets or incomes made them unqualified to pay the mortgage. Houses found buyers on the expectation that rising prices would bail out borrowers who spent more than they could afford. It looked like a bubble to me, and I said so.

In Las Vegas that year I attended a conference on mortgage securitization. The toxic and reckless subprime mortgages were plain to see. My own research showed that cheap debt and lax credit requirements were funneling money into a real estate bubble. Afterward I rented a car and set out to visit Death Valley, a below-sea-level lunar-like landscape where gold miners used to die by the scores in scorching summer heat while digging for the shiny precious metal. On the way I discovered a man-made death valley that sharpened my concerns about debt.

The road out of Las Vegas cut smack through a brand-new community. House after brand-new house sat empty in vast lots. Not a soul lived in them. No lights were to be seen. No cars. No families. The "community" was a graveyard instead of the town the developers must have imagined. Reckless greed had produced that housing bubble: the same motive that in Von Stroheim's classic film *Greed* leads two protagonists to beat each other to death in the Death Valley desert.

Despite clear evidence of a real estate bubble putting borrowers and lenders at risk, so-called experts dismissed fears. I pounded the same drum a few months later in a keynote address to economists at an event hosted by the International Monetary Fund (IMF).

Upticks in the cost of oil and some softening in home prices were visible but not yet too dramatic. I warned nevertheless that a huge financial crisis lurked on the other side of a real estate bubble. It would end in home mortgage defaults wiping out lenders and investors who had flocked to securities that bundled risky mortgages. While most experts relied on top-notch bond ratings from rating agencies mired in conflicts of interest, I predicted losses in the hundreds of billions of dollars for hedge funds, investment banks, commercial banks, vital financial institutions, and gobsmacked homeowners.

I stepped off the stage to tepid applause. The panel's moderator said aloud, "I think perhaps we need a stiff drink." That drew a laugh from a skeptical audience. The speaker after me noted that my predictions did not use mathematical models. He rejected my analysis as mere hunches of a perennial pessimist.

In February 2007 I stressed my concern again, on a panel on the global outlook at the annual World Economic Forum in Davos, Switzerland. Denial was still powerful. US Federal Reserve chairman Ben Bernanke had declared that a housing correction was due, but he ruled out any dire spillover effects. He foresaw no financial crisis, much less a systemic threat to the banking system. I respectfully disagreed, warning instead that we should brace for a bumpy ride and a global — not just US — financial crisis. I changed few minds so far as I could tell. Instead, I gave my critics more ammunition to call me Dr. Doom, a moniker that ignores my outspoken faith in progressive and inclusive capitalism when sound judgment, good policies, and moral principles prevail.

My reception affirmed that even the prominent experts at Davos may not see trouble before it's too late. It's a classic bias in human thinking: most of us never want to imagine the worst. We are optimists by nature. Personally, I find the zeitgeist at Davos every year to be a contrarian indicator of the future. If everyone in the Davos set believes something will happen — good or bad, as it may be — they are highly likely to be wrong.

Consensus groupthink often rules among the world's elites. The same event gave me another chance to voice my contrarian perspective. My second Davos presentation probed the future of the European monetary union with an eye to the risks ahead. My fellow panelists Jean Claude Trichet, who headed the European Central Bank at the time, and the Italian finance minister, Giulio Tremonti, expressed confidence in a sound and sustainable monetary union. My assessment was far less sanguine. I underscored the extreme danger of excessive debt and loss of competitiveness of some members of the union that could splinter the eurozone.

If low growth with large trade and fiscal deficits continued, I warned, Italy, Greece, Spain, and Portugal would face a crippling debt crisis by the end of the decade. My remarks visibly agitated the Italian finance minister. Introduced as someone who would share the American perspective, I reminded the audience that I was born in Turkey and grew up in Milan, Italy. So there I was telling Italy's finance minister that my adopted country would, over time, be in grave danger of financial collapse. Before I finished he could stand it no longer. "Roubini," he shouted, "go back to Turkey!" News reports called the outburst "Tremonti's Temper Tantrum."

Three years later, Greece was bankrupt and the other PIIGS (Portugal, Italy, Ireland, Greece, Spain) were in a severe financial crisis. And it took yet two more years before Greece embraced tough deficit restrictions. At that point, Greece restructured and reduced its public debt while also receiving a 200-billion-euro bailout package from the European Commission, the European Central Bank (ECB), and the IMF, dubbed the Troika.

Greece barely survived that crisis—but it was only a prelude. Italy owed ten times more public debt, making it too big to fail and too big to rescue. The eurozone might be able to survive without Greece. But losing Italy, Europe's third largest economy, would put an end to the dreams of eurozone planners.

Earlier in 2007–8, the Great Financial Crisis had erupted in the United States, this time driven by profligate consumer debt. Homeowners defaulted, banks shuddered and failed, stock markets collapsed, assets vanished, lenders balked, companies closed, and jobs vanished. Central bankers huddled with treasury officials and bank industry executives to stop the bloodshed.

No one enjoys seeing vast dislocation and the pain it causes. I did not welcome the vindication of my doom saying. The economist who invited me to speak to the IMF said that in 2006 I sounded like a madman. When I returned to speak again two years later, with housing prices in free fall across the United States and mortgage providers in peril, he said I was greeted as a prophet.

After so much upheaval and prodigious finger wagging you'd think we'd have mended our loose ways. But debt is too seductive.

Countries, corporations, and households all borrow, either to invest or to consume. Investment into new public or private capital pays for things that last long into the future. Using public debt, countries invest in ports, roads, bridges, and other infrastructure. In the private sector, corporations invest in the machinery, software, and computers to produce more goods and services. Households borrow to invest in homes or in education. Borrowing to invest can make good sense as long as the return on the investment is higher than the cost of financing it. Borrowing to consume, on the other hand, uses debt to plug recurring bills or deficits that operating income should cover.

Experience teaches prudent public and private borrowers a golden rule: borrow to invest, not to consume. In principle, borrowing to consume is riskier than borrowing to invest. When loans persistently cover stagnating salaries, budget deficits, discretionary items, or vacation expenses, borrowers are starting down a rough and slippery road that may lead to bankruptcy.

But overborrowing to pay for overpriced assets also imposes hefty risk. Nothing produces frothy asset bubbles faster than cheap debt pouring into the marketplace. If, for example, a hasty borrower spends billions on a fiber-optic network when prices are spiking, officials might convince themselves that they are investing in the future. Unless foreseeable revenue can service the debt, however, those investments may hurt companies or even put them out of business. As many learned after fiber-optics first appeared, investing in bloated assets with excessive leverage and cheap money leads to asset booms and bubbles, with busts and crashes close behind.

A boom-and-bust pattern has been well chronicled since the publication of *Extraordinary Popular Delusions and the Madness of Crowds* in 1841. In it, Scottish author Charles Mackay probed the human tendency to run amok in pursuit of quick profits, dating back to a mania for tulip bulbs as expensive as houses in seventeenth-century Holland.

Debt and financial crises erupt not only in emerging economies that are fragile. The financial history of recent decades is littered with economic and financial crises in advanced economies, too. When poor judgment sweeps investors, debt acts like a steroid.

We always embark with noble intentions. When the Nixon administration severed the US dollar from the price of gold in 1971, allowing the dollar to float as a currency based on market demand, it eased the financing of larger fiscal and trade deficits fed by the Vietnam War. The gold-exchange standard had been designed after World War II to safeguard global monetary stability. Nixon's decision had short-term benefits, but longer-term risks. The five decades since then have seen paralyzing vicissitudes in advanced economies (let alone emerging markets): stagflation in the seventies; a US real estate bust leading to a savings and loan banking crisis in the eighties; a Scandinavian banking crisis in the early nineties; a European Exchange-Rate Mechanism currency crisis in 1992; the Japanese great stagnation and deflation since the nineties after the collapse of its real estate bubble; the collapse of Long-Term Capital Management (LTCM) despite two Nobel laureates at its helm in 1998; the internet boom and subsequent bust and corporate defaults of the early 2000s; the housing and credit boom-and-bust leading to the Global Financial Crisis beginning in 2007; the eurozone crisis of the early 2010s; and of course the COVID-19 crisis of 2020. Each cycle resulted in more public and private debts.

I had my first exposure to a world-class debt disruption while working for the International Monetary Fund in 1984, my first summer internship in Washington, DC, while doing my PhD at Harvard. Excessive debt was smothering Latin American countries that had invested vast sums to modernize infrastructure and increase government spending during an oil boom. In New York and London, the Broadway musical *Evita*, loosely based on the second wife of Argentine dictator Juan Peron, was playing to sold-out audiences. In the real world, once again, Argentina would play a featured role in a debt crisis. The Latin American debt crisis exploded in 1982 but its seeds were in overborrowing by the region's governments in the 1970s.

In that decade oil prices spiked, given two geopolitically induced oil shocks in 1973 and 1979. Also, experts saw no end to rising global oil demand. Because commodity-based Latin American currencies looked risky to foreign investors, oil-rich countries (and even some in Latin

America with limited energy exports) ran up steep sovereign debt tabs — to finance sharply rising government spending and investment — by borrowing in the world's safest currency, the US dollar. A bond or loan repaid in pesos might lose value overnight versus a benchmark because of depreciation and inflation. One dollar today, on the other hand, is worth one dollar tomorrow. When oil fetched hefty prices, everyone prospered. Until 1980 ample oil revenues surpassed the rising cost of mounting debt tied to a floating rate benchmark. In a friendly climate, creditors and borrowers had their cake and ate it too.

But in 1980, interest rates reached nosebleed double-digit levels, a strategy that Paul Volcker — the Chair of the Federal Reserve — deployed to fight inflation driven by soaring oil prices. Ballooning debt service on foreign loans started to outstrip export revenues. The need to service foreign debt in dollars drained the dollar reserves in these emerging markets. In urgent need of more US currency to keep foreign creditors at bay, Argentina, Mexico, Brazil, and other Latin American oil producers scrambled for solutions, including more debt and borrowing.

When oil prices collapsed in 1982 — as the United States was in a deep recession — the game ended. Oil economies stalled, deficits mounted among OPEC nations, and choking debts festered. Treasury departments around the world, but especially in Latin America, strained to find dollars to meet interest payments. Dollar interest rates spiked. When principal amounts came due, countries without cash or access to fresh capital lacked options. Defaults multiplied. Lenders took huge hits. Global debt markets faltered. The International Monetary Fund, an institution created to resolve crises, stepped in with emergency loans. This was a debt crisis that pales next to the 2008 Great Recession and to the megathreat we currently face, yet it was highly damaging in Latin America.

Growth stalled throughout the region for a decade in the 1980s, the "lost decade" of growth for Latin America. Hyperinflation, when inflation climbs at double-digit rates each month, flared in Argentina. Relative stability did not resume until the 1990s, when creditors swapped bank loans for new bonds with lower face amounts or lower interest payments.

In fits and starts Latin American countries made peace with lenders. Then, after a short breather and a currency crisis in Mexico in 1994–95, East Asia demonstrated a new and different form of debt crisis in 1997–98. Four previously healthy and successful economies in Asia were going belly up. Most analysts were surprised because the typical emerging market crises were in the Latin American mold: a surge in public foreign debt followed by collapsing demand for a crucial commodity.

In East Asia, budget deficits and public debt were very low. Sovereign debt was well managed. They appeared to be doing things right! These economies featured high savings and prudent fiscal authorities. Dubbed the Asian Tigers, South Korea, Malaysia, Indonesia, and Thailand were touted as models of economic transformation. They nurtured a cadre of dynamic companies with global reach—but as it turned out, those companies were fueling their own growth with massive levels of debt, often in foreign currency. Private debt can be just as destructive, if not more so, than public debt.

At the time, I was trying to track both private and public debt levels. At Yale University where I was a faculty member, I built a website that tracked news and furnished analysis for thousands of academics, firms, and investors. The governments in East Asia were not profligate borrowers, as everyone could see. But corporate borrowers, real estate developers, and banks, egged on by growth-obsessed government agendas, compelled healthy companies or real estate firms to take on excessive risk, at times by absorbing companies shuddering toward failure.

To finance expansion, the private sector tapped foreign lenders. Borrowers in emerging markets saddled themselves with overvalued assets, much of them in real estate and the corporate sector. These volatile assets produced revenue in local currencies but required payment, rain or shine, in dollars and Japanese yen. The currency mismatch between dollars and yen, on the one hand, and (for example) the Thai baht, doomed those speculative investments. The fallout soon engulfed not just the Asian Tigers but banks and investors worldwide.

Under pressure to boost export revenues as their trade deficits surged, the Asian Tigers were forced to let their overvalued local currencies depreciate sharply, a practice that lowers the prices of exports to make them more competitive. This launched a race to the bottom: it took more and more local currency to pay lenders in dollars and yen. The real cost of foreign debt skyrocketed far beyond stated interest rates. Borrowers went bankrupt and took lenders with them. Shortfalls in the private sector spilled over into the public sector when countries emptied their pockets to offset lost taxes and bail out corporates and banks amid rising deficits.

While following the East Asian crisis in 1998, I received an email from Janet Yellen, who chaired the White House Council of Economic Advisers during the Clinton administration. She invited me to fill a job opening on the council.

I welcomed the opportunity to help develop policy aimed at restoring and reinforcing global economic stability. I spent the next two and a half years in Washington, first at the council with chair Yellen and then at the Treasury Department. I advised Treasury under secretary Tim Geithner and secretary Larry Summers on dealing with successive financial crises rooted in profligate debt. We watched crises rattle Russia, Pakistan, Brazil, Argentina, Ecuador, Turkey, and Uruguay, and even advanced economies, when Long-Term Capital Management, the biggest US hedge fund, went belly-up in 1998 after the Russian economy suffered its first post-Soviet recession. It was quite an education.

Once again, I found myself following events in Argentina. By 1991, Argentina pegged its exchange rate at one Argentine peso to one US dollar. Lenders relaxed their concerns and reopened foreign loan desks because they had confidence that the peso would be stable. Argentina wasted no time — it began to accumulate public debt. While working at the White House and Treasury from 1998 to 2000, I devoted many hours to evaluating Argentina's predicament. Exhausting debates centered on the advisability of a bailout or letting Argentina go bankrupt. Seeing no other solution, I lobbied for devaluation, default, and restructuring, the path Argentina eventually took in 2001.

I don't blame Argentina alone for its disastrous economic policies.

Lenders were complicit when a string of negative external shocks hit the country. Emerging markets often get in trouble when the Fed hikes interest rates rapidly, or the price of exported commodities falls sharply—or both. In international courtrooms I testified for a decade to help Argentina fend off aggressive lawsuits by vulture investors after the default in 2001.

When they mobilize to fix problems, government policy makers often lay the groundwork for future crises. Economists single out "moral hazard"—shorthand for economic bailouts that induce borrowers and investors to throw caution to the wind. Why worry about risk if someone else will shoulder your losses? Policy decisions have many unintended consequences, not least the subprime mortgage imbroglio that turned into the Global Financial Crisis of 2008.

During the savings and loan crisis of the 1980s, when speculative real estate loans caused innumerable small financial institutions to go belly-up, regulators formed the Resolution Trust Corporation, which bundled risky assets for sale to investors with sturdy risk appetites. Savvy buyers saw high returns on risky real lending and snapped up fire-sale bargains. A subprime industry took off. Creative minds on Wall Street started turning sows' ears into silk purses. With the hasty blessing of debt rating agencies paid by debt issuers, risk appeared to vanish. This pattern set the table for home buyers to go hog wild in the following decade, goaded by lenders with few standards and no scruples.

Fast forward to today. The COVID-19 crisis initially led to the worst global recession since World War II. The pandemic rocked a global economy already burdened with enormous amounts of private and public debt. In advanced economies the response featured unconventional monetary, fiscal, and credit easing under the presumption that a cash infusion could get most households and firms to the other side of an income or revenue shortfall. In formal economic terms, these borrowers were illiquid but solvent.

Expecting the pandemic to recede once vaccinations could begin, governments injected vast sums to help illiquid businesses keep their lights on. Nevertheless, there were casualties. Many companies, small and large, suffered. In the process, public and private debts mounted. The solution demanded still more increases in private and public debt, facilitated by central banks printing money ("quantitative easing" and "credit easing") at a faster pace than during the crisis of 2008.

The poorest developing countries lacked capacity for aggressive fiscal and monetary stimulus. Overwhelmed creditors applied financial triage that separated insolvent borrowers likely to fail from illiquid borrowers poised to survive with minimal assistance. The latter group needed urgent help to keep going. Absent resources to provide broad assistance, emerging markets and poorer developing economies suffered "pandemic depressions" that froze formal economic activity. Global lenders felt the pinch. Indeed, 60 percent of low-income economies still have significant debt vulnerabilities. And according to the United Nations up to seventy poor developing economies may face default in the next few years given the confluences of the calamities that are currently hitting them.[8]

Some governments and international agencies let the poorer countries suspend debt service. Private creditors generally pushed back against calls to lower their claims. Competing proposals increased the lending capacity of the IMF and other global multilateral official lenders to provide subsidized loans to fragile economies at high risk of a debt crisis. Vulnerable emerging and developing economies remained fragile into 2021 and 2022 even after global economic growth recovered from the severe COVID-19 induced recession. Many of these countries did not have developed health care systems and lacked access to cheap vaccines. Without enough credibility in financial markets to loosen their monetary and fiscal policies, their high debt levels mushroomed as a share of GDP as their incomes sank.

In 2022 a spike in energy, commodity, and food prices hit emerging and developing economies that were not commodity exporters. The specter of food shortages, hunger, and even famines loomed for dozens of millions of poor people in fragile developing economies. The risk of outright default spiked, starting with Chad, Ethiopia, Sri Lanka, Somalia, and

Zambia. As World Bank president David Malpass warned in April 2022: "Developing countries are facing multiple overlapping crises, including the pandemic, rising inflation, Russia's invasion of Ukraine, large macro-economic imbalances, and energy and food supply shortages. These are causing massive reversals in poverty reduction, education, health, and gender equality."[9]

Advanced economies with ample resources have let risk run amok. A new alarm bell sounded in 2021 when self-styled investors took on debt to buy shares of GameStop, a brick-and-mortar video game retailer undermined by online game delivery. Using leverage provided by an online stock trading service, they bid up stock prices far beyond levels that earnings could justify. The motive: beat short sellers whose strategy counted on GameStop's demise.

This was a boom-bust-crash scenario in miniature. A debt bubble fueled an unsustainable asset bubble. When GameStop and other shares returned to earth, small investors suffered massively. Indeed, many meme stocks—shares of a company that gained a cult-like following through social media—lost over 70 percent of their value in 2022 from their 2021 bubble valuations. A similar boom-and-bust cycle occurred in 2021-22 for cryptocurrencies, another asset class with no intrinsic value and whose bubble was driven by the FOMO (Fear of Missing Out) frenzy of retail speculators. Many experts brushed off these episodes as a fleeting departure from rational judgment. But can we overlook the fact that the US government had just sent checks to millions of adult Americans? Is this how some of them spent the money? Millions were day trading and gambling their little savings in meme stocks or crypto assets with no fundamental value. It did not help them and did not help the economy as policy makers had intended. Their money just vanished into thin air, leaving behind debts and a commemorative sweatshirt with an image of the Fed chair as a Christ figure ringed in a halo of golden light, as the *Times* reported. "In place of the Bible, the gospel he holds declares, 'Recession canceled, stocks only go up.' "[10]

Democratizing finance by easing access and lowering cost of credit opens floodgates that seldom get the scrutiny they deserve. In the early 2000s, consumers raced to buy homes with cheap debt. Detailed postmortems fill the six-hundred-page *Financial Crisis Inquiry Report* and many more accounts. Now thanks to low rates and trading apps that resemble video games, uninformed investors have new reasons and new ways to borrow. They are touting stocks out of touch with fundamental value and cryptocurrencies with no intrinsic value. And like home mortgages requiring only a signature, the new invitation to disaster lures people with low income, scarce assets, unsatisfying jobs, and limited skills. Stranger still, politicians on the far left and on the far right have united to give starry-eyed borrowers more rope to hang themselves.

How might the Mother of All Debt Crises play out in the coming decade? Much as the world has changed over the last century, the past furnishes a chilling window on the future.

As Europe labored to repay debts incurred by World War I, the Spanish flu of 1918 killed more than 100 million people, pummeling economic output. Nevertheless, euphoria followed in the shape of the Roaring Twenties, a time of great economic, financial, and technological innovation, including the first televisions, radios, phonographs, talking movies, vacuum cleaners, mass-produced automobiles, and electric traffic signals. A rising stock market overshadowed signs of financial bubbles, excessive credit, and debt accumulation. As we all know, it ended badly. Misguided policies after the Crash of 1929 led to the Great Depression of the 1930s.

History may not repeat itself—but it often rhymes. Signs abound of another Roaring Twenties. Massive monetary, fiscal, and credit stimulus is feeding financial asset bubbles in global markets. The real economy that produces goods and services is poised to boom for a while, fed by debt arising from low interest rates, ample credit, and enormous economic stimulus by governments.

The party will go on until reckless speculation becomes unsustainable, ending with the inevitable collapse in bullish sentiment, a phenomenon called a Minsky moment, named for economist Hyman Minsky. It's what happens when market watchers suddenly begin to wake up and worry about irrational exuberance. Once their sentiment changes, a crash is inevitable as an asset and credit bubble and boom goes into a bust.

Booms and bubbles always precede busts and crashes, but the scale this time far exceeds all precursors. Advanced economies and emerging markets are burdened with more debt than ever. Potential growth is low in advanced economies, and the recovery from the COVID-19 recession has been bumpy and will slow further over time. Policy makers have tapped every resource in monetary and fiscal arsenals. Little dry powder remains. The next act in this economic drama will not resemble others.

No one can predict what exactly will trigger the next shock even if the bear market in many equity markets in the first half of 2022 signaled that the latest asset bubble was nearing an end. There are plenty of candidates: a massive market bubble bursting as in 1929; a surge in inflation forcing central banks to tighten monetary policy in a draconian way, leading to an unsustainable rise in interest rates; pandemics worse than COVID-19 as zoonotic diseases transmitted from animals to humans become more frequent and virulent; a corporate debt crisis stemming from a credit crunch as interest rates rise; a new housing bubble and then bust clobbering homeowners and lenders; a geopolitical shock like the war between Russia and Ukraine in 2022 escalating and becoming more severe, leading to further spikes in commodity prices and inflation; other geopolitical risks; and the rising risk of another global recession triggered by the confluence of the above risks. Alternatively, we might see a return to protectionism or a decoupling between the United States and China as the two countries careen toward a geopolitical collision. Italy could eventually go bankrupt and start the collapse of the eurozone. Populists seizing power might mismanage their economies with nationalistic policies and piling on more unsustainable debts. Global climate change might furnish the tipping point when regions of the earth become uninhabitable.

When one or multiple shocks trigger a severe recession and financial crisis, the traditional responses that used to mitigate them will not be available. Absent a backstop, bankruptcies of highly leveraged households, corporate firms, banks, and other financial institutions will sweep away savings and other assets, leaving only debts. Assumptions about wealth will crumble. What we owe, not what we own, will govern our status.

Governments under stress will be less able to service debts as interest rates now rise. Central banks will need to decide whether to allow governments to go bust or instead wipe out debts with a bout of high inflation, a form of default on the debt. We may see this impact first in the eurozone, where member countries do not have their own central banks to fend off local monetary crises.

Emerging markets with high debt and weak currencies face crushing consequences. When exports fail to generate enough income to pay foreign creditors, local currencies will weaken or collapse. If this free fall causes domestic inflation to spike as economies shrink and currencies are debased, we can expect an economic tar pit that hedge fund luminary Ray Dalio calls "inflationary depression." Instead of exporting goods or commodities, struggling emerging markets will export citizens hoping for better lives elsewhere.

Even China is vulnerable to a string of global defaults. In recent decades rapid Chinese growth had kept its massive public and private debt sustainable. But the recent slowdown in growth and excesses of private debt—as in the real estate sector burdened with overleverage and overcapacity—have already led to stresses as some large real estate firms are on the verge of default and bankruptcy. But a severe worldwide recession would shrink China's export markets and trigger protectionism against goods from China, precipitating a recession and a debt crisis as problematic as anywhere else.

This contagion will travel across borders from sector to sector. Monetary policies and fiscal stimuli enacted since the Great Recession might blunt its progress, but we are running out of monetary and fiscal bullets, and multinational institutions and countries with large amounts of debt rest on shaky foundations. Small businesses and individuals will have to reset economic priorities to remain viable. Governments will curtail vital services. We are in a deep hole and the water is rising.

The debt crisis may be the worst we've ever faced. But it is just one of the megathreats coming toward us. What happens when it is compounded by severe policy and behavioral failures, both public and private?

Chapter 2

Private and Public Failures

Happy borrowers are all alike, the author of *Anna Karenina*, Leo Tolstoy, might have said, but each unhappy borrower is unhappy in their own way. Borrowers who repay debts move forward. Unhappy borrowers, by contrast, fail to meet obligations for reasons as varied as the ill-fated projects that grind to a halt still owing money.

It is true for individuals and also for governments. When national governments wobble on the verge of default, they need a hand to steady themselves and regain their footing. That assistance requires public international institutions—such as the IMF and the World Bank—sympathetic enough and sturdy enough to absorb the costly economic consequences of errors, policy mistakes, misjudgments, and bad luck. Despite the fact that the total wealth in the world today is vastly greater than at any time in the past, robust help is getting harder to find. The deepest sources of capital—the governments of major powers—are themselves burdened with debt.

Curing debt crises is possible but most solutions require strong medicine and excruciating rehab. Bailouts inject vital cash in exchange for crippling concessions. Restructurings dislocate workers and pummel investors and still may not work. Inflation shrinks the real debt load over time but savings erode and costs soar. Capital taxation squeezes owners of real and financial assets. Financial repression hands the tab to a profligate financial sector adept at shifting the burden to everybody else.

Austerity sounds prudent until it triggers a severe recession. Economic growth furnishes the only welcome solution, but its prospects are dimmest when debt smothers initiative. In this chapter, we will consider seven strategies and why so many end up making problems worse instead of better.

Bailouts of insolvent agents cannot restore economic health any more than two sober friends make a drunk friend sober by standing him upright: socializing unsustainable private debts often leads to unsustainable public debts. Just consider Argentina, now at risk of a fifth default since 1980. Successive accords with creditors have restored Argentina's access to international capital markets in each instance, yet they have also set the stage for more debt crises. Coming to Argentina's rescue in 2016, the International Monetary Fund warned about "pervasive macroeconomic imbalances, microeconomic distortions, and a weakened institutional framework."[1]

Jump forward to October 2020. Less than two months after reaching yet another deal with lenders, a high official reported that Argentina's public debt was increasing relative to its gross domestic product. Instead of improving, the country's risk rating worsened. This alarming trend spurred an Argentine economist to warn in the Official Monetary and Financial Institutions Forum that his country was "on the brink, again."[2]

Argentina forms the rule these days more than an exception. Gaping deficits, unfavorable balance of payments, and an insatiable appetite for debt have propelled many countries toward default. Ask treasury officials in Greece, Italy, Spain, Lebanon, Turkey, Ecuador, Ethiopia, Chad, Zambia, and Sri Lanka, to name a few. But don't rule out anybody. During the administration of former president Donald Trump, the president himself entertained in public the notion of default as a quick way to shed the national debt, as if the United States were a family-owned real estate business with shoddy management and a less than pristine reputation.

Let me be very clear: *I am not anti-debt.* Debt is useful to finance investment and in cases where sound economies feature stable currencies, manageable debt ratios, favorable balance of payments, and rising incomes. Growing output measured in gross domestic product can keep debt manageable. When economies are humming, authorities can focus on fine-tuning policies that spur economic growth. Prudent debt in combination with economic growth improves life today without burdening future generations. Borrowing in bad times, like a recession, can make it less severe and can be absolutely fine if primary fiscal surpluses (budget balances net of interest payments) are run in good times, to stabilize and reduce debt ratios.

A mostly happy environment prevailed for seven decades after World War II that nudged the industrialized world into cooperation instead of conflict. Robust economic growth brought industrialized countries out of the massive debt that the war had incurred. Yet underneath that placid surface, beginning in the 1970s, incentives began to shift. Slow at first, the pace of that shift has steadily accelerated under the much-hyped banner of globalization.

Emerging markets now compete to produce goods at the lowest cost. Embracing concepts like offshoring, multinational companies race to reduce costs. They abandon domestic facilities and move jobs to low-wage regions. Rising wealth in emerging markets lifts millions out of poverty and hikes consumer expectations. To accommodate demand, growing companies and competitive countries tap global debt markets.

As individual and household debt skyrocket, many workers in advanced economies suffer under a global wage race to the bottom. In once flourishing communities, lower incomes spur rising credit card debt. Credit card balances in the United States now swamp savings. Household economics drive the national economy. Shrinking household income for many means lower tax rolls. No longer employed in full-time jobs with benefits, workers get caught between declining purchasing power and soaring health care and education costs. Citizens facing economic duress impose a big tab on local, state, and federal resources as rising income and wealth inequality trigger political and economic populism.

Credit pays an increasing share of food, housing, clothing, secondary education, and much more that consumers want or need. Municipal debt subsidizes public schools and local services, while national debt funds national priorities from health care to warships. Up and up debt climbs, at all these levels, without enough growth to pay interest and principal.

To keep consumers spending, lenders and regulators loosen access to student debt, credit cards, mortgages, and more. Bankers invent new and riskier ways to borrow money. Their incentives encourage borrowers to pile on yet more debt.

Easing the gap between sagging incomes and rising consumer aspirations looks somewhat different in European economies with lavish social welfare programs. Instead of encouraging borrowers to take on private debt, they furnish a wide range of free or subsidized public services. The tab for health care, education, pensions, unemployment benefits, and welfare largesse lands on national balance sheets, not on households, without commensurate taxes to pay for them. These voter-friendly policies inflate budget deficits and public debt faster than private sector loans.

Although less willing historically to bear the cost of social benefits, the United States threw caution to the wind in the wake of the global financial crisis and the COVID-19 pandemic. Republicans often cut taxes while in power, pretending to try to pair them with cutbacks in spending and entitlement programs, and usually failing. Democrats often pay for generous social agendas without increasing taxes enough to underwrite them. Either way, the ratio of public debt to economic output in the United States is quickly catching up with Europe's.

In our book *Political Cycles and the Macroeconomy,* the late economist and friend of mine Alberto Alesina and I explored the impact of partisan conflict on financial crises. By dissecting tendencies on the left and the right to pump up budgets before elections, we discovered that such a practice leads to large budget excesses in industrial economies no matter who's in charge. Since then, these biases have become much more pronounced and rigid.

It's hard to see how borrowers and lenders will break a habit that scratches an irresistible itch. High interest rates used to give borrowers pause. Sustained low interest rates erased until recently the harsh memory of double-digit inflation last seen four decades ago. Few consumers under sixty years old recall such a climate. In 1981, home buyers signed up for mortgage rates pegged at 10 percent. Since those days, amnesia set in. As inflation receded, attitudes toward cheap debt began to echo *MAD* magazine's devil-may-care mascot, Alfred E. Neuman: *What, me worry?*

It matters exactly how governments and private sector agents borrow. The absolute numbers are one thing, but the tools that produced those numbers are themselves cause for alarm. Three epic mismatches have compounded the predicament we are in now.

Short-term loans taken by government or private agents might save a few bucks thanks to lower interest rates than longer-term loans, but at a high potential cost. If a liquidity crisis hits, and those loans come due, they are hard to refinance. A maturity mismatch (that is, having short-term liabilities and longer-term illiquid assets) can be fatal, as the Wall Street firms Bear Stearns and Lehman Brothers learned in 2008. When lenders refuse to replace a maturing loan with a new loan, then households, companies, and governments may run short on cash they need to operate. Lack of liquidity may correct itself if creditors willing to refinance in times of debtor distress or bailouts by governments can plug a temporary shortfall. But if cash-strapped borrowers must sell assets at fire-sale prices to pay creditors, they may be heading straight to insolvency and they may go belly-up.

Borrowing in a foreign currency can also appear cheaper than borrowing in the local currency at higher interest rates. But there's a treacherous catch to this tool, as well. Exchange rates tied to a foreign currency like the US dollar widen an emerging market trade deficit when the currency is pegged at an overvalued level and/or exports fetch lower prices, as when the price of commodities exported by that small economy falls. Then, if that currency peg to the US dollar collapses because of an untenable trade deficit, the dollar debt of a small emerging market rises in real terms. Indeed, if Argentina borrows from abroad in US dollars and its currency then depreciates, the real value of such a foreign currency debt expressed in local currency—the peso—sharply increases; this is what is referred to as the balance sheet effect of currency mismatches. These currency mismatches—borrowing in foreign currency when your income or assets are in local currency—make life untenable in less developed nations. The value of debt denominated in a foreign currency and associated debt service soars; debtors with their income and assets in local currency go bust.

Capital structure risk is a third crucial factor that borrowers must weigh. Companies often finance new investments with loans or with proceeds from the sale of stock. The ratio of debt to equity capital can suddenly matter when a firm is in trouble. In good times, companies can often sustain sizable debt. Faced with a crisis, however, that debt can become lethal.

The ratio of debt to equity has a large impact on households that pay interest on homes that earn no income. Prudent ratios of debt to home equity keep monthly mortgage payments affordable. Mismatches—with too little equity in an investment—invite default in hard times, a rude lesson for many homeowners with near zero or negative equity in their homes when the housing market tanked in 2008.

Countries, like companies and households, must mind their balance of debt and equity. When payments abroad for imports exceed receipts at home from exports, countries record a current accounts deficit. They can plug the deficit with debt, often supplied by foreign lenders, or with foreign direct investment that is like an equity rather than a debt financing. Much as treasuries like to reduce interest burdens, they often prefer debt because foreign equity investments surrender at least some control over natural resources, state-owned enterprises, power grids, and other private assets and firms.

Private borrowers maximize debt for two primary reasons. Like public treasuries, they prefer to retain control of assets. Tax considerations also lure them to lenders even if more debt adds risk. Once touted as a mark of peak financial form, meaning ultra-low debt ratios, triple-A credit ratings have lost their luster at strong companies that would rather exploit tax advantages to boost earnings. In the 1980s, bonds below investment grade, better known as junk bonds, fueled an appetite for hefty debt loads.

As borrowers learn, a loan is a contract. Interest must be paid in good times or bad, and maturing debt must be retired when due or else refinanced with a new loan. Equity investments, on the other hand, collect a share of dividends that issuers can raise, lower, or eliminate as conditions require. Mounting debt may not alter a company's market value any more than the size of a mortgage changes the value of a house, but by nudging homeowners, companies, and countries closer to insolvency, capital structure risk matters a great deal. We all share in the cost.

Maturity mismatches, currency mismatches, and capital structure mismatches all exacerbate the risk of insolvency. They make it easier for borrowers to amass debt beyond the restraints of current income, often all the way to restructurings and default.

The Global Financial Crisis of 2008 jolted borrowers and lenders, and it should have caused a fundamental reassessment of the potential risks of large debts. Some people did get religion, at least for a moment. Experts gave lip service to the importance of safeguards. Bank regulators tightened rules. Rating agencies became more transparent. The US Federal Reserve and other bank regulators engaged in rounds of "stress testing" of major banks.

Highly leveraged households and banks reduced their debts, either by saving more or defaulting on part of their liabilities, but other agents— governments, corporate firms, shadow banks (financial institutions less regulated than banks)—started to borrow much more. Instead of easing global risk, policy makers and some parts of the private sector resumed their old bad habits of overborrowing.

Geologists know that mountains can go only as high as gravity permits before the weight above begins crushing rocks below. A similar principle should limit debt capacity. Alas, there is no corresponding gravitational limit to human behavior. As debt levels climb, risk appetites recalibrate.

Every borrower can measure risk. Comparing interest rates between two bonds that mature at the same time tells investors which one is riskier in terms of its default risk. More risk increases interest rates, or yields. Because the US government is unlikely to default, its notes and bonds furnish a risk-free benchmark yield. Borrowers that cannot bail themselves out by printing money — households, corporations, cities, states, or countries — must offer a higher yield to their debts to attract lenders. The spread between two yields — the risky borrower versus the safe one — flags the credit risk — that is, the risk of default.

Let's say a company named MegaCorporation issues a ten-year bond with a 6 percent yield. If a ten-year US Treasury bond pays 2 percent, the spread is 4 percentage points. It means investors aren't willing to buy MegaCorp's bonds unless those bonds are returning that much more than a safe Treasury bond. The higher the spread, the more the market is expressing doubt in the bond issuer's solvency. Instead of muting demand, higher spreads lure investors seeking returns that compensate for default risk. More and riskier debt piles on as higher spreads increase the eventual risk of default.

When spreads get too high — close to double-digit levels — the marketplace is declaring that debt levels are becoming unsustainable. That news increases instability. If MegaCorp had hundreds of millions in debt already, when that debt is due, lenders might raise interest rates or refuse to lend. As weakness proliferates, lenders get cold feet about lending to anyone at risk of widening spreads. Once a wave of fear begins, no one can apply the brakes.

What's true of MegaCorp is true of national governments and countries. And when they face a debt crisis, governments and corporations must choose among bad options.

Bailouts by lenders of last resort generally come with strings attached. Managers of corporations must submit to intense scrutiny and constraints on spending and capital allocations. National governments, who often borrow from the World Bank or the IMF, face strict "conditionality." In exchange for loans, they must commit to fiscal austerity and/or structural reforms to make the underlying debts more sustainable.

Lenders try to make a distinction between a company or a government that just needs to get through a temporary liquidity crisis versus one that is fundamentally unhealthy and insolvent. Here, governments have an advantage over corporations. Some of them truly are too big to fail, and the IMF is likely to bail them out to avoid systemic effects on global financial markets. But that doesn't mean there won't be a lot of risk and pain involved in any rescue, as conditionality rules.

When debtors turn out to be insolvent rather than just illiquid, they become zombies that cash handouts cannot resuscitate. Zombies mean big trouble. "Zombies are stirring as the Fed creates a monster debt problem," the *Sydney Morning Herald* warned in June 2020.[3] "Zombie companies are hiding an uncomfortable truth about the global economy," the investigative research website Yahoo News reported in March 2020. Cash flow at nearly 17 percent of the world's forty-five thousand public companies could not meet interest costs over three years through 2020, according to data reported by FactSet.[4] Indeed, given cheap borrowing costs, thanks to central banks' unconventional policies, many corporate firms — already highly indebted — borrowed more during the COVID-19 crisis and became bigger zombies. Their overborrowing came home to roost in 2022. Monetary policy tightening by the Fed sharply increased the spread that "high yield" bonds paid relative to safe bonds, thus vastly increasing the borrowing costs of leveraged firms that rely on "junk" bonds. Then, defaults started to increase.

Bailing out zombies just delays inevitable bankruptcy, which is good news only for the lawyers charging by the hour. At some point, MegaCorp will face a bankruptcy and restructuring. The restructuring process can be painful for many lenders and many workers. Not all lenders are treated equally in a typical restructuring. Creditors whose claims come to maturity early may be able to collect their debts in full before default occurs. Creditors with less clout and longer-term claims are often forced to settle for a fraction of their claims, increasing their own exposure to insolvency.

A doom loop ensues. Banks, corporations, and households bailed out by their governments only increase the size of public debt—putting the state at risk. Conversely, because banks, corporations, and households own the new public debt, a nation at risk of bankruptcy exposes the private sector to bankruptcy too. This doom loop animated the eurozone crisis between 2010 and 2015. And that was with far less public debt in the balance than now exists, after the COVID-19 crisis.

Misdirected bailouts pose another kind of existential threat. When borrowers take risks with the confidence that someone will come to their rescue, there is what economists like to call "moral hazard." If you feel confident the government will bail you out if a risky bet fails, why not go for it? The higher the risk, the higher the potential return, and there may be no downside. If you win your bet, you get to keep all the chips; if you lose it, someone else picks up the tab and you live to bet another day. When taxpayers are on the hook, moral hazard privatizes gains and socializes losses.

Ironically, there is one controversial but popular solution to high debt problems: take on yet *more* debt, to stimulate growth. Economists have debated the merits of economic austerity versus fiscal stimulus for more than a century.

The so-called Austrian school of economics prefers a solution rooted in austerity when debts and deficits are high. In brief: spend less, save more. It's the kind of advice that any household should heed: if you can trim your spending to avoid running up your credit cards, you'll be in a much healthier state. But when it comes to governments, the rules are not the same as for households. Governments have options that households do not. They can issue bonds, and they can increase the money supply. They can stimulate demand.

The disciples of the legendary British economist John Maynard Keynes argue against the Austrian school. Pointing to the Great Depression, these economists advocate for reviving a sluggish economy with borrowed cash. Keynesians argue fiscal stimulus can prevent painful and damaging depression and insolvency. Keynes recognized the paradox of thrift. When one household owes more than it can manage, prudent families cut spending and increase savings as much as possible. But if every household scrimps and saves in an economic downturn, the collective absence of economic activity will send growth into a nosedive. Then the government must act as the spender of last resort.

In 2007, during the Global Financial Crisis, the IMF aligned with Austrians. It insisted on fiscal restraint by countries coping with too much debt. To some observers, IMF stood for *It's Mostly Fiscal*, shorthand for putting a lid on spending to ease financial disarray. Today, the consensus has swung to the other extreme. The new post–COVID-19 conventional wisdom says: spend more to resolve debt problems. If you don't, you'll face a deeper recession and even surer likelihood of default.

The difference between Biden advisors now and Obama advisors in 2009 illustrates an about-face in the United States. The loudest voices surrounding President Obama argued for a lid on spending to exit the Global Financial Crisis. Prevailing wisdom in the Trump and Biden administrations saw more danger in spending too little than in spending too much. Thus, we have much larger budget deficits today than after the Global Financial Crisis.

The United States and many other economies are prepared to spend and use unconventional monetary policy—a form of bailout—to restart economic activity. One zippy acronym is ZIRP—zero interest rate policy. A broader policy goes under the banner of quantitative easing or credit easing, which allows the Federal Reserve to inject cash into the economy by purchasing public and private debt, even debt on the fringes of investment grade. Those policies push short rates and long rates lower. Europe and Japan have actually implemented NIRP—negative interest rate policies. As a result, the equivalent of some $18 trillion in government bonds, with maturities of up to ten years in Europe and Japan, had a nominal negative return in 2021: lenders paid borrowers to hold their lent money. In some Scandinavian countries even the interest rate on home mortgages was negative.

To be sure, lavish "helicopter drops" of cash have offset the worst impact of an economic shutdown. Advocates like to talk about the virtues of Modern Monetary Theory, or MMT for short. MMT seems to amount to governments running large, permanent fiscal deficits with money printed by the central bank, an extreme variant of quantitative easing. To skeptics like investor Jim Rodgers, who worries about corrosive effects, MMT stands instead for "More Money Today."

Just as I am always wary of the Davos consensus view of any big question, I am wary of the emerging new consensus around MMT. Of course, I understand that when rates are near zero or negative, governments can increase spending and debt, boosting national economic growth, without facing ballooning debt-service costs. But that magical thinking cannot last forever. Gaping deficits today are causing debt ratios to rise despite those low prevailing interest rates.

Absent a powerful and lasting level of economic growth, some sort of event will eventually lance the worldwide debt bubble. The COVID-19 pandemic has pushed us close to the brink. The next shock is likely to push us over.

Wiping out debts sounds like good news for debtors, but then you are wiping out creditors also. Many creditors these days are ordinary people with savings accounts and 401(k)s. The public debt of the government is owned by households directly or indirectly—directly when savings are in government bonds; indirectly when savings are deposited in banks that buy government bonds. If banks go bust or if the government defaults, then how will banks pay depositors? This is the doom loop all over again.

Defaults as a way of resolving debt problems are ugly business. They cause many complications. First you see a credit crunch. Then banks collapse. Credit dries up. Corporations go bust. People lose jobs. Households lose their incomes and homes. The stock market tanks. It's not as if the Mother of All Defaults is a nice biblical moratorium where you erase all debt. It's going to be nasty. Compared to a default and restructuring, a bailout is preferable when the debtor—whether private or public—is short on cash but fundamentally sound, meaning illiquid but not insolvent. But when insolvency looms, a default and debt restructuring is the unavoidable option. Orderly ways to unscramble difficult debt crises include collective action clauses that force holdout creditors to accept restructuring terms accepted by a majority of creditors.

Borrowers that owe a lot to foreign lenders will feel the economic pain most. They may scramble, litigate, and innovate with some success, but not forever. Strapped Latin American nations enjoyed a small victory way back in the 1980s by convincing companies like Whirlpool to purchase chunks of dollar-denominated debt and then exchange it for local currency over its market value, a win for Whirlpool and a win for Brazil, which needed dollars to retire its foreign debt.

At current levels of debt, however, such small victories are merely rearranging deck chairs on a sinking ship. When emerging markets cannot pay foreign debts, options vanish. Unavoidable defaults shut off access to global capital markets. Without access to capital, economies contract. Local currency becomes worthless. Printing more money invites inflation and hyperinflation. Poverty proliferates. Governments that cannot provide for their populations do not last long. Chaos opens the door to empty promises by authoritarians armed with populist slogans and freelance militias.

Advanced economies are not invulnerable, as history has shown repeatedly. It's worth noting that in 1899 cautious investors sought safety in one-hundred-year bonds issued by the Habsburg Empire that ruled Austria-Hungary. When the anarchist Gavrilo Princip assassinated Austria's archduke Ferdinand in June 1914, an act that ignited World War I, sovereign Habsburg bonds were still holding their value relative to other European bonds. In other words, no experts saw the end coming. Within four years, the Habsburg Empire was history. Two decades later, the postwar debt and reparations bills that nearly smothered Germany helped usher in World War II.

Strong economies that borrow in local currency have options not available to emerging-market nations that need to borrow in a foreign currency. They can avoid default by using their own currency to repay lenders; that is, they can use money printed by the central bank. They can continue to borrow. Initially, more monetary issuance may shore up economic stability. But eventually, that remedy can turn toxic. Inflation creeps back and eventually amounts to a form of default as we will discuss in more detail in Chapter 5. Just like a default, inflation transfers wealth from creditors and savers to debtors and borrowers. The United States and other advanced economies that borrow in their own currency don't need to go through a formal default when their debt becomes unsustainable. Instead, inflation can shrink the real value of long-term fixed interest rate debt, a kinder and gentler form of default.

Indeed, inflation transfers wealth because the link between bond prices and bond interest rates, or yield, famously resembles a seesaw. When interest rates go up, bond prices go down, and vice versa. When inflation surfaces, lenders demand higher rates of interest. A ten-year bond that pays 1 percent interest to investors has less appeal when rates go higher. Why earn 1 percent for years when another bond earns more? If I lend to a government at 2 percent for ten years when inflation is 1 percent, then the real return on my investment is 1 percent. But if ex-post (after the fact) inflation turns out to be 10 percent the real return is *negative* 8 percent.

Sensitivity to interest rates governs monetary policy. Sitting on top of towering debt with low interest rates restrains the inclination to raise rates, a step that would cause the value of bonds to fall. But those low rates encourage borrowing and reckless leverage, causing a bigger debt problem down the line.

Alternatively, policy makers can impose "financial repression." The mechanism is complex, but the bottom line answers the prayers of politicians who want to raise cash without riling too many voters. Governments direct large financial institutions to bail out small businesses, households, and even distressed banks. It amounts to a stealth tax on the financial sector. Monetary, fiscal, and credit easing and bailouts reached a record level in 2020. "This, ultimately, will be seen as the route to fund all sorts of politically necessary ventures including green initiatives, because guarantees cost governments nothing beyond a contingent liability, should the assets turn bad," the *Financial Times* reported. "An age-old solution to such problem credit would then be to lend more money, to keep debtors current on both interest and principal. The shaking of the money tree has only just begun."[5]

Would proposed solutions to the debt crisis sound complete without calls to tax individual wealth? Alluring as it may look to people without wealth, downsides lurk. If authorities tax accumulated wealth or impose lofty tax rates on super-high incomes, tax avoidance may increase and proceeds still won't approach amounts needed to ease the global debt load. And taxing labor to reduce debt levels is often politically impossible when many workers are income strapped and already facing high tax rates.

Every single remedy to high debt levels brings its own costs: the paradox of thrift, the chaos of defaults, the moral hazard of bailout, the wealth taxation that hurts the wealthy and may lead to less private capital investment, the labor taxation that hurts the most vulnerable, unexpected inflation that wipes out the wealth of creditors. That is why we have arrived at the new "consensus" of MMT, as if it were a free lunch. Keeping interest rates low and continuing to pile up debt has become the path of least resistance and the softest way to redistribute wealth/income from savers/creditors to borrowers/debtors. But by definition, easy money feeds more debt. Easy money also leads to asset inflation, and eventually to bubbles. There will be a reckoning. It could come in the form of a great crash, bursting the bubble and triggering default, or inflation, or even stagflation.

The way things are going, past debt crises are just a shadow of the crises that lurk ahead. We don't want to face the truth; we are in a collective state of denial. We don't want to tighten our belts or admit that the future lacks opportunity to grow incomes, much less concede that our purchasing power is likely to decrease.

I wish it were not so, but the Mother of All Debt Meltdowns looks inevitable, either via inflation or outright default. Choose your poison. We're speeding toward it on greased rails. We cannot succumb to inertia or presume that we'll get through another debt crisis as we have before. This time, I'm sorry to say, we have to expect far worse.

Anyone who imagines that a collapse of this magnitude will only harm lenders and borrowers—banks will suffer, but my household will be fine—should remember just how much risk exists in the world, not just economic and financial, but also geopolitical. Debt crises have consequences well beyond the realm of economics. Indeed, while serving on the President's Council of Economic Advisers during the summer of 1998, I attended meetings to deal with the Russian debt crisis and default. One meeting took place in the Situation Room in the basement of the White House, often depicted in television shows as a high-tech bunker. In fact it's a dilapidated basement that has not been updated or refurnished for decades. The secure space allowed us to talk with senior military officials. We were all concerned that Russia's deterioration could lead to a breakup of the country, which in turn could put some of its nuclear weapons in the hands of bad actors. Default and deadly weapons make for dangerous bedfellows. And again in 2022 a Russia with nuclear weapons was close to default as sanctions froze its foreign assets. Similar worries surfaced when we were weighing the case for assisting Pakistan in 1999, another country with both crushing foreign debt and nuclear weapons. Working together, the US Treasury and the IMF helped Pakistan avoid economic collapse and restructure its foreign debt, but its debt levels remain precarious even today.

Attention to geopolitical constraints helps me battle groupthink. When the consensus view on Wall Street expected Greece to leave the eurozone (Grexit) in 2015, it was in part because the hawkish German finance minister Wolfgang Schauble was advising Chancellor Angela Merkel to let Greece go rather than bankroll a bailout. My contrarian view argued that a compromise to avoid Grexit would be reached by Greece and the so-called Troika that comprises the European Commission, the European Central Bank, and the International Monetary Fund. I believed Greece would test the Troika's resolve but that Germany would not pull the plug and risk a collapse of the monetary union. That's exactly what occurred: Greece got a large $200 billion bailout deal with the Troika in exchange for austerity and reforms; thus Grexit was avoided.

My assessments weigh more than strictly economic and financial factors, for instance the geopolitical consequences as millions of refugees in Turkey massed at the border with Greece, Europe's doorway. I seek hopeful signs and signs of trouble. Those who label me Dr. Doom fail to see that I examine the upside with as much rigor as the downside. Optimists and pessimists both call me contrarian. If I could choose my nickname, Dr. Realist sounds right.

Today, we can see enormous amounts of debt wherever we look. Yet, like an iceberg, much more implicit debt lies below the surface. We know precisely how much money binds lenders and borrowers. We cannot measure the implicit cost of salvaging unfunded elderly health care and pension liabilities, the costs of climate change, the costs of future global pandemics, and other untold liabilities. Our debt crisis would still be terrible even if it was the only megathreat we faced, and even if our policy makers were as wise as Solon. Yet it's much worse.

All of our lessons from history have been based on a world of growing population, with growing labor pools to help local economies climb out of trouble. What happens when population growth peaks, labor pools decline, and fewer workers support an aging population? Those unfunded liabilities are the megathreat we analyze next.

Chapter 3

The Demographic Time Bomb

During the Great Depression the industrialized world had a long list of severe problems. Commerce nearly ground to a halt. Bills went unpaid. Businesses failed. Financial institutions collapsed. Unemployment exceeded 25 percent. Bankrupt farmers and homeowners posted FOR SALE signs on their property. Uncertainty reigned. Lost faith in prosperity gave rise to totalitarian and militarist regimes in Germany, Italy, Spain, and Japan that promised greatness and crushed political and human rights. Nervous American leaders in that climate valued stability over long-standing democratic principles. Senator William Borah, an Idaho Republican, proposed handing "dictatorial power within the Constitution for a certain period" to Franklin Roosevelt.[1]

While big companies borrowed to stay in business, governments borrowed to fuel economic activity. Exhibit A: the New Deal. Program after program injected cash into the economy. We built roads and bridges, revitalized banks, fed the hungry, and mobilized artists to enrich our cultural heritage.

Bleak as conditions were, in vital ways we were healthier when soup lines snaked around city blocks. Why? The global economy shuddered but did not crumple. A crashing stock market and hungry people obscured two critical advantages compared to today. Industrial nations had low debt and lots of room to grow. The United States could borrow money and eventually pay lenders back from rising tax revenues. Social Security (passed in 1935) and Medicare (passed in 1965) made sure that retired workers would have pensions and health care. As long as the workforce kept growing, those programs had growing funding, even as the number of retired workers was also growing.

But those very programs have turned into traps, as demographic trends have reversed. Today, with growth hard to come by, we face the suffocating weight of unpaid bills for Social Security and health care. Not even World War II created so many implicit liabilities relative to economic output. The burden now is larger than ever and we're pushing it uphill against a stiff wind.

Members of Generation X in their forties or fifties have decades of work ahead. Social Security payments depend on the condition of the Old Age and Survivors Insurance (OASI) Trust Fund. Current projections anticipate insolvency—the fund running out of assets—in 2033, a date that COVID-19 advanced by one year.[2] Anyone who expects to retire after that date may see only about 76 percent of the benefits that they are owed.[3] Retirement will depend mostly on personal savings, and that bodes badly for the golden years. The Federal Reserve finds that nearly four in ten Americans could not afford to replace a major appliance.[4] A bit more than half of Americans have $5,000 or less in savings; a third have $1,000 or less.

Have you noticed that commercials on cable networks such as Fox News or CNBC are overwhelmingly aimed at senior citizens? Ads selling Viagra, pain relievers, and hair-loss supplements signal one thing clearly: our demographic trap has arrived.

An alarm has been ringing for decades, but we keep ignoring it. Imagine waking people up to grim news. That's my job. As an economist attuned to upheaval, I see no alternative. I'm marshaling the evidence and making as much unwelcome noise as I can. We have slept at our peril. I hope enough of us will wake up, pay attention, connect the dots, and prepare for the consequences.

Chapters 1 and 2 looked at explicit debt—that is, contracts between borrowers and lenders. But another kind of debt dwarfs car loans, home mortgages, credit cards, personal loans, home equity loans, public debts, and the like. The official, explicit debt tab actually pales in comparison to *implicit* debt: all the foreseeable financial obligations in our future.

Most implicit debt stems from two principal sources: providing financial safety nets for aging workers and mitigating the destructive consequences of global climate change. This chapter will focus on the former; Chapter 10 will address the latter.

Not enough money exists to deliver on the financial promises that have been made to current workers and the swelling numbers of retired workers in advanced economies—and now even in some aging emerging markets such as China, Russia, and South Korea as well. How will we pay these massive costs, which by the way must accommodate global migration patterns? Raising taxes cannot do it. Payroll taxes on current workers to finance the pensions and health care of the retired and soon to be retired would need to be increased enormously, and yet cannot guarantee enough resources for the health care and pensions of current younger workers when they retire. Printing enough money will trigger inflation or eventually hyperinflation. Reneging on promises to retirees and soon-to-be retired workers—even lengthening the retirement age—invites political unrest. To make ends meet we increasingly rely on the only remaining alternative: additional debt we can never repay. Caveat emptor—this won't end well.

"Nature abhors the old," Ralph Waldo Emerson wrote when the industrial revolution was in its youth. Modern observers are reaching the same conclusion for reasons that the author of *Self-Reliance* could not have foreseen.

Many workers in advanced economies are approaching advanced and retirement age, especially in Japan and Europe but also the United States.

I have no beef with getting older. No one escapes it. But an aging workforce can trigger spiraling problems in economies where growth has peaked. Aging reduces the supply of workers and slows down productivity as investment in new machines declines. Financial promises—pensions and health care—divert increasing chunks of national income to an older population. As jobs move abroad and robots proliferate, advanced economies employ fewer workers who must support growing ranks of retirees.

If the trend continues, and I see no reason it won't, we can forget a future that continues centuries of social progress from one generation to the next. Instead of buying goods and building nest eggs for young families, the paychecks of active workers will be more and more devoted to maintaining safety nets for the elderly. Lower rates of spending and savings by younger generations will pump the brakes on economic growth.

Nobel laureate Milton Friedman, an economist fiercely opposed to government intervention, sounded one of the first warnings. Way back in 1980, he railed against a looming crisis when we had more time to avert it.

> What you have is a system under which people are being taxed today to pay benefits to the people who are receiving them. So far those people who are receiving payments have received much more than the actuarial value of what they paid. That's because you've had a growing working force, you've had higher wages being paid. Wage tax has gone up very sharply but the number of recipients is growing relative to the number of people paying. That's why social security is in so much financial trouble. That's why the so-called reserve has been getting smaller and smaller and that's why you have all the agitation for congress to do something to make social security financially responsible.[5]

What's puzzling is that nothing has changed, despite mounting evidence over decades that the threat is real. In 2012, *The Clash of Generations* authors Laurence Kotlikoff and Scott Burns calculated for the United States the difference between *official* public debt and *true* indebtedness when unfunded obligations are included. They call this difference the fiscal gap. Official debt, they determined, was then $11 trillion.[6] True debt was a whopping $211 trillion. They sounded the alarm, but policy makers did nothing.

Ordinarily, when total debt becomes equal to a country's annual economic output, or gross domestic product (GDP), macroeconomists grow concerned. In the United States today, a decade after *The Clash of Generations* was published, the fiscal gap measures *fourteen times* GDP. More stunning still, they found, the fiscal gap "is twenty-two times the official debt that now has everyone's attention." This does not bode well. "If the United States goes broke and descends into economic chaos and generational conflict," they wrote, "the whole world will suffer, probably in ways none of us can, or want, to imagine."[7]

Of course, estimates of the fiscal gap are somewhat exaggerated because they don't consider the fact that GDP grows over time. Many of the liabilities due decades from now will be financed by that larger output. But even scaling for future higher incomes, the gap between what the government has promised and the resources it will have when the bill comes due is massive by any standards. And the US economy is healthier than many others. The situation elsewhere is much worse.

Giant fiscal gaps are now part of the global economic landscape. "Aging is a Europe-wide phenomenon," the World Bank has warned. Consider one example: Poland. In 1950, half the population was less than twenty-six years old, still youthful. Today the median age is approaching forty and on its way to fifty-one in 2050. A graying population is also shrinking. Poland is projected to have 32 million people in 2050, 6 million fewer than in 1995.[8]

Long before COVID-19 arrived, World Bank researchers expected demographic shifts in Poland to trim per capita GDP by more than a third over a decade. Their report flagged the funding of Poland's pension system as a key concern—despite a full restructuring undertaken a decade earlier to bolster capacity. The report also forecast more demand for round-the-clock social care services over extended periods, posing significant boosts in expenditures. "The children who are born in today's Poland stand a good chance to live until 100," the report noted. It also asked, but did not answer, the pivotal question of how to pay for expanded services.

Across developed nations, statistics expose a treacherous imbalance. Instead of going to young workers, an increasing share of the national income must preserve standards of living for retirees. The skewing gets worse every year as payrolls and working-age populations shrink and old-age liabilities balloon. If young workers do not yet resent surrendering their futures in order to bankroll retirees, they eventually will. Watch for headlines declaring generational conflict between young and old.[9]

Instead of moving forward, we have slipped backward. In 1960, there were five active workers for every retired and disabled worker in the United States. The ratio slipped below 3 to 1 in 2009 and is headed toward 2 to 1 by 2030, according to the Social Security Administration.[10]

The situation in the United States was dire, but not as dire as in Europe, thanks to immigration that until recently helped to increase the US labor supply. The total US population is not yet decreasing, even though birth rates are well below the so-called replacement rate of 2.1 children per woman. The continuing influx of immigrants from Asia, Central and Latin America, and elsewhere, helped the total population to grow, albeit very modestly. Nonetheless, more retirees in the United States will swell Social Security rolls to 73 million beneficiaries, nearly twice the number that received payments in 2010. The value today of unfunded obligations that will come due in the future exceeds $5 trillion, more than two and a half times the ambitious jobs bill proposed in 2021 by the Biden administration.

Japan has one of the oldest populations in the world, as birth rates are very low and life expectancy is very high. Before COVID-19 the Japanese government estimated that retirement income would be only 61.7 percent of preretirement wages given the unfunded pay-as-you-go pension system; that pension-to-wage ratio is estimated to fall to 51 percent by the late 2040s and could fall below 40 percent in the 2050s under some worst-case scenarios.[11] Legacies of comprehensive social welfare programs leave Europe and Japan with the steepest hills to climb. Aging in those regions is occurring faster than in the United States while pension promises are overall more generous than in America. Safety nets that were the envy of workers a generation ago heap mountains of debt on current and future generations.

The United States is close behind Europe and Japan in a race that bestows no glory on its winners. The problem isn't just with the federal government. A crucial measure of implicit debt highlights the difference between the assets all fifty states collectively hold in their pension systems and how much they owe. According to the Pew Charitable Trusts, the collective shortfall in state pension funds has climbed to a record $1.2 trillion.[12]

Pensions for state government employees make up only a fraction of claims on public coffers. Add retirement and health care costs for hundreds of thousands of federal, state, and municipal workers, including teachers, and the increase in unfunded liabilities goes sharply up. Then there is the private sector. Pension plans with fixed payouts have disappeared in many industries, but they are still an issue — and the government has promised to support them via the Pension Benefits Guarantee Corporation. Right now, underfunded private sector plans could leave taxpayers on the hook for $185 billion, and that's a best-case scenario.

National health expenditures are climbing even faster than pension commitments. In 2020, spending on Medicare, Medicaid, private insurance, hospitals, physicians and clinical services, out-of-pocket costs, and prescription drugs grew by nearly 10 percent to $5.4 trillion. That's $12,530 per person, or almost 20 percent of the US gross domestic product. The federal government shouldered more than a third of this giant tab and households a fourth. State and local governments picked up just over 14 percent, according to the Centers for Medicare and Medicaid Services.[13]

These financial pressures are destined to increase. Through 2028, national health spending in the United States is on pace to grow at an average annual rate exceeding 5 percent. Projected enrollment growth will cause Medicare to sprint ahead of other national health costs.

A 2010 paper published by the National Bureau of Economic Research exposed one landmine that is poised to explode. "The Growth in the

Social Security Disability Rolls: A Fiscal Crisis Unfolding," by David Autor and Mark Duggan, found that Social Security insures more than 80 percent of non-elderly US adults against the risk of disabling physical or mental illness, a much higher number than in the past.[14] They attribute the rapid expansion in payments to three factors: Legislation lowered the benefits threshold for workers with back pain, arthritis, and mental illness. Added tax benefits for disability income added incentives for workers to seek benefits. And a steep increase in working women expands the pool of insured workers. The authors noted than when cases go to appeal, judgments favor plaintiffs three-fourths of the time.

Thus, the unfunded liabilities deriving from aging and a pay-as-you-go welfare system for the elderly — pension, health care, disability benefits, and other services — are huge and exploding over time, especially in advanced economies but now also in some aging emerging markets. One estimate is that the unfunded or underfunded government pension liabilities in the top twenty economies that are members of the Organisation for Economic Co-operation and Development (OECD) are about $78 trillion; this is an estimate for pensions only, not health care or disability.[15] Clearly, implicit debt is a major time bomb and a severe megathreat.

Solving the aging dilemma vexes politicians and policy makers. No solution will please everyone, nor can anyone guarantee that draconian solutions will restore balance. Agendas must collide.

All plans to ease implicit costs entail some form of default on promises to influential interest groups. Obviously, you can't simply deprive retirees of benefits they believe they have earned. AARP, with 38 million members, won't be shy in its opposition to any such proposal. Raising the retirement age is a political minefield.

Adjusting the retirement age would compound unfairness. Ample data show that white-collar workers outlive blue-collar workers who, on average, start working before they are twenty and die by seventy. Why should they subsidize white-collar workers who finish college and graduate school in their twenties and are more likely to collect Social Security for two decades or more? Alternatively, the government could tax payrolls more. Young workers are likely to balk, fearing a loss of wages today and an empty cupboard when they retire. Shrinking workers' take-home pay could ramp up pressure on employers to keep workers whole, squeezing bottom lines in the corporate sector.

One option for solving the funding problem would tax a group with few voters: the wealthiest citizens who exercise their influence on legislators with lavish campaign donations. Taxing billionaires has appeal in some progressive circles, but it too may be ineffective if not counterproductive. Taking even hundreds of billions of dollars from billionaires would still fall far short of implicit liabilities that are in the trillions. Moreover, no one has better accountants who can find ways to subvert hefty taxes than billionaires. Bankrolling friendly politicians is always popular. If all else fails, billionaires who oppose higher taxes, and some who do not, can move to new jurisdictions, lowering tax rolls instead of raising them.

Unfunded liabilities will balloon as more workers qualify for the safety net and political will falters. Taming Social Security, known as the third rail of politics, is so perilous that almost no politician dares to propose reductions.

Longer life expectancies and new medical technologies, once a dream of visionaries, now pose a nightmare. Advanced economies created social safety nets when many workers were dying before retirement age. We fixed that problem at a cost no one foresaw. Retirement at age sixty-five starts a stream of pension benefits that may last for decades, far exceeding any Social Security taxes. Keeping older people healthy imposes the most draining costs on the health care sector. The question arises yet again: How will we pay all these bills? Ducking the answer has turned a festering problem into a volatile megathreat that can explode over the next two decades.

Note also that aging worsens any unfunded liability by driving the potential growth of any country lower. Indeed, given any trend in productivity growth (output per worker), a smaller working population reduces potential growth proportionally. Also, productivity growth may fall with aging. A lot of productivity growth depends on investment into new productive capital, but the investment rate falls as you have fewer workers. Thus, even productivity growth can fall over time as you have less investment. No wonder that Japan—the advanced economy with the greatest aging rate—has faced stagnant growth for most of the current century.

So, how to boost potential growth? One partial solution would accelerate the immigration of young workers.

Indeed, were growth robust and jobs plentiful, immigration might partly solve the aging problem that besets advanced economies. More young workers earning salaries could contribute to Social Security and health care funds. More consumers would fuel demand, spurring income growth that eases current and implicit debt burdens.

Immigrants pouring into the United States used to populate factory floors and service businesses that needed talented, industrious workers. Economic growth hinged on their arrival. The Statue of Liberty welcomed the world's tired, poor, huddled masses yearning to breathe free. How times have changed. Anti-immigration fever would place a new sandwich board on Lady Liberty, one that reads "no vacancies."

As an immigrant to the United States, I hate to imagine closed doors. Like millions of others raised abroad, I saw America as a land of opportunity. I arrived in 1983 to pursue graduate studies, but work kept me here as an academic, then as a policy maker, then as an entrepreneur with an economic consultancy. That consultancy grew to more than fifty employees, many of whom, like me, were immigrants. New workers have a superb track record of creating wealth. A *Forbes* magazine headline declared in 2018: "55% of America's Billion-Dollar Startups Have an Immigrant Founder."[16]

Economist Dani Rodrik advocates policies that encourage developed nations to welcome immigrants. Why? Because research links immigration with higher economic growth rates. Skilled workers head for regions where growth and productivity are strong and wages higher. Motivated immigrants become entrepreneurs who build new businesses, a trend especially visible in the lucrative high-tech sector. Meantime, immigrants send income home via remittances that help stabilize those economies. The bottom line, says Rodrik, is that freer immigration has a much more positive net impact on global domestic product than liberalizing trade, movements of capital, or financial services.

According to standard economic theory, free trade helps global welfare. The same is true for free trade in people, via open-border immigration policies. Suppose you have two countries. One has a lot of workers and little capital. Wages will be low. The other country is more advanced and has a lot of capital and fewer workers. Wages will be high. When labor can move freely, wages tend to equalize. Someone with the same intelligence and potential skills in the United States or Europe will have four or five times higher income than the equivalent person in Nigeria or Bangladesh. The catch is that average wages in advanced economies with higher initial wage rates will tend to fall; that explains part of the resistance to immigration.

Ludwig von Mises, who inspired generations of austere economists in the Austrian school and many modern conservative politicians, embraced immigration. By forcing people to endure economic hardship, von Mises believed that barriers to immigration led ultimately to war in Europe.

Nevertheless, convincing voters in advanced economies to side with immigrants is a tough sell. The reasons are no mystery. Wages have stagnated for low-skilled workers—both blue-collar and service workers— and migration tends to reduce them further. New immigrants put pressure on public services from schools to housing to health care, stirring more resentment. Migrants who speak different languages and come from unfamiliar cultures provoke a social backlash, especially when nativist politicians malign them for partisan purposes.

In eras past, migrants who sought work in new countries competed for jobs with native-born people. Nowadays, they compete with algorithms. Artificial intelligence erects a thoroughly modern barrier to immigration. As robots replace factory and office workers, including many with professional credentials, immigrants with skills may not find work and will be increasingly unwelcome as they compete for even scarcer jobs.

Businesses in developed economies rely increasingly on robots and AI as a way to deal with fewer workers, given the aging population.

In Japan, where the average worker is older than elsewhere in the industrial world, the solution to aging is not migration. Instead, Japanese employers have accelerated the move toward robotics and automation. Employers worldwide are likely to go the same route, putting algorithms to work instead of humans. Workers from abroad competing for fewer jobs—as technological unemployment surges—will exacerbate the backlash against immigration. Indeed, the migration policies of the Biden administration have ended up being not very different from those of the nativist Trump administration: faced with an influx of economic, climate, and political refugees from Central America, Biden ended up restricting entry into the United States. But, as we will discuss in later chapters, the incipient flow of potential migrants from poor countries to richer ones will swell in the next few years as global climate change, failed states, personal safety, economic underdevelopment, and poverty surge over time. Alas, the gates and borders will be closed to them, not just in Japan but increasingly in the United States and Europe too.

The picture is grim, I am sorry to report. Even if advanced countries can absorb unprecedented numbers of immigrants, promises of pensions and health care to older workers will become untenable in the foreseeable future. Public and private borrowers will compete for funds. Countries that can print money will keep the presses rolling. Others will default abruptly or experience high inflation, inviting social chaos that spurs conflict and accelerates emigration.

So, what should governments do, faced with all these pressures? There is one overwhelming temptation: pump out money. Throw money at every problem. Make it easy for consumers to borrow. Pass spending bills so that governments can borrow more massive sums. Chapter 4 probes this timeless temptation. Thanks to levels of debt and demographic challenges, money printing leading to more cheap borrowing and boom-bust cycles now poses a megathreat.

Chapter 4

The Easy Money Trap and the Boom-Bust Cycle

To see where financial crises originate, step back from the dozens of recent headlines that expose poor judgement in the leadership ranks of central banks, who are charged with maintaining economic stability. Heated debates over the means to control inflation or ease unemployment routinely miss a sad truth: top policy makers make upheaval inevitable.

When Parker Brothers introduced the board game Boom or Bust in 1951, both concepts resonated. The global economy was entering a legendary post–World War II boom, but the Dow Jones Industrial Average was still two years away from returning to its peak price before the Great Crash in 1929. Game players bought and sold properties at prices subject to random economic news. A roll of the dice changed boom times to bust — or vice versa. The winner was the player who did not go bankrupt.[1]

Board game players cannot read an economic climate that depends on a roll of the dice. The real world is infinitely more complex, but it does furnish lots of clues about boom-and-bust cycles. When loose monetary policy makes money too cheap for too long, you don't need Sherlock Holmes to detect excessive risk of a coming bust as the bubble eventually bursts. Attracted by low interest rates, homeowners gorge on debt to pay their bills. Individual and corporate investors borrow vast amounts to acquire financial assets they cannot otherwise afford. Governments borrow to finance huge budget gaps. Central banks print money and ease restraints on lending. Regulators take long lunches. If this behavior doesn't shout danger ahead, I'm not sure what does. Yet as history records, this pattern goes unheeded much of the time, even by experts.

To resuscitate economies stalled by COVID-19 and already drenched in debt, the Fed, other central banks, and fiscal policy makers threw caution aside. They embraced monetary, fiscal, and credit policies much looser than those implemented after the Global Financial Crisis of 2008. What are the unintended consequences when loose money and transfer payments bankroll profligate risk takers? Ask former star money manager Bill Hwang, whose portfolio strategy sounded like a story right out of 2008. Hwang made headlines when Archegos Capital Management went bust in early 2021.

This Wall Street implosion began—once again—by underestimating risk. Archegos took enormous stakes in total return swaps, a contract that exchanges a fixed rate payment for "total return" payments based on the income and capital gains that an underlying asset generates. Swaps help aggressive investors disguise highly leveraged equity positions that exceed regulatory thresholds. Shrewd calls can generate fat gains, but when large, highly leveraged positions unravel abruptly they can rattle the market.

Overexposure to tumbling tech stocks in Asia sent Archegos scrambling for cash in April 2021. An attempt to liquidate a leveraged position in ViacomCBS clashed with a stock offering. Shares flooding the market caused the price to drop. News traveled fast. Wall Street lenders issued margin calls, demanding repayment of large loans. Archegos could not comply. Goldman Sachs reportedly seized capital and others soon followed. "This so-called forced liquidation set off a bloodbath," CNN reported.[2] Caught in the downdraft as the boom deflated, Archegos went bust. Lenders recorded losses in the billions.

So much for lessons taught by the Great Recession and the massive bailouts it had required. The Archegos collapse ranks as "one of the most spectacular on Wall Street," the *Financial Times* reported.[3] Five global banks swallowed losses exceeding $10 billion, their penalty for too much faith in a bubble.

Archegos is far from the only player that became too enamored of risk as borrowing costs became dirt-cheap. Its debacle came within weeks of news that regulators seized Greensill Capital, an investment firm that proposed financing arrangements for risky start-up companies, including makers of a nuclear submarine, and facilities used in the Muslim pilgrimage to Mecca, the *Wall Street Journal* informed readers. "While some of Mr. Greensill's more speculative ideas never got off the ground, they illustrate the scale of his ambition and his high tolerance for riskier investments," according to the *Journal*.[4]

A report from Bloomberg captured the heady climate as the first round of COVID-19 began to recede. It described a cryptocurrency trader in Hong Kong napping on his beanbag to get through eighteen-hour days handling orders for digital assets as a massive bubble formed; a "ferocious" auction in Wellington, New Zealand, where prices for houses blew way past historical valuations; and a hedge fund manager in New York mulling credentials of a thirteen-year-old job applicant who claimed a four-fold return on his investment. "Cheap money, gushing in from the world's major central banks," Bloomberg reported, "inflated assets and reshaped how we save, invest and spend."[5]

Add to the frothy mix a new fad for publicly traded special purpose acquisition companies, or SPACs. Formed with no inherent business, they exist to acquire or merge with companies that sell goods or services.

"Over the past year, SPACs, once considered a flaky sideshow in the finance world, have become the driving force of capital markets and deal-making," the *Financial Times* reported in May 2021. "'Blank-cheque' companies backed by well-known figures on Wall Street, as well as celebrities and sports stars, have raised eye-watering sums of money, creating a $142 billion pool of capital looking for merger targets."[6]

One high-profile deal proposed the merger of Momentus, a space transportation start-up, and Stable Road Acquisition Corp., a SPAC. Pitched as "a unique and compelling opportunity for investors" to invest in outer space, Momentus claimed that revenues would exceed $4 billion in 2027, the *FT* reported. Projections envisioned a fleet of robotic vehicles servicing large spacecraft. A Securities and Exchange Commission investigation into the merits of statements put the deal on hold and alerted investors to give all SPACs more careful scrutiny — or look elsewhere.

If one sector dims, another takes its place. Investors hungry for risk can gorge nonstop. "A new breed of day traders chasing thrills in the intense ups and downs of markets is asserting its dominance again, sending shares in popular stocks surging while crypto currency prices wilt," the *Financial Times* reported in May 2021. Said one analyst who tracks retail investing flows, "In the past, day traders tended to focus on particular themes or stock sectors. But the new generation tended to 'rotate in different asset bubbles' across global markets."[7]

The historical record is crystal clear: Whenever you have a casino full of nearly free money, it leads to a volatile bubble. No sign is clearer than the price investors pay for expected earnings. The price-earnings (P/E) ratio divides the price of a share of stock in a company by its earnings per share. If the shares change hands for $100 and the company expects to earn $10 a share then the P/E ratio is 10 to 1. Fast-growing stocks fetch bigger P/E ratios because investors count on growth to provide higher returns on their investment, but future growth is never certain. Bigger P/E ratios signal more hope — and more risk. That's why ratios vary widely by sector.

Since 1950, the average P/E ratio across all sectors has generally floated between 10 and 20. In post–COVID-19 euphoria, however, familiar benchmarks looked tame. Ratios for S&P 500 companies rose above levels that preceded the 1929 crash and rivaled that of the dot-com bust in 2000, reaching well into the 30s. Ratios in the red-hot tech sector reached stratospheric levels, into the 50s and above. Another signal comes from exotic investments. A piece of digital art fetched $65 million. Cryptocurrencies that were effectively "shitcoins" with no intrinsic value reached stratospheric values until 2021. The buzz of crypto, decentralized finance (DeFi) and non fungible tokens (NFT) gave FOMO to retail suckers—

investors hoodwinked by insiders in this unregulated Wild West. A firm whose only asset was a delicatessen in New Jersey with slim revenues rocketed to $100 million in market value.[8] Home prices followed suit as apartment dwellers raced to trade urban ambience for suburbs and backyards.

Flawed human judgment—like "irrational exuberance" and excessive risk taking—connects the Great Depression, the savings and loan crisis, the dot-com bubble, and the financial crisis of 2008. It's a weakness we cannot correct. Investors should have learned three times over to rein in suicidal tendencies. But as the saying goes, success on Wall Street requires two components: a rising market and a short memory. Instead of real steps to promote stability, we were hurtling yet again toward a self-inflicted boom-and-bust cycle, this one more punishing than its predecessors.

With interest rates at zero for too long, financial markets became a casino where free money fed a monster asset and credit bubble. Quantitative and credit easing reduced the borrowing costs for public and private borrowers. A fiscal stimulus became excessive and bailed out zombies. It propped up stocks, especially growth and tech stocks, home prices, private equity, SPACs, crypto assets, meme stocks, government bonds, high yield and high grade corporate bonds, exotic credit instruments such as collaterized loan obligations (CLOs), shadow banks, and hedge fund investments. Fed bailouts starting in March 2020 drove the price of every type of asset through the roof.

The bubble eased in late 2021. This massive monetary, credit and fiscal stimulus pushed the inflation rate to levels not seen since the early 1980s. Central banks—starting with the Fed—acted at first as if the rise in inflation was temporary. When it turned out that inflation was persistent, central banks at last applied the brakes at their disposal. They wound down QE and credit easing and began to hike interest rates.

The monster asset bubble of 2020–21 started to burst as money and borrowing at zero rates became history. By May 2022, public equities sank into bear market territory, when prices fell more than 20 percent. Highflying growth and tech stocks that populate the Nasdaq index imploded. The rout engulfed the robust FAANG group that comprises Facebook, Amazon, Apple, Netflix and Google. Even venerable blue chip stocks wilted.

Bad news proliferated. Meme stocks fell by over two-thirds from nonsensical 2021 peaks. The crypto market swooned. Bitcoin plummeted 70 percent from an all-time high months earlier. Flimsier cryptocurrencies fell even further by 80 percent or more. Bubbly SPACs sputtered and deals fizzled. US government bond yields tripled to 3 percent. Credit spreads above and below investment grade widened sharply, unsettling the global bond market where more than $100 trillion resides.

In early 2022, the Fed and other central banks finally signaled that rising inflation required much tighter monetary policy. That yanked the punch bowl. Asset prices sank in response to interest rate hikes aimed at taming inflation. When monetary restraints fanned fears of a recession, prices for risk assets slid further.

Macroeconomists are not game designers, although it might look that way. We build models on a grand scale, using imaginary concepts that aggregate all the factors that drive production and consumption, also known as supply and demand. We nudge variables like prices, taxes, wages, and exchange rates to see what happens. We seek combinations that promote growth while dodging calamities that arise from flawed judgment and bad luck. We attempt to balance inflation that comes from excessive increases in the money supply and deflation that at times may derive from a severe recession and a credit crunch. We monitor long- and short-term bond yields along a curve that informs us about expectations of future rates. We watch data for evidence that low unemployment signals higher inflation ahead. Like a board game, rules apply. Unlike a board game, the rules can evolve and the consequences are real.

Booms and busts do not occur randomly. Unfortunately, the commonsense narrative about them, which is accepted wisdom in many quarters, is wrong. It goes like this: We begin with a happily growing economy. Robust animal spirits propel rising stock prices—until something turns those animal spirits negative. After scant warning, a crash follows. It's the madness of crowds, from irrational exuberance to irrational panic. Anxiety paralyzes demand. Corporate revenues fall. Workers lose jobs. Recession and deflation loom. Without massive intervention to spur demand, the economy tumbles into a death spiral.

This narrative rests on two prominent flaws. First, it ignores short-sighted monetary and regulatory policies that actually encourage bubble-and-bust cycles in the first place. Second, it fails to weigh developments in the global economy that can defeat the best intentions of policy makers. The traditional narrative kicks blame for crises down the road—there isn't much you can do about the madness of crowds. Yet that narrative actually feeds a mega debt supercycle that will pummel all our assumptions about wealth preservation and growth.

When recessions or financial crises occur, macroeconomists always try to guide economies clear of a Great Depression. No one wants a repeat of the 1930s. Countless movies and books have documented that terrible time, from breadlines and bank runs to ruined investors leaping from window ledges on Wall Street. In an economist's lexicon, the Depression saw deflation at its ugliest.

Although markets were already unsettled, the stock market crash on October 24, 1929, dubbed Black Thursday, marked the start of the Great Depression. In an instant, fortunes vanished. Steep losses in the bluest blue-chip stocks continued for a week. Stunned investors and consumers postponed purchases. Aggregate demand for all goods and services fell. As revenues declined, companies shed jobs. Incomes fell. Demand dropped further. More jobs vanished. Viable companies ran short of cash and failed. A crash turned into a depression.

The crash should not have led to a fiasco of such magnitude. It could have been limited to a stock market event with a minor recession to follow, were it not for a misguided response by authorities who favored austerity. Let the economy repair itself, in other words. Its leading proponent in the United States during the Hoover administration was secretary of the treasury and prominent banker Andrew Mellon. He voted to let strapped consumers, banks, and businesses go bankrupt, allowing deflation to "cleanse" the system of weakness. In Mellon's view, institutions with cash shortfalls deserved to fail.

Since then, policy makers have learned that they can intervene and help boost the economic system when it is threatened with a crash and/or a recession. Central banks can pump money into the system, and Congress can increase spending.

Since World War II, deflation has seldom gripped developed nations. It has surfaced for short intervals in the United States and Europe. Only Japan has experienced prolonged deflation. After 1990, its economy entered a stagnant twenty years remembered as the "lost decades." Growth swooned. Consumption was weak. Wealth drained out of the formerly robust economy. Standards of living flattened.

Citizens in healthy economies are accustomed to inflation. Prices rise and bills increase every year. But we expect wages, incomes, savings, and investment to grow as fast or even faster. When that happens, inflation gives borrowers a helping hand.

If annual inflation is, say, 2 percent, the long-standing target for most central banks, then a dollar loses 2 percent of its real value each year. It's the same as needing two additional cents per year to remain whole. If MegaCorp borrows $100,000 for new machinery, at the end of the year the debt's real value has decreased to $98,000. So long as economic growth at MegaCorp keeps pace with inflation, the real debt burden keeps shrinking. After ten years of 2 percent inflation, the real purchasing power of the original loan would fall below $81,000.

Now imagine that MegaCorp, a proxy for all suppliers, has agreed to pay a nominal 3 percent interest to borrow the money. In real terms, inflation offsets the nominal interest rate. The interest rate adds 3 percent each year to the real debt but inflation subtracts 2 percent. Thus, Mega-Corp can subtract the rate of inflation from its rate of interest to compute the real economic cost of borrowing. In this illustration, the real cost to borrow subtracts two percent from three percent, yielding one percent in real borrowing cost.

Actual inflation fluctuates constantly, of course, but the principle is constant. With solid real income growth and inflation, debt-to-income burdens ease as long as debt doesn't rise faster than nominal income growth. However, inflation is not a panacea for towering debt. Steeper inflation might erase debt faster, but at the cost of imposing unsustainable interest rates on new borrowers and borrowers who must roll over their debt.

Deflation works in the opposite direction. Every dollar borrowed has higher real value than the same dollar when it is repaid in the future. A phenomenon called *debt deflation* wallops borrowers.

The real value of debt grows *more* burdensome. Suppose MegaCorp takes out a loan at 3 percent and deflation is 2 percent. Forget the windfall that inflation bestows. The real cost of borrowing *adds* the rate of deflation to the rate of interest. Real borrowing cost at MegaCorp would go to 5 percent a year, a five-fold increase. True, interest rates will fall over time. But borrowers who lose their jobs and businesses with tighter cash flow often lack the option to refinance at lower rates. Defaults loom instead. Millions endured this scenario in the Great Depression.

Franklin Roosevelt ushered in a new regime when he became president in March 1933. "The country needs and, unless I mistake its temper, the country demands bold, persistent experimentation," FDR declared. "It is common sense to take a method and try it: If it fails, admit it frankly and try another. But above all, try something."[9]

With demand for goods and services at a near standstill, the spender of last resort, Uncle Sam, intervened at last. FDR lobbied for a host of new laws under the New Deal. None was bolder than the National Industrial Recovery Act of 1933 (NIRA). It authorized federal regulators to fix prices and wages, establish production quotas, and restrain companies from forming alliances, steps aimed at promoting financial recovery.

A way out of the deflationary spiral required more than regulatory actions, some of which were eventually found unconstitutional by the Supreme Court. Authorities in the United States and other advanced nations had to make more money available by loosening or easing the money supply. More money in circulation created more money to spend; more spending lubricated the economy. Uncle Sam printed money and ramped up borrowing. Every dollar printed or borrowed eventually landed in someone's pocket or bank account. In some circles this monetary action is anathema, but most economists agree that monetary and fiscal stimulus in the thirties arrested a devastating deflation.

The painful lesson was clear, and John Maynard Keynes spelled it out in *The General Theory of Employment, Interest and Money,* his epic tome that shaped economic strategies for battling deflation and depression. He endorsed massive monetary and fiscal stimulus that put money in the hands of consumers. Spending lifted revenues for businesses, which then hired more workers.

Keynes has enduring value, to be sure, but we forget too easily that the Depression was not an innocent mistake visited on the world by chance. It's not as if all of a sudden for no reason people became pessimistic about the future, stopped spending, animal spirits vanished, and bad things happened.

What if the reason why we experienced a monumental collapse in demand cannot be pinned to spontaneous pessimism? Why else might people appear to turn pessimistic all at once? Because conditions were ripe, thanks to the asset and credit bubble leading up to the Crash.

Our economic house did not catch fire spontaneously in 1929. Metaphorically speaking, we were smoking in bed and far too confident. During the Roaring Twenties — an era that followed the deadly Spanish flu pandemic of 1918 — the stock market soared to record heights. Some leaders predicted affluence without end. When John Brooks, a long-standing writer of the Annals of Finance column in *The New Yorker,* chronicled the 1920s and '30s in his "true drama of Wall Street," he called it "Once in Golconda" because Golconda was a legendary region of India where every visitor became rich.[10]

Demand drove stock prices up and everybody wanted in. There was also a credit bubble: people were buying cars, homes, and appliances on credit, in record numbers. Those giant speculative bubbles had few guardrails. Unscrupulous insiders pooled their money to boost stock prices, then got out as less informed investors rushed in. Prominent bankers gambled depositors' money on stocks. Some ended their careers in prison.

Money was indeed loose. Leading up to the Crash anybody could buy one hundred dollars of stock with a few dollars of savings and the rest on margin, meaning borrowed money. Margin debt exploded. Debt and leverage soared. When the party ended and the bubble burst it left numbed investors with empty bank accounts and ruinous debts. Nest eggs vanished, spending slowed, and bankruptcies proliferated. Absent intervention to bolster demand, the effects snowballed into a financial crisis.

Boom-and-bust cycles tend to follow this familiar pattern. We've spent essentially the last forty years reacting to every shock and crisis triggered by a bubble gone bust the same way. We created more easy money, easy fiscal, and easy credit. That's why global debt ratios climbed from 2.2 times GDP in 1999 to 3.2 times in 2019. They kept on rising—to 3.5 times GDP—after the COVID-19 crisis. In advanced economies the ratio was already 4.2 in 2019 and still rapidly rising. The sum of public and private debt in the United States during the current peacetime recovery has surpassed its peak during the Great Depression or its high after the debt buildup during World War II; but today we are not following a depression or a major war. This trend is ominous and unprecedented.

In a typical bubble, loose monetary and credit policies cause excessive borrowing. All that cash chases financial assets. Historical benchmarks lose meaning. Sobriety succumbs to FOMO: fear of missing out. Prices soon fly past underlying value, fueling the wealth effect: as assets appreciate, apparent wealth spurs more buying of assets and spending on goods and services. Bloated demand affects homes in the same way. You borrow; you buy a home. More buyers follow suit. People want to buy homes before prices go even higher. Prices of homes soar. The collateral looks better. Homeowners can borrow more with less equity at riskier loan-to-value ratios.

Waste accumulates as more spending, more output, and more construction and wasteful capital spending boost bottom lines and tax revenues, keeping everybody happy at first. Eventually, this house of cards reaches a point where it is hopelessly unstable and then it collapses. Busts and crashes have several triggers. A very loose monetary policy during a bubble provokes overheating and inflation, forcing central banks to end cheap money policies. Supply chain interruptions caused by geopolitical maneuvering, foreign wars, or pandemics can send dominoes tumbling. These negative supply shocks reduce growth and increase the cost of production. Alternatively, animal spirits can wax and wane with little or no explanation, triggering outcomes last seen in the bubble of 2020-2021 followed by the bust of 2022.

Fragile economies and flawed policies are vulnerable to demand and supply shocks that arise in a world full of economic, political, and social friction. Shocks can trigger inflation or deflation with little warning. No one will forget the COVID-19 pandemic, a textbook negative demand—but also supply—shock that shut down consumption almost overnight. Positive demand shocks, by contrast, spur robust hikes in consumer sentiment, spurring higher consumption. They disrupt markets by spiking demand for something new. Electric cars and digital phones furnish classic examples.

On the production side, positive supply shocks occur when productivity gets a sharp boost from favorable changes in technology, labor supply, or regulation. Recall the internet's impact on efficiency in the workplace. Conversely, sudden drop-offs in production cause negative aggregate supply shocks—such as the ransomware attacks that shut down major US suppliers of oil and beef in 2021 or more severely the Russian invasion of Ukraine that spiked a wide range of commodity prices. Anyone old enough to remember lines at gas pumps during the 1970s knows what a global oil-supply shock looks like. Even the COVID-19 crisis was a combination of a negative demand and supply shock as we shut down economic activity to stop the spread of the virus.

Blaming crashes and recessions on random and unpredictable shocks beyond our control has led experts and policy makers to view subsequent crises through the wrong lens. There are random and unpredictable shocks in life, but that doesn't mean we can't face them honestly and prepare for a world in which we know they happen even if we don't know when.

To assert—like former Citicorp chairman Charles Prince, Moody's Corporation shareholder Warren Buffett, and Goldman Sachs Group CEO Lloyd Blankfein—that the housing bubble and ensuing bust were "unanticipated" shocks beyond the grasp of most Americans, or a "hurricane," ignores evidence and history. Consider the findings of the *Financial Crisis Inquiry Report*, an exhaustive anatomy of the events leading to the 2008 recession:

In fact, there were warning signs. In the decade preceding the collapse, there were many signs that house prices were inflated, that lending practices had spun out of control, that too many homeowners were taking on mortgages and debt they could ill afford, and that risks to the financial system were growing unchecked. Alarm bells were clanging inside financial institutions, regulatory offices, consumer service organizations, state law-enforcement agencies, and corporations throughout America as well as in neighborhoods across the country. Many knowledgeable executives saw trouble and managed to avoid the train wreck. While countless Americans joined in the financial euphoria that seized the nation, many others were shouting to government officials in Washington and within state legislatures, pointing to what would become a human disaster, not just an economic debacle.[11]

We have met the enemy, *and it is us*. Any other conclusion unleashes more risk and misapplies remedies. If you insist that the housing bubble came out of nowhere—pure "animal spirits"—then you might think it's perfectly fine to do anything, anything at all, to counteract its effects.

Central banks cut interest rates and print money. Fiscal authorities spend more, cut taxes, and increase transfers to firms and workers. The line between monetary and fiscal policy became blurred when central banks and fiscal authorities bailed out households, banks, and firms with cash shortfalls. Never mind the borrowing spree that put the economy *in extremis* in the first place, now another borrowing and spending spree ensued. More public debt piled up on top of large and growing private debt. As money becomes more plentiful, the difference between prudent borrowing and reckless borrowing blurs. Inhibitions weaken so long as asset prices are rising. Hope springs eternal and risk looks less risky.

It's a conundrum. Once a crisis erupts, there is no sure way out. Policy makers and regulators are damned if they do and damned if they don't. If they don't act, the system may crumble and a new depression may ensue. If they do act, flooding the economy with money, credit, and fiscal stimulus, they are piling on more public and private debt. Solvent businesses benefit but so do zombie corporations, households, banks, and shadow banks that bog down a more healthy and sustainable recovery. Giving more drugs to an addict in withdrawal reduces the short-term pain but makes the addiction worse or even fatal over time.

Cheap money through the mechanism of low interest rates, credit and fiscal stimulus ends up seeding subsequent asset and credit booms and busts. Each cycle reaches an inflection point with more debt until we find ourselves where we are today, in debt as far as the eye can see.

Now we are trapped. No solution is painless. Reducing debt would leave borrowers with less to spend on goods and services. Growth would slow or even stop. Raising interest rates would make debt service chokingly expensive for firms, banks, workers, and governments. Paying more in interest would divert cash away from growth-oriented investments, crippling future performance. Many firms would face bankruptcy. Debt-burdened governments might resort to higher taxes or lower spending and transfers, compounding stress in the private sector. A severe drag on growth might further unsettle the debt markets and unnerve the stock market, prerequisites for a crash when bubbles are present.

Across the developed world, we have created a megathreat by building up debt with loose money, credit, and fiscal policies. So what can authorities do? Sadly, they are almost forced to encourage borrowers, because otherwise the *"debt trap"* will slam shut at a high cost to everyone.

There is always an excuse to say hey, we're in danger of a crash, open the money, credit, and spending spigot to avoid deflation and recession. But before we do so, we should ask why crashes occur. The answer is not flattering: Crashes occur because in good times we are not smart or prudent. We do not encourage enough saving in the private and public sectors. We let lending and borrowing go crazy. We allow financial cycles to run amok until the music stops. Then we're in a bad way. What may appear to be an unforeseen shock is actually a predictable consequence of financial excesses of debt, leverage, and bubble.

We must exit this relentless boom-bust cycle if we hope to avoid a more terrible crash. We're hardwired to ramp up risk at the wrong times. Rising inflation won't rescue us from massive debt or shock us into better behavior without a collapse. It hasn't so far.

A wiser strategy starts by reappraising *de*flation or lowflation (shorthand for inflation below target). The moment regulators see or imagine deflation or lowflation they think it's bad, but that is not always the case. I agree with researchers at the Bank for International Settlements in Switzerland, where central bankers regularly convene. "Our survey of history suggests that deflations of the past fall into three broad categories: the good, the bad and the ugly," they wrote in a 2005 paper entitled "Deflation in a Historical Perspective":

In the century before World War I, price levels in many countries declined as often as they rose and, moreover, falling prices were not always associated with recessions. Indeed many deflation episodes were "good" in the sense that they were associated with productivity-driven economic growth.[12]

Policy makers regularly mischaracterize the causes of inflation. They label inflation rates below "target" (that is, in recent decades, below 2 percent) as unforeseeable declines in aggregate demand. Central bankers jump to the conclusion that bad deflation or lowflation is always at fault and dangerous. Thus, they keep interest rates stubbornly low while also continuing unconventional polices like buying long-term assets. Seeing signs of persistent economic weakness, they persistently encourage borrowing and spending that fuel déjà vu all over again.

There is an alternative scenario. Not all deflation or lowflation of the last twenty years has been *bad deflation*. Much of it reflects progress in technology, trade, globalization, migration, and a rising supply of labor worldwide as China and emerging markets joined the global economy. For an extended period, this good deflation put downward pressure on prices. Until 2021 as the pandemic waned, inflation hovered below the 2 percent target set by most advanced economies' central banks.

Flawed assumptions compound deflation's impact. Misdiagnoses apply the wrong tools and objectives. Suppose that deflation is good. Trade globalization, better technology, and ample labor supplies ease prices without harming economic health. The actual inflation rate approaches zero. Yet central banks all cling to an article of faith, that 2 percent is the proper nominal target for the inflation rate. Alarms sound. Central bankers fear that deflation and lowflation are dangerous. Then they trot out the same unconventional responses: lowering interest rates to zero and below; buying financial assets from the private sector under the banner of quantitative and credit easing; relaxing credit restrictions; and taking debt off the hands of private sector lenders. Once invoked, these policies are hard to reverse. They can remain for years, even decades, with unsatisfactory returns, as officials at the European Central Bank and the Bank of Japan can attest.

Rather than accept good deflation or lowflation as a new normal, central bankers try to cure a problem that requires no solution. They spur borrowing, because more borrowers competing for loans nudge interest rates closer to their 2 percent target. They get their wish, but it's not only unnecessary; it's counterproductive. Excess credit launches the next bubble.

This manic pattern has persisted for decades. In 1966 the Dow reached the 1,000 level and again in 1968, a burst of enthusiasm for stocks pushed it to almost 1,000 in December of that year. Investors were in love with boutique stocks of companies that sold leather boots and electronic gadgets. Conglomerates, companies that bought up other companies to maximize earnings irrespective of business lines, also stole the limelight. But after teasing investors, the Dow Jones Industrial Average went into a slide — down 36 percent to 631 in May 1970 — and would not close above 1000 again until 1972. Although the recession that began in 1969 was mild, the Federal Reserve eased monetary policies in 1970 to spur growth.[13]

Officially, oil shocks triggered two stagflationary recessions in the mid- to late 1970s. Yet with a closer look, we can see that there were fiscal and monetary roots to the crisis; it wasn't all OPEC's fault. Paying for the Vietnam War led to large fiscal and trade deficits. A fixed exchange rate for gold exposed the United States to demand for gold by foreign creditors. Rather than surrender gold reserves, the United States exited the gold standard in 1971. Other countries followed suit. No longer tied to the price of a precious metal, currencies began to float based on the economic strength and reputation of issuers free to print money at will. So the oil shocks hit a world where monetary and fiscal policies were already too loose and inflation was rising rapidly. The policy reaction was to increase interest rates less than the rise in inflation, thus keeping real rates negative. Central banks remained behind the curve and that response unhinged inflation expectations without easing high unemployment, a textbook description of stagflation.

By July 1974 the die was cast, the *New York Times* reported:

How to cure Wall Street's acute case of the jitters? There is no shortage of remedies being offered by both private and public confidence healers. The need was particularly great early this week when the Central National Bank of Cleveland raised its prime interest charge to its most creditworthy corporate borrowers to 12¼ per cent, and most major banks moved up to 12 per cent. The stock market, reciprocally, plunged.[14]

It took an ugly double-dip recession in 1980–82 with super-tight monetary policy engineered by Fed chairman Paul Volcker to wrestle inflation down to low single digits in the 1980s. Nothing since then has required such tight policies, thankfully. The Volcker remedy was painful worldwide, especially in Argentina and other Latin American countries that borrowed heavily when high oil prices seemed permanent. Growth on that continent stalled for a decade as most of its nations went bust in 1982 in what became known as the Latin American Debt Crisis, which triggered a lost decade of growth.

Winning the battle with inflation has a long-lasting dark side: it reinforces overconfidence. The American and global scars from the double-dip recession led to easy money and credit after 1982. By the time President Reagan ran for reelection in 1984, the next credit bubble was heating up, fed by loose regulations of lending to real estate. Indeed, a recession in 1990–91 followed a real estate bubble that took down lenders, mainly hundreds of savings and loan institutions (S&Ls) ill equipped for the real estate lending risks they assumed.

Congress gave thrift lenders the rope to hang themselves by passing two pieces of legislation that heightened competition with Wall Street. Depository Institutions Deregulation in 1980 and the Garn–St. Germain Depository Institutions Act of 1982 released thrifts from restrictions imposed during the Depression that capped interest on savings and checking accounts.

Accustomed to issuing and retaining home mortgages and paying depositors a lower rate than borrowers paid, most savings and loans were no match for nimble financial firms geared to buying, selling, and trading residential and commercial mortgages, many of them speculative.

The need for financial institutions that cater to home buyers spawned the thrift industry a century ago. Lenders operating as savings and loans or savings banks sold mortgages and kept them until they matured. A sleepy business performed a useful service while commercial banks lent money to companies with revenue.

Then Wall Street learned how to create and trade securities based on the income from thousands of mortgages. Constrained by regulation and culture, thrifts could not compete. When inflation spurted in the seventies they owned mortgages with below-market interest rates, losing money every day. A lid on their interest rates deterred new deposits that funded new mortgages. Wall Street and commercial banks, meanwhile, seldom owned mortgages for more than an instant before selling them to investors.

When interest rates eased and real estate began to boom, thrifts suffered a fatal blow. They raced into the boom by lending in the hottest markets. When the boom became a bust, those that survived could only limp out.

The short-term economic damage looked relatively brief and mild compared to the stagflation of the prior decade. Regulators closed insolvent thrifts and moved assets to more stable institutions. Most depositors were protected. Yet long-term carnage was coming; it just took a while to unfold. The real estate bust pushed the Federal Reserve to slash policy rates to 3 percent from 8 percent from 1989 to 1992, a tectonic shift as interest rates go. The Fed kept rates low to accelerate job growth that did not happen fast enough to help President George H. W. Bush win his 1992 bid for reelection against candidate Bill Clinton.

The 1990s are remembered as the beginning of the period of Great Moderation: "good lowflation" arose chiefly from the internet and its sweeping boost to productivity, keeping a lid on price increases that usually accompany low unemployment and stable growth.

Yet outside the United States, the 1990s featured global financial instability and crises fed by loose monetary policies. Following vigorous deregulation of its banks, Sweden and other Scandinavian economies experienced turmoil that foreshadowed the global financial crisis. "Banks, mortgage institutions, finance companies, and others now entered a new environment where they were free to compete on the domestic credit market," according to author Peter Englund in a report on the Swedish banking crisis:

> The impact of the deregulation was immediately apparent. The rate of increase of new lending from financial institutions, which varied between 11 and 17 percent per year during the first half of the 1980s, jumped to 20 percent in 1986. Over the 5 year period, 1986-1990, lending increased by 136 percent (73 percent in real terms).[15]

As in the United States, Swedish legislators and policy makers stood aside despite record low unemployment and prices rising faster than in other countries. The Swedish stock market posted a 42 percent gain for the year in 1989. Days later, a major Swedish finance company with extensive exposure to real estate could not roll over its short-term loans vital to daily cash flow, a scenario that would topple major Wall Street firms in 2008. "The crisis spread to the whole market," Englund reported, "which dried up in a couple of days."

Five of Sweden's finance houses defaulted on their short-term loan programs in 1990. Two of six major banks eventually failed to meet capital requirements and received bailouts. A third bank defaulted.

Next came upheaval in Europe's exchange rate mechanism (ERM), the means by which pounds sterling, deutschmarks, French francs, Italian lira, and other currencies set their relative values before the euro displaced them. "The dress rehearsal for the ERM crisis was staged in Scandinavia," concluded the authors of a report published by the economics department at Princeton University.[16] Once again, overvalued currencies across the United Kingdom and Europe—that were associated with large trade deficits spawned by loose monetary and fiscal policies—set events in motion.

There were troubles, too, in Mexico when its semi-fixed currency collapsed in late 1994 and 1995, and shortly afterward in 1997, when massive private sector foreign debt sent East Asian currencies into free fall. Soon afterward, currency and other balance of payments and debt crises hit a wide range of emerging market economies, including Ecuador, Brazil, Russia, Argentina, Turkey, Pakistan, and Ukraine. "Against obvious differences in their dynamics and underlying causes," wrote the authors of the Princeton report, "the currency crises of the 1990s are alike in sharing a rapid and 'contagious' propagation of speculative waves from the original country or group of countries under attack to an entire region having (perceived) comparable macroeconomic features."[17] This publication appeared in 1998—ample warning, you'd think: a full decade before the global financial crisis.

By 1996 the new internet was leading to an economic boom and a rapid rise of the new internet stocks on the tech-heavy Nasdaq market. This was the beginning of the dot-com bubble. The Fed could have tightened monetary and credit policy to slow borrowing that inflates a bubble. But it did not, and its restraint thrilled stockholders who hoped the good times would never stop. Events half a world away ended the festivities. A currency crisis in Asia and unexpected default by Russia roiled global markets. Capital dried up.

Without the liquidity essential to keeping them afloat, highly leveraged hedge funds felt the squeeze. Long-Term Capital Management (LTCM) led the pack with investments valued at nearly one hundred times its net worth, the equivalent of owning a $1 million home with a $990,000 mortgage. When financial assets lose value, hedge funds need to cover losses. In the case of LTCM it was devastating and contagious. Its failure exposed the entire US financial system to a crash and recession. Desperation forced the Fed to arrange a private bailout of LTCM by all its creditors—major US and foreign banks. Then with the economy already overheating in the thrall of dot-com stocks, the Fed actually cut interest rates to stabilize wobbly financial markets roiled by LTCM.

Yet again, monetary easing, intended as a solution, fueled a bubble. The Nasdaq shot higher to the applause of investors posting huge gains. It was beyond time to remove the punchbowl by tightening access to credit, yet the Fed resisted doing so.

By now, any stock in a company with any claim to a digital future was red-hot. Do you remember Pets.com and Webvan, or Worldcom and Global Crossing? With so many companies skyrocketing in paper value, the phrase "irrational exuberance" was coined by economist Robert Shiller. The dot-com craze popped in 2000, erasing three-fourths of the market value of technology stocks listed on the Nasdaq. By 2002, a time frame that included the deadly attack on the World Trade Center, the Dow Jones Industrial Average tumbled by 43 percent.

The dot-com bust led to the demise of many firms—tech and otherwise—that had loaded themselves with debt. The stress also exposed sloppy management and shenanigans that skirted or broke rules. Corporate scandals featured a string of highly visible collapses by Enron, WorldCom, and Tyco, companies leveraged to the max.

Yet once again, the Federal Reserve hit the gas. The rate with immediate impact is the rate at which the Fed lends money to member banks every day. In just a year, the so-called fed funds rate tumbled to 1 percent, a historic low, from 6.5 percent. The rate remained at 1 percent for two years until the recession formally ended after eight quarters of growth in the GDP.

Rates eventually began to climb, but only at a snail's pace compared to the abrupt drop. It took three years for the fed funds rate to reach 5.25 percent in 2006. Meanwhile, borrowers flocked to new asset sectors. Housing and subprime loans surged in popularity. Low rates and regulators on siesta fostered a climate of anything goes by aggressive lenders.

Is it any wonder that low interest rates and lax supervision produce reckless behavior? Enter the mass marketing of mortgage securities with dubious creditworthiness. Myriad accounts—including my own book *Crisis Economics*—tell the story that caused millions of homeowners to default in 2007–09, hundreds of banks to fail, and prominent Wall Street firms to close their doors.

But what did the Federal Reserve do to rescue the economy from the global financial crisis? It lowered interest rates to zero, meaning it pays no interest on reserve funds it holds for banks against their loan portfolios. It also started and amped up quantitative and credit easing by purchasing long-term bonds and residential mortgage-backed securities. By assuming ownership of these securities, the Fed furnished banks with cash to expand lending at low rates. The race was on, and its ethos was not complicated: lend more, borrow more, and let the devil take the hindmost.

When a first generation of quantitative easing ran its course, others followed: QE1, QE2, QE3. Successive rounds featured looser restrictions. Seeing no end, investors started joking, but only half in jest, about "QE-infinity." As money floods into assets that central banks used to abjure, massive bailouts loom. Bravo, if you enjoy more boom-and-bust cycles.

The dust from the global financial crisis had barely settled when households, businesses, and governments availed themselves of low interest rates and started pushing debt to still greater levels, capped by a massive $1.5 trillion Trump tax cut in 2017 that spiked the US federal deficit to more than a trillion dollars per year in a year of good economic growth. While banks were being more carefully regulated, shadow banks proliferated, creating financial arrangements that kept risk beyond the scope of regulators and fed a corporate debt bubble. From 2014 on it was the time when corporate debt exploded, especially among risky and leveraged firms as well as "fallen angels," a term for companies whose high debt caused their credit ratings to plummet from investment grade to junk bond levels.

Non-bank financial institutions created new forms of risk lending. Covenant-lite loans had weak protections for lenders in case of default. Collateralized loan obligations (CLOs) that securitized bundles of corporate loans resembled infamous securitized collateralized debt obligations (CDOs) of the subprime crisis. Toxic schemes make risky debt fashionable in the short run but soon wreak havoc. By 2019, before the COVID-19 crisis, even the Fed and the IMF were sending warnings about the rising and risky forms of corporate borrowing.

Here we go again, starting the next bubble that down the line will precipitate the next crash and bust. Exit ramps seem closed. In the years immediately preceding the pandemic, central bankers maintained loose policies because inflation was deemed to be too low. Did they forget what happened after the global financial crisis? Under a de facto fourth round of quantitative easing, in 2019 the Federal Reserve increased the amount of money in circulation and reduced interest rates well before the COVID-19 crisis, as a trade dispute between the United States and China slowed growth.

After the Global Financial Crisis other advanced economies jumped on the bandwagon. They unveiled their own unconventional monetary policies. In Europe and Japan, policy rates slipped below zero. They went negative, meaning central banks are paid by banks to hold cash reserves instead of paying interest rates.

Boundaries keep expanding. Besides allowing the purchase of public bonds, monetary policy in Europe and Japan permits central banks to buy corporate bonds. In Japan, even stocks and real estate assets are permissible. If you still don't believe the world is awash in too much cash, by 2019 the equivalent of $17 trillion resided in government and private bonds, with maturities up to ten years with negative nominal yields—meaning the yield borrowers promise to pay is negative. In other words, lenders pay borrowers to borrow, rather than the reverse.

At long last the Fed had started lifting interest rates slowly, in mid-2017. The plan was to reach 3.25 percent in 2019. Yet private and public borrowers held so much debt that small upticks in the interest rate jolted them. A pivotal gap widened between the interest rate on benchmark Treasury securities—that is, those with no risk of default—and bonds with equivalent maturities from issuers who did bring a risk of default. It signaled anxiety by lenders. Credit spreads spiked for corporate borrowers. The stock market fell by 20 percent in the fourth quarter of 2018. That's what caused the Fed to go back for more quantitative easing, and to stop raising rates. They were trapped—they couldn't stop feeding the beast.

Indeed, by January 2019 the Fed reversed its course. Chairman Jerome Powell announced that the Fed would pause rate hikes and quantitative tightening. A few months later the recovery started losing steam. Exotic financial securities that go by names like repurchase agreements (repos, for short) got locked out of capital markets. The Fed braced for a downturn in the usual way. It cut rates below 2 percent and resumed quantitative easing. Almost a year before the COVID-19 crisis changed everything, the Fed could not stomach even a modest dose of policy tightening. Instead, it stepped right back into a debt trap.

COVID-19 was a shock no one could have predicted precisely, although the risk of some sort of pandemic was already on the minds of medical experts. In March 2020 the stock market plunged, millions of Americans lost their jobs, and the economy threatened to seize up, with every lender hoarding cash, and no money circulating to keep the economy moving. To their credit, regulators worried about overhanging debt. But their hands were tied. Banks, shadow banks, hedge funds, private equity funds, broker dealers, small and medium businesses, and mortgage holders could not pay lenders, given their high debt burdens. Debt markets tottered. The only option for the Fed was to keep the money coming fast and furious at a speed and pace and extent much larger than ever, greater even than 2008.

By late 2020 and 2021 we were emerging from the pandemic with tons of debt, fiscal deficits spiking, and looser monetary policy than at any time in history. Have policy makers learned their lesson? Yes and no. They have signaled renewed inclination to finance huge deficits by printing money instead of issuing debt. Besides quantitative easing and zero interest rates, policy makers seem to want to make debt monetization a permanent feature of central banking.

Where will that approach lead? To bubbles everywhere ready to burst: stocks, cryptocurrencies, hedge funds going crazy on risk, uninformed investors taking on short sellers over GameStop, millions of Gen Z and Gen X day traders spending their meager savings and fiscal transfers to bet on stocks, private equity groups and corporations borrowing like never before and, to top it off, housing prices going through the roof. And stock prices rose by about 100 percent between their bottom in March of 2020 and the end of 2021, with P/E ratios well above historical averages.

I don't mean to imply that no one is minding the store to stop bubbles from getting too big. On the contrary, many smart people are trying to do just that. It's an immense challenge. The problem is not inattention, ill intention, or negligence. It's the fact that every decision in the macroeconomic sphere has gigantic stakes attached. The wrong call can cause a lot of damage.

To mitigate damage, a welter of rules and regulations has emerged since the global financial crisis. The traditional focus on maintaining sound individual financial institutions has turned by necessity to a larger realm. "Keeping individual financial institutions sound is not enough," the International Monetary Fund has warned. "Policy makers need a broader approach to safeguard the financial system as a whole. They can use *macro-prudential* policy to achieve this goal." That's a fancy way to say, let's think about the aggregate picture, not just the moving parts.

There are two types of macro-prudential intervention that the Fed thinks about. One is permanent. It says to build up walls of capital so that even if the bubble bursts, banks will survive. It's a way to brace for trouble. This is a structural approach to macro-prudential policy.

The other approach is cyclical. It says that as the buildup and frothiness of private sector debt rises, we can curtail dangerous credit cycles by imposing greater restrictions on borrowing. The cyclical approach tries to decompress bubbles before they become volatile. It relies on precise timing—and timing always spurs a lively debate. Who can say if the peak is a week away, a month away, or a year away? This makes regulators reluctant to intervene. No one wants to curtail growth, not even the Federal Reserve, whose job has traditionally been to do just that before the party gets too heated. Where booms and busts are concerned, structural solutions prevail. You might say that macro-prudential regulation favors drainage systems over floodgates. This is shortsighted and not sustainable.

Moreover, history suggests that macro-prudential policies cannot stop a bubble when monetary policy is too loose for too long. Authorities must raise interest rates to stop bubbles from forming in the first place. But the ideology of all major central banks resists using monetary policy to prick a bubble. They rely instead on unproven and ineffective macro-prudential policies that usually don't work even when tried. Thus, we keep on feeding the debt supercycle. And while loose policies cause asset bubbles in the short run, in the medium term they eventually lead to inflation of goods and services, as the next chapter will show.

Keynesian and Austrian-school economists offer competing solutions in the boom-bust drama. Keynesians favor intervention; Austrians favor austerity and debt restructuring or reduction over bailouts. If you are purely Austrian at the beginning of the bursting of a bubble, where there's a collapse of aggregate demand, you might end up with another great depression, as history shows.

I prefer a middle course. My view has always been that policy makers should be Keynesian at the beginning of a cycle, when there is illiquidity. Yet they should not stay Keynesian forever because the buildup of easy money, easy credit, and easy fiscal eventually precipitates the next boom-and-bust cycle. They must break the addiction to easy money.

Look at the new crop of central bankers. A few years ago we had outstanding economists like Ben Bernanke and Janet Yellen heading the Federal Reserve, Mario Draghi at the European Central Bank, and Mark Carney at the Bank of England. They were central bankers with cachet and with advanced degrees in economics. Even so, they were stuck in the debt trap. After the Greenspan put we got the Bernanke put, the Yellen put, and now the Powell put. Tactics vary but all have the same bottom line: when debt and equity markets wobble, central banks will come to their rescue.

If central bankers schooled in economics and boom-and-bust cycles are locked in a debt trap, it's even harder to be sanguine without seasoned economists in command. The watch has changed. In 2021, former law-yers Christine Lagarde and Jay Powell ran the European Central Bank and the Federal Reserve. Martin Bailey at the Bank of England came from banking operations, not a background steeped in monetary policy.

So what have central banks become when the fig leaf of their inde-pendence has been ripped off as debts mount? They have strayed from a rigorous focus on the long-term big picture. Instead, they take cues from politicians and leveraged investors who cater to every wind of change. When short-term goals dictate policy, they lean heavily on easy money and credit because that is what voters want and leveraged markets need to avoid crashing.

The macro economy is no game and experts should never look at it that way. But it's also fair to say that a misdiagnosis has been harmful. We've wandered into a conundrum by following the rules in the wrong way. Easy money and credit and loose fiscal policies won't save us from relentless boom-and-bust cycles. They will cast us into a debt supercycle. We need to adjust the rules to stop this debt trap. If we don't, nobody wins, and everybody will crash and lose during the next mega-crisis.

So far we have dissected a pattern of parallel macroeconomic threats that can trigger severe short-term market disruptions and recessions. We've been there before. Now we're entering uncharted territory where threats converge. Should that occur, expect much more alarming conse-quences, namely, the worst period of stagflation that the world has ever seen.

Chapter 5

The Coming Great Stagflation

Fears of economic misery conjure the Great Depression for most people.

We teeter now on a different precipice: not depression, but stagflation. Recall the 1970s, a decade that featured bubbles, busts, an end to the global gold exchange standard, devaluation of the dollar, mounting debt, risky financial innovation, monetary and fiscal experimentation, and oil supply shocks driven by geopolitical shocks. It all culminated in double-digit inflation, stubborn unemployment, and persistent recession. That is the corrosive condition known as stagflation, or stagnation with inflation.

As economic headaches go, the seventies checked nearly every box. But who remembers all that upheaval? The world since the seventies has looked very different, at least prior to the Great Recession of 2008. For thirty years, we faced brief and mild recessions and relatively quick rebounds. Even taking the Great Recession into account, we have enjoyed four decades of robust employment and mostly positive growth, accompanied by low inflation. A stream of innovations, globalization, immigration, weak labor and unions, and billions of workers from China, India, and other emerging markets helped improve productivity and kept a lid on prices.

This congenial climate earned a label: *the Great Moderation.*

After wrestling stagflation under control in the early 1980s, most experts expected the Great Moderation to last. The Federal Reserve could always turn the money supply spigot on or off to achieve desired results. Lower interest rates and looser credit could spur growth and avoid deflation. Higher interest rates and tighter credit could cool overheating, excessive growth, and rising inflation.

"One of the most striking features of the economic landscape over the past twenty years or so has been a substantial decline in macroeconomic volatility," former Fed chairman Ben Bernanke declared in February 2004.[1] He credited multiple factors that altered the structure of the financial economy. He also predicted the continuation of this Great Moderation — just three years before a major upheaval struck.

The Global Financial Crisis of 2007–9 soon challenged the idea that all was under control. But did it change anything fundamental about how central bankers and policy makers approached their jobs? The chaos was blamed on greedy lenders and shadow bankers, reckless home buyers, lax regulators and credit rating agencies, mispricing of risk, and myopic government agendas aimed at boosting home ownership. Couldn't we just tighten up a few loopholes, perform some stress tests on banks, pass new financial regulations, and continue on our merry way?

Some critics noted deeper problems. William A. Barnett, the Oswald Distinguished Professor of Macroeconomics at the University of Kansas and a director at the Center for Financial Stability in New York, gave a blunt assessment of one such problem — the data available to the regulators — in his book *Getting It Wrong: How Faulty Monetary Statistics Undermine the Fed, the Financial System, and the Economy*. About the idea that the Fed really knew what it was doing, he responded:

It was not true. It was all a myth. There were no great improvements in monetary policy design, which was based fundamentally on the same approach used for over half a century. The sources of those appearances of improvements were developments outside the Federal Reserve system. The one genuine, noteworthy change in Fed activities was the decline in data quality. When more and better data were needed by the private sector, as the complexity of financial products grew, the quantity and quality of Fed data declined.[2]

Indeed, the growth of nontransparent, complex, hard-to-price new financial derivatives in mortgages and credit—among other markets—created mushrooming, toxic financial instruments whose risks were hard to measure and assess. But the Global Financial Crisis was driven by much more than the lack of good macro data. Experts love to dissect trouble in the rearview mirror. Most pause at trouble ahead. They dismissed me in 2006 when I warned that a giant housing and credit bubble put the entire global financial system in peril. I showed them the data to no avail. I feel the same pushback now when I warn about the risks ahead.

While others debate whether inflation has staying power, I say: brace for stagflation that combines recession and high unemployment with high inflation that stifles job growth. Conditions are ripe. Easy money inflates the price of assets and goods while spiking credit growth, but massive debt rules out policy responses that can curb inflation. Forty years ago the Federal Reserve raised policy rates to almost 20 percent. That solution, draconian in 1980–82 when it caused a severe double-dip recession, would be worse than draconian. It would be fatal today, given the debt trap we are in now. With inflation simmering and surging, any persistent policy rate changes that reduce growth and increase the cost of money to fight inflation can shock us back into stagflation and a debt crisis if other negative supply shocks emerge.

People looked at me as if I'd lost my senses when I spoke about the risks of stagflation, as I did starting in 2021 in a series of articles,[3] just like after my presentation in 2006 at the IMF. Heads nod but nothing changes. Instead of connecting the dots right in front of them, audiences say, *we need a stiff drink.*

What they need is the philosopher George Santayana. "Those who cannot remember the past," he famously warned, "are condemned to repeat it."

We have reached the tipping point of a debt supercycle. Loose monetary and fiscal policies now court disaster. Recession and high interest rates will hobble all but the sturdiest institutions, banks, global corporations, and countries. Runaway inflation will pummel advanced economies as well as emerging markets. Structural deficiencies will become existential threats. If Italy collapses again, and Germany opts not to bail Italy out, then *sic transit* the eurozone.

Global consumers and investors have been conditioned over four decades to expect growing worldwide markets amid tame inflation. Will they be able to handle prolonged stagflation? I doubt it. Profits will tumble. Payrolls will fall. Wealth will vanish. Growth will cease. We will reckon with an observation by Sir Jonathan Stephen Cunliffe, a former Deputy Governor of the Bank of England for Financial Stability. "Money," said Sir Jon, "is in the end a social convention that can be very fragile under stress."[4]

The seventies tested this fragile social convention. To measure stress, economist Arthur Okun invented the misery index: a simple addition of the percentage rate of inflation with the percentage rate of unemployment. "What better gauge of our economic misery," asked the popular syndicated columnist Sylvia Porter, "than the murderous squeeze on us resulting from a simultaneous rise in joblessness and soaring living costs?"[5]

If inflation is 2 percent and unemployment is 4 percent, the misery index equals 6. The misery index—then in the high double digits—helped candidate Jimmy Carter replace Gerald Ford. Four years later, with the misery index even higher, candidate Ronald Reagan convinced voters to elect him and ditch Carter.

Prepare to revisit the seventies and dust off the misery index. In 2022 the misery index was back to double digits in spite of a low unemployment rate as inflation got above 8 percent. We are due for lasting turmoil.

Remembering the past can help us predict what will happen in the future.

The seventies began on the heels of robust economic growth after World War II, tempered by two ultra-expensive initiatives: the war in Vietnam and the war on poverty along with the expansion of the welfare state. Investors who expected the seventies to resemble the two previous decades soon experienced disappointment. Economists Charles Goodhart and Manoj Pradhan label the period from the end of the Korean War until 1973 "a golden age for macroeconomics." Monetary and fiscal strategies produced expected results. "It all then went horribly wrong in the 1970s."[6]

Things went to pieces because large budget deficits had financed the Vietnam War and the domestic social programs of the Great Society. Overspending leading to economic overheating nudged inflation upward. In response, the Federal Reserve only modestly raised interest rates to stem rising inflation. In the ensuing recession in 1970, output shrank only a little, by less than 1 percent. A mild recession ended in November 1970. And yet its impact persisted.

In the stock market, the Dow Jones Industrial Average, after nearly closing above 1,000 in 1968, was hovering below 800 in November 1970.[7] These were not glory days for the markets and the economy.

Labor was unified, muscular, and ready to rumble. Strikes and work stoppages paralyzed key industries. The Bureau of Labor Statistics counted 5,716 strikes in 1970, involving 3 million workers.

These conditions produced inflation, not jobs. Ordinarily, low unemployment means the economy is humming. Something was odd, however. Demand for goods, capital, and labor tends to promote inflation. Conversely, inflation falls if unemployment is high because workers have less bargaining power over wages and firms don't have much pricing power as demand is weak. "Despite the persistence of unemployment at roughly 6 percent since last November," the *New York Times* reported in May 1971, "inflation still dogs the American economy."[8] Inflation then exceeded 4 percent.

President Richard Nixon fashioned an economic package as his reelection campaign approached. It was designed to stimulate US industry "with the clear hope this will produce many more jobs and cut that menacing unemployment rate," the *Iowa City Press Citizen* reported in August 1971.[9]

A dominant postwar dollar pegged to gold gave the United States bragging rights, but it imposed a competitive disadvantage on domestic companies competing abroad. Companies based in countries with weaker currencies and high productivity growth, notably Germany and Japan, could sell competitive products for less, an edge that China enjoys nowadays. Exports grew weakly as imports increased. Spending outpaced the country's income. Thus, a trade deficit ballooned.

When the United States runs a trade deficit it borrows from abroad to finance the gap in the balance of payments. Foreigners accumulate claims in dollars. Whether claims reside in the United States or abroad does not matter. They are liabilities owed ultimately to foreign creditors by US residents.

American dollars had been backed by gold since 1945. Yet that backing was a confidence builder more than a practical mechanism—in fact, the United States could not exchange all existing dollars for the gold in its vaults. When the French government called the US bluff and requested gold in exchange for its dollar assets at the fixed exchange rates of $35 per ounce, the United States balked. Top advisers warned President Nixon that the fixed exchange rates had to go. The gold-exchange standard regime was no longer sustainable, given the persistent US trade deficits. At first, President Nixon suspended gold redemptions. Then, in 1971, he exercised the nuclear option: the United States stopped pretending and exited the gold-exchange standard. From then on, the dollar would be a floating currency, with exchange rates for other countries' currencies determined by the free market.

Without a gold standard to restrict the money supply, the United States had new policy options. It could print money, cut interest rates to encourage lending, and let the dollar weaken over time. Moving from fixed to floating exchange rates caused dollars to lose value *vis à vis* other currencies. Surging imports got more expensive. Increased prices fed inflation.

In this new climate, a group of stocks flourished. Investors poured their faith into so-called one-decision blue chip stocks with resilient earnings and P/E ratios. Once bought, there was no need to sell them. These were supposedly timeless, rock-solid companies like General Motors, Exxon, Coca-Cola, IBM, Xerox, Pfizer, and Polaroid. "The delusion was that these companies were so good, it didn't matter what you paid for them; their inexorable growth would bail you out," *Forbes Magazine* explained.[10]

Dubbed the Nifty Fifty, a handy moniker more than a precise list, their price to earnings multiples soared far above levels than historical valuations warranted.[11] As *USA Today* later recounted, "Their popularity among institutional and individual investors sparked a quantum shift from 'value' investing to a 'growth at any price' mentality that resurfaced with a vengeance in the tech-stock bubble a quarter century later."[12]

In January 1973 stocks succumbed to rising prices, stubborn unemployment, increasing interest rates, the end of the postwar monetary agreement, and the Watergate scandal that would force Nixon to resign in August 1974. The Dow Jones Industrial Average ended September 1974 just shy of 608, down 36 percent in a year and just ten points above the close in July 1962.[13] The Nifty Fifty were not spared. Their prices tumbled along with the market as a whole.

And then came a jolt that altered the global landscape and still reverberates today. In October 1973, conflict between Israel and its Arab neighbors—the Yom Kippur War—mobilized the Organization of the Petroleum Exporting Countries (OPEC). Twelve Arab nations imposed an oil embargo against the United States and other Western countries that enjoyed friendly ties with Israel. The embargo led to a tripling of oil prices in a matter of months, spiking an already rising inflation and triggering a severe recession in 1974–75. Nations shuddered. Consumers panicked. Firms lurched on the verge of default.

Americans who remember the '70s can vividly recall long lines at gas stations. I remember visiting London with my father in the winter of 1974. It was the holiday season. Piccadilly Circus was dark. All the festive lights were off or dimmed, including Christmas trees. Oil-dependent countries were under siege. Fuel prices shot up and other prices and wages followed. The Justice Department and the Council on Wage Stability initiated studies of skyrocketing prices, notably for sugar, which outpaced increases for all other foods.[14] Even the prices of sugar-free drinks rose. Overall in 1974, inflation spiked for the first time in decades to a double-digit rate, 11.4 percent.

The times were unforgiving, in some dimensions worse even than the Great Depression, according to columnist Sylvia Porter. She blamed inflation. "In one sense, this has been the worst slump of all. For in 1929–1932, prices at least fell too along with incomes—but this time, they galloped at the start of the decline and even now, 18 months later, are still climbing at an intolerable rate."[15]

Sharply rising interest rates garnered news in July 1974 in the *New York Times*. "The need was particularly great early this week when the Central National Bank of Cleveland raised its prime interest charge to its most creditworthy corporate borrowers to 12¼ per cent, and most major banks moved up to 12 per cent. The stock market, reciprocally, plunged."[16]

Attempts to control inflation had a dismal track record. In a 1971 televised address when inflation was still modest, President Nixon imposed a freeze on all prices and wages for ninety days. He formed a Pay Board and a Price Commission to weigh the merits of any increases. A pause in inflation spiked supply shortages. Nixon wanted to suppress inflation while running for reelection. Inflation refused to comply. It surged again in early 1973. Nixon reimposed price and wage controls in June. That failed again. As Daniel Yergin and Joseph Stanislaw explain in *The Commanding Heights*, their classic book on the period: "Ranchers stopped shipping their cattle to the market, farmers drowned their chickens, and consumers emptied the shelves of supermarkets."[17]

Then the oil shock and embargo of 1973 struck, leading to a more severe recession. President Nixon resigned in August 1974, ending the Watergate scandal. In October, President Gerald Ford enlisted every American in the battle against inflation with the WIN (Whip Inflation Now) motto and related pin buttons.

All the president's horses and all of his men could not put the economy back together again. WIN was a flop. Inflation whipped the administration into sinking popularity rather than the other way around. The misery index kept notching new highs and soon ended Mr. Ford's administration.

Enter Jimmy Carter, who had no good permanent solution, even if he had been catapulted into power by a surge in the misery index and the Watergate scandal. Inflation eased a little, thanks mainly to the severe recession of 1974–75 that paused wage demands. Growth resumed in 1976. Inflation and unemployment remained stubbornly high. Prices kept rising. Incomes could not match the pace. "The rules considered inviolable for generations don't work any more," wrote the pundit Paul Harvey in June 1977. "We are still bedeviled by too much inflation and too much unemployment at the same time."[18]

Stagflation became a household word that few could comprehend. "Economists have viewed stagflation the way a physicist would view an object suspended in midair in violation of the laws of gravity — as a scientific obscenity," wrote Columbia University sociology professor Amitai Etzioni in a column for *Businessweek*. "And being unable to understand stagflation they have, of course, encountered difficulties in trying to find ways to deal with it."[19]

Etzioni urged economists to weigh factors other than supply and demand. "To suggest that stagflation is a mystery merely indicates that one has elected to view the world through narrow econometric lenses rather than more widely through social and political as well as economic ones," he wrote. "There is a problem here, but if there is a mystery, it is in the eye of the beholder, not in the real world."

By early 1979 the Islamic revolution in Iran led to a second oil shock, another oil embargo, another spike in oil prices, even higher inflation, and a return to outright stagflation. While fiscal and monetary policy had remained loose after the first oil shock, feeding the inflation rate, inflation nearly doubled to 13.3 percent in 1979. And then, finally, came the decisive intervention: besieged by critics, Carter chose inflation hawk Paul Volcker to head the Federal Reserve.

Volcker attacked inflation as directed: with relentless, single-minded focus. To slow loan demand, the Fed cranked up the fed funds interest rate to 20 percent. Borrow at that rate and interest will exceed the value of a loan in less than four years. No business or homeowner can sustain such a pace. The draconian monetary tightening, in tandem with the oil shock, did halt inflation. But at a steep cost. It precipitated a double-dip recession in 1980 and 1982, the first of which (along with the Tehran hostage crisis) cost Jimmy Carter his job.

In June 1981, a *New York Times* headline posed the question on most minds: "Reagan: Can He Cure Inflation?" The new president inherited thorny challenges: double-digit inflation, double-digit interest rates, lagging savings and investment, sluggish productivity growth, chronic unemployment, and slipping competitiveness in global markets. "These problems add up to a complex economic disorder known, for want of a better term, as stagflation," the *Times* reported. "Mr. Reagan's campaign for the Presidency was based chiefly on his commitment to break the hold of stagflation on the American economy."[20]

Breaking that hold tested nerves on an epic scale. "This year will mark the start of an experiment to resolve a national economic crisis that is comparable to the program begun by the New Deal nearly half a century ago," said the *Times*, calling stagflation "in many ways a more baffling problem than depression."[21] President Roosevelt had one job: get Americans back to work—at any cost. Mr. Reagan had to solve chronic inflation in combination with unemployment and sluggish growth.

The painful answer came in the form of keeping interest rates at nosebleed levels, bringing the second dip of the double-dip recession. When the air traffic controllers went on strike, Reagan fired them all—sending a message that no union workers were irreplaceable. That helped dampen wage demands. But ultimately, it was Paul Volcker's crippling interest rates that brought inflation rates back down from their stratospheric heights. Reagan finally declared victory over stagflation in 1983.

What ultimately explains the stagflation that the United States and other advanced economies experienced in the 1970s? The short answer: oil shocks together with a misguided policy response that released restraints on inflation expectations.

Oil shocks, like all negative aggregate supply shocks, reduce potential growth and increase production costs. That puts pressure on companies that use oil; they must trim payrolls and/or raise prices. Loose monetary policy lowers the cost of capital, helping companies maintain payrolls until demand resumes. But it feeds further costs and price increases.

In the late 1960s, the Phillips curve furnished a way to align inflation and unemployment targets. It hinges on an inverse relationship: inflation in wages and prices stays low when unemployment is high, chiefly because workers lack the power to negotiate higher pay and firms lack the power to boost prices. The curve follows a path where inflation and unemployment levels move in opposite directions. In theory, setting monetary and fiscal policy to affect demand will move inflation and unemployment in desired directions along that curve. Higher inflation leads to lower unemployment rates; lower inflation leads to higher unemployment.

That's the neat theory, at least. The reality is thornier. Good intentions in the form of loose monetary policy can backfire, especially when unemployment exceeds a basic structural level (sometimes labeled NAIRU, or Non-Accelerating Inflation Rate of Unemployment) where a typical amount of economic and technological change keeps some job seekers out of work at all times. That level tends to fluctuate within a narrow range, certainly under 5 percent in the United States. Yet when a negative supply shock occurs, that level is higher, and attempts to keep employment at pre-shock levels will only cause higher inflation by increasing inflation expectations.

Milton Friedman earned a Nobel Prize for exposing a shift in the Phillips curve. If loose monetary policies try to push unemployment below its normal, structural level, inflation expectations rise. Workers and firms seek increases in wages and prices that suppress demand. Less demand means fewer jobs. Unemployment sees no improvement, but inflation increases. So the long term Phillips curve is vertical. The unemployment rate needs to be at its structural level and any attempt to reduce it below that level will cause ever rising inflation.

OPEC delivered two major supply shocks that shifted the Phillips curve. Policy missteps compounded their ill effects. Traditional economic theory recommends financing temporary shocks—pumping up the money supply, lowering interest rates and providing a debt-financed fiscal stimulus—and adjusting behavior to permanent shocks. If I lose my job but I'm likely to find another in a few months, then it makes sense to borrow funds and continue my normal spending until I get back on my feet. If, however, the job loss is permanent and replacing my income is unlikely, for example, because of a health issue that impairs my productivity, then my lifestyle and spending must be adjusted to match my new circumstances. Otherwise, I'll go bankrupt.

The oil shocks were permanent—OPEC was a new force that would continue to act as a bloc, for the most part. That increased the real price of oil on a permanent basis and reduced the future growth of oil importing economies. That also raised the structural level of unemployment. The right policy response should have accepted those unpleasant facts. Tight monetary and fiscal policies, rather than loose ones, could have prevented runaway inflation. Had tighter monetary and fiscal policies prevailed, the oil shock would not have caused wages and prices to spiral across the board. Growth would have stumbled, and unemployment might have ticked up, but economies would have averted successive years of corrosive inflation.

Instead, the United States and other advanced economies reacted as if oil shocks were temporary, so they increased interest rates less than necessary to control rising inflation and financed the shock with loose fiscal policies. We did not adjust expectations about permanently lower living standards, but rather, we financed and fed the permanent shock. Loose monetary and fiscal policies encouraged borrowing to sustain employment and consumption. The ugly result, as Friedman predicted, produced higher inflation and stubborn unemployment, the roots of stagflation.

Are we now really heading again toward higher inflation and stagflation? Mounting evidence began suggesting as much in 2021 to anyone following the financial news. Inflation, the precursor to stagflation, flared up thanks to the COVID-19 shock, which was both a negative supply and demand shock. The COVID-19 recession led to massive and unprecedented monetary and fiscal stimulus in 2020–21 that, together with global supply chain bottlenecks, commodity price surges, and a shrinkage in labor supply, nudged inflation rates to levels not seen since the 1980s. Things got worse in 2022, when some observers hoped that the fading of the COVID-19 contagion would reduce the supply bottlenecks that cause inflation. Instead, the Russian invasion of Ukraine raised the price of commodities that Russia and Ukraine supply: oil and natural gas, industrial metals, fertilizers and agricultural goods. Then the Omicron variant of COVID-19 struck China. A draconian Zero-COVID policy forced the shutdown of entire cities that are major hubs for business, trade and transportation. This further clogged global supply chains. When goods are scarce, prices rise. Inflation climbed in advanced economies and emerging markets. Severe droughts heightened concerns about access to food, a prescription for volatility. Poor crops in Russia and Ukraine and a drought in parts of the Middle East sparked food riots in 2010 that launched the Arab Spring.

"The Fed Is Risking a Full-Blown Recession," a *Bloomberg* editorial declared in 2021.[22] The drumbeat was also unmistakable at BlackRock, the world's largest asset management company. Its CEO raised the alarm about inflation — while rewarding staff with an 8 percent pay raise. Rising rents looked like a warning flag to the chief investment officer at Pimco, the largest actively managed bond fund in the United States.[23]

Meanwhile, inflation-protected bond funds, designed to protect investors when interest rates rise, posted record inflows.

CNBC noted a 40 percent surge in the cost of agricultural commodities, the biggest jump in a decade for global food prices. Deutsche Bank called rising inflation a global time bomb. "In a forecast that is well outside the consensus from policy makers and Wall Street," CNBC reported, "Deutsche issued a dire warning that focusing on stimulus while dismissing inflation fears will prove to be a mistake if not in the near term then in 2023 and beyond. The effects could be devastating, particularly for the most vulnerable in society."[24]

Economist Larry Summers, a former treasury secretary, applauded key aspects of the Biden administration's aggressive economic stimulus goals. But he also advised caution and criticized excessive fiscal stimulus. "There is a chance," he wrote in the *Washington Post*, "that macroeconomic stimulus on a scale closer to World War II levels than normal recession levels will set off inflationary pressures of a kind we have not seen in a generation, with consequences for the value of the dollar and financial stability."[25]

Some reports nurtured hope for sustained moderation. "A Key Gauge of Future Inflation Is Easing," the *Wall Street Journal* reported at the end of July 2021. It cited a University of Michigan survey which found that inflation expectations looking one year ahead hit a thirteen-year high in July. "A more-reassuring message comes from their expectations for five to 10 years from now: That came in at 2.9% in early July, down slightly from 3% in May and close to the average of 2.8% in surveys from 2000 to 2019."[26] But then inflation expectations rose again by the second half of 2021 and into 2022 as commodity prices rose further and inflation reached a level of 8.6 percent by May.

For the record, I don't hang my hat on these inflation expectations. They are wrong most of the time, usually because they fail to anticipate the kinds of aggregate supply shocks that loom directly in our path.

Warning signs resist accurate interpretation. Even experts require course corrections. Harvard professor and former IMF chief economist

Kenneth Rogoff tried to ease concern in a *Financial Times* op-ed with the title, "Don't Panic: A Little Inflation Is No Bad Thing." He reckoned that after a decade of lower than expected inflation, a pendulum swing in the other direction might be welcome. "US inflation today is much more like good news than bad," Rogoff wrote. "Prices are rising mainly because the US economy is doing vastly better than seemed possible a year ago."[27] But a few months later he wrote a new column about the rising risks of stagflation.

Seeking to dispel alarm as inflation picked up in the spring of 2021, Federal Reserve vice chairman Randall Quarles stressed the resilience of an economic framework equipped to cope with slow growth and simmering inflation. "I am not worried about a return to the 1970s," he declared even as a bloated Federal Reserve balance sheet displayed a record and unprecedented increase.[28]

"Bridgewater's Prince Rejects Return of the 1970s," the *Financial Times* reported in June. Co-chief investment officer Bob Prince at Bridgewater Associates, the third-largest hedge fund company in the world, counted on sturdy deflationary forces to moderate any upward movement in prices.[29]

But then, in early 2022, as analysts hoped that the stagflationary impacts of COVID-19 would start to gradually fade, Russia attacked Ukraine and Chinese production shut down in response to another COVID-19 surge. The initial reaction to this stagflationary shock—a moderate pace of policy normalization by the Fed, the ECB, and other major central banks—under the excuse that the shock and the resulting inflation may be temporary and that monetary policy cannot do anything about negative supply shock—fed further inflation and its expectations in a repeat of the 1970s policy mistake: throughout 2021 central banks risked falling behind the curve in the fight about inflation, only to wake up too late to the reality of persistent inflation in 2022.

Call me contrarian, but hearing prominent experts *say it ain't so* increases my alarm.

When trouble is imminent, I often wonder why very smart people brush off the downside. In 2020–21 we poured massive amounts of money and fiscal stimulus into a financial and economic system already awash in cash and credit, sending asset prices into the stratosphere, yet investors with the most to lose fear not for too long. I see disaster; they see money on the table. To a portfolio manager I know well, cheap money looks like a snow cone on a hot summer day. Consume it before it melts. So long as money is cheap, he planned to invest like crazy. And if things go awry? Risk of failure is *de minimis* when the government acts as a backstop under the banner of quantitative and credit easing.

Far from worrying about stagflation and wrecking a party, Blackstone CEO Stephen Schwarzman predicted an "avalanche" of private investment opportunities. He told *Bloomberg* that he foresaw owners bailing out ahead of new taxes to pay for massive economic stimulus. In this climate, Blackstone and two partners paid $30 billion to close one of the largest leveraged buyouts on record.[30]

With prices for homes and stocks soaring in the United States and across advanced economies, consumers also threw caution to the wind. Borrowing and spending surged, thanks to a massive rise in COVID-related savings and pent-up demand.

As risk climbs and debt accumulates in public and private sectors, everyone clamors for more. It's addictive. "Inflation is just like alcoholism," warned Milton Friedman. "In both cases, when you start drinking or when you start printing too much money, the good effects come first and the bad effects only come later. That's why in both cases there is a strong temptation to overdo it, to drink too much and to print too much money. When it comes to the cure, it's the other way around. When you stop drinking or when you stop printing money, the bad effects come first and the good effects only come later. That's why it's so hard to persist with the cure."[31] A bad case of hangover from an economic and financial system addicted to liquidity is ahead of us. The Fed has spiked the punch bowl and let the party go on rather than take the punch bowl away as it should.

For most of 2021 there was a heated debate on whether the surge in inflation—to 7 percent at the end of 2021—was temporary or persistent. The Fed and many Wall Street economists argued that it was temporary. Economists such as Larry Summers, Olivier Blanchard, and Mohamed El-Erian were in the persistent inflation camp as they argued that economies were overheating. I was also in the latter camp, but I argued in several articles that stagflation—not just inflation from overheating—was looming over the horizon.[32] By early 2022 even the Fed threw in the towel and agreed that the inflation surge wasn't transitory. But by then inflation and inflation expectations were de-anchored and the Fed was behind the curve. Then the Russian invasion of Ukraine further spiked the inflation rate. The US inflation rate surged to 8.6 percent by May 2022 and remained well above the 2 percent target of the Fed and other major central banks; and inflation expectations remained stubbornly high.

In 2021, the key economic debate featured "team transitory" versus "team persistent." They sparred over the rise in inflation in advanced economies. Was it temporary or more permanent? As the year progressed, "team persistent" prevailed. By 2022, even the Fed and other central banks finally gave up the misguided view that inflation was transitory.

However, the debate soon took on a new dimension. Finally, monetary authorities in advanced economies scrambled to prevent inflation anxiety from provoking more inflation, a so-called de-anchoring of inflation expectation. With the sole exception of the Bank of Japan, where inflation remained stubbornly low, central banks phased out quantitative and credit easing and increased interest rates. They insisted that tighter policies could restore inflation to the 2 percent target rate without causing a recession, the textbook description of a soft landing.

But policy makers face a quandary. When stagflationary shocks occur, rising inflation and slowing growth hamper prospects for a soft landing. If central banks care about inflation more than growth, they should hike rates and tighten financial conditions sooner and faster. But precipitous monetary policy tightening can invite a hard landing, meaning unemployment and recession. Favoring growth over inflation concern poses the opposite dilemma. A wait and see attitude dominates.

Authorities may not react in time to tame inflation while trying to avert a recession.

So the great debate of 2022 was whether central banks—at last committed to fight persistent inflation—would be able to achieve a soft landing or whether actions would precipitate a hard landing. I belong to the hard-landing camp. The policy response came too late. Thus I see the probability of a recession in advanced economies at 65 percent by 2024.

In normal times, global supply chains support growth. In unsteady times, negative supply shocks cause a lot of harm. A report from the consulting firm Accenture found that 94 percent of Fortune 1000 companies saw supply chain disruptions arising from the pandemic,[33] and delays persist.

A negative supply shock in only one sector—oil and energy—unleashed stagflation in the seventies. Twelve Arab states imposed the first oil embargo in October 1973 to punish allies of Israel. Another one in 1979 followed the Iranian Islamic revolution.

Today I count on the horizon not one, but eleven potential global negative supply shocks that loom over the medium term. Each one affects all the others. They all reduce potential growth, reduce the potential economic output, and increase the costs of production with inflationary consequences. Each is a potential megathreat. Multiple shocks in the coming decade would not surprise me. Together with loose monetary and fiscal policies and staggering levels of debt, they will precipitate stagflation that could make the seventies look like a warm-up act. These stagflationary negative aggregate supply shocks are:

1. Rapid aging of populations will disrupt developed and emerging markets. The shrinking pool of young workers will force employers to boost wages to fill jobs. In addition, active workers save and produce. Retirees tap savings to cover living costs. Thus, aging distorts the ratio of spending to production with inflationary impact. Rising costs and slower growth spell stagflation.

2. For decades, migration from the global poor South to the global rich North has helped employers fill jobs without significant

pressure on wages. In the current global political environment, draconian restrictions on migration will strip employers of that option when workers press wage demands. Wage inflation will accelerate.

3. Deglobalization, protectionism, and inward-oriented policies intended to protect workers and firms will punish economies rather than bolster them. By restricting global trade in goods, services, capital, technology, data, and investments, they will impose higher import prices, rising costs of production, and will sap growth.

4. Reshoring of manufacturing may improve supply chain security, but shifting production from low-cost emerging markets such as China to friendlier but higher-cost developed markets ("friendshoring") will spur cost and price increases. When security replaces efficiency in allocating capital, costs of productions will rise. Expect price increases, supply bottlenecks, and unintended consequences when narrow nationalistic politicians reverse globalization.

5. Fierce competition between the United States and China is already becoming a cold war. Two-way trade restrictions and tariffs may be opening salvos with many more to follow, especially in technology, trade in goods and services, investment, data, and information. Why is this stagflationary? In the vital realm of 5G networks alone, Western-based systems cost 50 percent more than Chinese alternatives. We spurn the Chinese options because of national security concerns, but it's a costly decision. Or take microchips. Demand by China has caused price spikes and shutdowns of auto factories that need chips. If China stakes its claim to Taiwan, capturing major chipmakers, a global supply shock would cause wider disruption than the oil shock in the 1970s. These alarming reverberations pale next to the consequences if Chinese claims provoke armed conflict with the United States on the issue of Taiwan.

6. Other geopolitical shocks deriving from the new cold war between China and its effective allies—Russia, Iran, and North

Korea—and the West are stagflationary. The Russian invasion of Ukraine spiked prices of energy, food, and other raw materials that are key in global supply chains and the consumption and production process. If eventually Iran goes nuclear—and it may if a possible temporary new deal with the United States is scuttled again by a Republican administration in 2024—then Israel will eventually strike Iran, because a nuclear Iran is seen as an existential threat to Israel. Such a conflict would trigger an oil shock as severe, if not worse than, the two in the 1970s. A restless and sanctioned North Korea is regularly saber-rattling and launching ballistic missiles in the waters between South Korea and Japan. If this confrontation were to escalate—and it will at some point, given the new cold war between four revisionist powers and the West and its Asian allies—it would disrupt global supply chains that have South Korea, Japan, and other Asian nations trading in those contested waters as the key industrial hubs of Asia. Geopolitical shocks—as we learned in the 1970s but forgot since then—are severely stagflationary. And we are now entering a geopolitical depression starting with the Russian invasion of Ukraine.

7. Global climate change will trigger stagflationary pressures in at least three ways.

   a. Vast tracts of the earth will face severe drought and become desert, lacking water. Regions far beyond the Middle East, North Africa, and sub-Saharan Africa are vulnerable. Lack of water is now crippling agricultural and livestock production across California and the Southwest United States, among many other regions.

   b. The trend toward decarbonization has caused underinvestment in fossil fuel development without yet sufficient increases in the supply of green energy. Energy prices are apt to rise so long as this imbalance persists, and closing the gap in ten years would require a fast track toward green energy, an unlikely scenario.

c. "Natural" disasters and the resulting human devastation will interrupt supply and production of vital goods. Many factories shut down when extreme weather events—floods as much as fires and drought—occur.

8. Global pandemics loom, as they are occurring with higher frequency and more severe virulence. Humans living in closer proximity with animals carrying pathogens (as animal ecosystems are destroyed by global climate change) and the melting of the permafrost in the Siberian tundra, exposing bacteria and viruses frozen for millennia, could make COVID-19 seem routine. Supply chains depend on healthy people to deliver goods and services, and they depend on open cross-border trade. Slowdowns and breakdowns jeopardize every stage of production, especially where inventories depend on just-in-time networks. And COVID-19—together with the war in Ukraine—has led to restrictions on the export of vital goods as countries try to achieve self-sufficiency in pharma products, PPE, food, and agricultural goods.

9. A justified rising backlash against income and wealth inequality favors pro-labor, pro-wage, and pro-union legislation and fiscal policies that can backfire, as in the seventies. As fiscal stimulus policies increasingly aim at protecting workers, the unemployed, and those left behind, wage growth may accelerate, causing higher inflation in a wage-price spiral.

10. Increasingly frequent and virulent cyberattacks disrupt supply chains, as gas pipelines and meat processing plants learned in 2021. Critical infrastructure is also vulnerable, not least power grids and our financial infrastructure. In August 2021, two federal agencies, NASA and HUD, barely passed evaluations of their digital security. Whether massive investment in cybersecurity will keep most industries secure for millions of customers remains to be seen. In the best case, upgrading and protecting vast systems will cost hundreds of billions of dollars and increase production costs. In the worst case, crippling cyberattacks will increasingly damage growth.

11. The weaponization of the US dollar—and, after the Russian war in Ukraine, other major currencies in countries allied with the United States—via the increased use of trade and financial sanctions risks undermining the role of the US dollar as a major global reserve currency and propels an inflationary disorderly fall in its value. In the 1970s, that inflationary shock was triggered by the end of the gold-exchange standard. History will remember the trade and financial sanctions imposed by the United States and its allies against Russia—starting with the effective freezing of most of its foreign reserves—as the trigger for Russia, China, and other rivals of the West to dump the US dollar as the major global reserve currency and the creation of an alternative to it that didn't depend on dollar accounting, dollar payments, dollar funding, and dollar store of value accumulation. Financial wars led by geopolitical shocks and changes in geopolitical power have for centuries led to the decline of some currencies as the global reserve currency and the rise of other ones. The decline of the US dollar and its ensuing depreciation will be highly inflationary and stagflationary as most commodities are priced in dollars, and a fall in the value of the dollar increases the dollar price of such commodities. Moreover, trade and financial sanctions triggered by geopolitical events massively disrupt—as they did in 2022—global supply chains that rely on dollar financing and payments and the smooth operation of global financial markets, starting with the functioning of SWIFT (the Society for Worldwide Interbank Financial Telecommunication) for international trade and financial transactions. Financial wars lead to stagflationary financial disruptions and eventual innovations that we will analyze in Chapter 6.

In part II, we will analyze in more detail many of these looming negative stagflationary supply shocks. In the decade ahead, the economic disruptions and damage from stagflation could be worse than in the 1970s.

During the seventies we had an inflation problem but not a debt problem. Private and public debt ratios as a share of GDP were a fraction of current levels. During the Global Financial Crisis of 2008, we were lucky. Too much public and private debt precipitated a financial crisis, but we did not have an inflation problem, as the shock to growth came from a collapse in demand following a credit crunch. Both times we got off relatively easy. Combine both problems, however, with a bubble gone bust; then we will be in brand-new territory in the coming decade: a global financial and debt crisis plus stagflation. That would be horrific. Extreme as this sounds, it is likely.

Optimists argue that we can still rely on technological innovation to trigger positive aggregate supply shocks and exert disinflationary pressures over time. That may be valid, but the impact of technological change on aggregate productivity growth remains unclear in the data for advanced economies. Those data show stagnant productivity growth. In any case, artificial intelligence, automation, and robotics are not an unalloyed good. If they improve to the point where they create meaningful disinflation, they would probably disrupt entire occupations and industries, widening already large income and wealth disparities. That invites an even more powerful political backlash than the one we have already seen—accompanied by stagflationary consequences.

We're now at the beginning of a series of aggregate supply shocks. Over time they will feed the risk of stagflation as well as massive debt crises. I'm not saying it's going to unravel tomorrow, or next year, even if stagflationary shocks are already mounting. It will happen in slow motion even if the disruptions of COVID-19 and the war in Ukraine were the first salvoes in this slow-motion unraveling. Yet we're in a fix. With the debt levels so large, trying to normalize interest rates might crash the bond and credit markets, the stock market, and eventually the whole economy. As shown in Chapter 4, central banks are in a debt trap. Their targets and their policy tools have become increasingly unconventional in a classic and terrifying case of mission creep.

The path of least resistance politically favors large fiscal deficits, and effectively monetizing the resulting debt by printing money. That approach will require large infusions of new money. Over time, these "helicopter drops" will allow inflation to wipe out the real value of nominal debt at fixed rates. But there's a hitch: most debt is *not* held at fixed rates. Thus, over time, inflation will cause real rates to rise. Increasingly onerous debt service will spark massive crises in public and private debt sectors. The debt trap where we find ourselves today will soon meet the inflation of tomorrow. If we need to come up with a name for the looming crisis, call it the Great Stagflationary Debt Crisis.[34]

PART II

FINANCIAL, TRADE, GEOPOLITICAL, TECHNOLOGICAL, AND ENVIRONMENTAL CATASTROPHES

Chapter 6

Currency Meltdowns and Financial Instability

When they work as intended, efficient monetary and financial systems support price and financial stability. The vast network of transactions operates smoothly across the globe, moving resources, finished goods, payments, and capital with minimal friction. Buyers, sellers, borrowers, investors, and lenders can count on central banks to restrain inflation and maintain stable currencies through shifting economic climates and business cycles. A stable currency—in the last century the US dollar—is the anchor of that international monetary and financial system, where transactions in goods, service, capital, labor, technology, and data require a stable and accepted global reserve currency to grease international trade and globalization.

That's the theory, at least. In practice, decades of financial experimentation and innovation have created a very different reality. Unconventional central bank goals and policies spurred by the Global Financial Crisis and the COVID-19 pandemic have flooded advanced economies with unprecedented sums of liquidity. Swift and dramatic action averted recessions, but at what long-run cost? And now financial warfare risks undermining even the global reserve currency role of the US dollar, the anchor of international monetary and financial stability. We have already discussed the challenges of inflation, stagflation and asset bubbles fed by cheap money. In this chapter, we'll look at a more subtle and insidious threat of financial instability and chaos.

Instead of throttling back on their experiments and applying due caution, central banks have accelerated mission creep in the last few years. What, exactly, is the role of the Fed and other central banks? Once upon a time, they cared only about price stability. Then they set their sights on growth and unemployment. After the global financial crisis they started to care also about financial stability. Now they have also embraced "average inflation targeting," using the tools at their disposal to try to reach an average rate of 2 percent over time, thus allowing the target to be overshot on a temporary basis. Are these goals all compatible? And what else is on their agendas? Recent speeches by central bankers routinely mention climate change and income and wealth inequality. No sane person disputes that these threats can rock the global economy, but asking central banks to fight politically charged battles opens a Pandora's box, taking their eye off the vital priorities that they are actually equipped to manage. Now, major currencies like the dollar are also being weaponized and used to achieve foreign policy and national security goals, such as the freezing of the foreign reserves of Russia and other financial sanctions in 2022. Similar financial sanctions have been imposed in the past on Iran and North Korea; they may be imposed on China if the rivalry between that country and the United States escalates significantly. Thus, central banks and treasury departments are now increasingly drawn even into the pursuit of foreign and national security policy. Ultimately, if central banks are undermined by their conflicting agendas and multiple goals, the value of our currencies is at stake.

"Why does the Fed think its regulatory authority extends to climate issues?" asked Alexander William Salter and Daniel J. Smith in a March 2021 *Wall Street Journal* op-ed entitled "End the Fed's Mission Creep."[1] They blame overreach by the Dodd-Frank Act that connected climate change to systemic risk in the financial industry. It's easy to see how trillions of dollars in climate-related costs can derail economies and why central bankers should worry about it, but it is more difficult to see what they can do about it.

Answering critics, central bankers frame climate change as a force they cannot ignore. "I don't see this as a main issue we are responding to with monetary policy on a day-to-day basis," San Francisco Federal Reserve president Mary Daly told an audience at an event convened by the American Enterprise Institute. "The central bank does have an important role in ensuring that banks are prepared for the direct risks from severe weather and from the globe's transition to new energy sources."[2]

Inequality is another serious problem that can tear social fabric apart and is now leading to political populism and economic nationalism. Moreover, the greater the rate of inflation, the greater the gap between haves and have-nots. Thus, easing income inequality has become another priority for central banks like the Fed. It now pursues a "broad and inclusive maximum employment" target where the term inclusive implies addressing inequality and the jobs of those left behind in a recession: women, minorities and the poor. But again, are all these priorities in conflict? Which ones will fall through the cracks?

Now the Russian invasion of Ukraine has led to a further mission creep of central banks that—with financial sanctions—are expected to support the national security goals of the United States and Western nations: weaponizing the US dollar, freezing most of the foreign reserves of the Russian central bank that are in part kept in central banks and financial institutions of the West, restricting the use of the SWIFT system of international payments. This sort of weaponizing of currencies for the pursuit of national security goals is the latest frontier of the mission creep of central banks, starting with the Fed.

This is a deeper problem that the Fed, in particular, faces, and it's a megathreat. For decades, the US dollar has been the "fiat currency" of the global financial system. It has been the most trusted of all currencies, and thus, the one that most countries wish to hold in foreign exchange reserves. That's a big advantage to the United States: the demand for dollars coming from its global reserve currency status implies that the United States can borrow for cheaper and longer to finance its ballooning twin fiscal and trade deficits. But what if the world loses confidence in the dollar, especially when the US twin fiscal and current account deficits are becoming larger while the US dollar is increasingly used as a weapon for foreign policy and national security goals? What if there are alternatives, including some innovative, all-new options that cut off the international reserve currency role of the dollar? As an astute commentator pointed out in the *Wall Street Journal* in March 2022 following the sanctions imposed on Russia, "Sanctions have shown that currency reserves accumulated by central banks can be taken away. With China taking note, this may reshape geopolitics, economic management and even the international role of the US dollar."[3]

In the private sector, innovation has reinvented finance. Private digital payment systems may challenge the vitality of banks, central banks, and the very currencies they produce. The outlook for banks could grow murkier if digital currencies were to potentially displace fiat money issued by governments. The crypto market is still relatively tiny, but it is growing fast. At the end of 2021, the value of digital currencies exceeded $2.5 trillion, up almost 100 percent in one year, even if highly volatile by day and month; indeed, by June 2022 that market value had fallen to $1 trillion given a sharp collapse of their price. In 2008, none of these currencies existed. Taking note, every major central bank has begun to explore the potential for central bank digital currencies (CBDC), a course with significant opportunities and some pitfalls.

All these financial innovations and other changes in financial markets lead to serious questions about the stability of the system in the face of megathreats. How much more unconventional will monetary policies become? What are the potential dire consequences of these experiments? Will fiat currencies survive as resilient stores of value, units of account, and mediums of exchange, or will policy actions debase them and financial innovation displace them? Will financial crises become more frequent and virulent? Will monetary unions such as the eurozone foster prosperity or eventual collapse? Will the US dollar retain its global reserve currency status or be replaced by the Chinese renminbi or other arrangements now that the dollar is increasingly weaponized? Will cryptocurrencies replace all traditional currencies, or will central bank digital currencies

(CBDCs) prevail and displace cryptocurrencies? Will high costs and inefficiencies doom venerable financial institutions and usher in decentralized finance built with blockchain technology? Or will centralized fintech—rather than DeFi—challenge traditional banks and financial institutions? These critical questions beg for sensible answers.

Data are still coming in. We can point now to tentative conclusions, but we absolutely must figure out the future of money, finance, and reserve currencies, stable or unstable as they may be. Two or three stumbles could trigger economic shocks that would quickly spiral out of control. If monetary and financial innovation leads to chaos and instability rather than a more stable monetary and financial system, we will indeed enter megathreat territory.

The ice has never looked thinner to seasoned observers like Peter R. Fisher, a former senior official in the US Treasury and the New York Federal Reserve. "I feel as anxious today as I've ever felt about the financial world," Fisher told the *Frontline* podcast in November 2021.[4] "The Fed has been pumping up asset prices in a way that is creating a bit of an illusion. I think the odds are now sort of one in three, very high, that we will look at this as an epic mistake and one of the great financial calamities of all time." And Ray Dalio, the founder of Bridgewater, the largest hedge fund, argued in 2021: "Fiat money eventually leads to the debasement of money."[5] And indeed the recent surge of inflation in 2021-22 following unprecedented money printing and fiscal stimulus seems to confirm this view. The financial sanctions imposed by the United States and its allies against Russia in 2022 also create greater monetary and financial uncertainty at the global level. Even modest monetary policy tightening by the Fed and other central banks caused significant turmoil in financial markets in the first half of 2022.

How did we get here? When economic historians name causes, most will agree that central banks' experimentation, misguided mission creep, weaponization of reserve currencies, and loss of independence had catastrophic consequences.

The Federal Reserve has come a long way from its beginnings. After three years of legislative wrangling, in 1913, the 63d Congress passed Public Law 63-43, "An Act to Provide for the Establishment of Federal Reserve Banks, to Furnish an Elastic Currency, to Afford Means of Rediscounting Commercial Paper, to Establish a More Effective Supervision of Banking in the United States, and for Other Purposes."[6] President Wilson signed the Act in December 1913, making the United States the last major economy to create a central bank. It replaced financier J. P. Morgan as the nation's pillar of economic strength and financial stability after another bank run, in 1908, revealed the weakness and instability of a system without a central bank.

The initial mandate of the Fed was only to maintain the stability of the American banking system. There were two ways to guard against repeated and destructive bank runs: first, to provide deposit insurance to every bank customer, and second, to create a lender of last resort that could help maintain the money supply and stable prices. Initially, the Fed was supposed to perform both functions; but later, in 1933, Congress created the Federal Deposit Insurance Corporation, or FDIC, to take over the former. Critics who feared excessive concentration of economic power in private hands breathed more easily—no longer would an individual like J. P. Morgan play such a powerful role in the nation's finances.

The Fed promoted stability through World War I, but it famously failed to prevent the Great Depression and arguably made it worse by refusing to step in to save banks and keeping a tight hold on the money supply. That policy mistake violated the mandate of the Fed. It was triggered in part by misguided views that bailing out illiquid but solvent banks and other private agents would promote moral hazard. In his memoirs President Hoover recollected that his treasury secretary Andrew Mellon advised him to "liquidate labor, liquidate stocks, liquidate the farmers, liquidate real estate. Purge the rottenness out of the system." The result was a disastrous Great Depression.[7]

It took the intellectual genius of the economist John Maynard Keynes to propose a way out of an economic morass. He argued that during recessions and depressions, when demand is low, central banks and fiscal authorities should help the economy end its slump through monetary and fiscal easing. So de facto, the Fed and central banks started to care about economic stability on top of financial stability, even before it became their formal mandate. It took World War II and massive federal intervention in the economy to put the United States back on a major growth spurt.

Over time, the Fed's mandate has vacillated between competing priorities. Because a valid public policy goal is to maintain maximum sustainable employment, Congress charged the Fed with a mandate on top of price stability: keeping a lid on unemployment.[8] When inflation and unemployment both worsened during the 1970s, senior officials said wait a moment; very loose monetary policies cause high inflation. We've all seen the cost of inflation. Let's make central banks independent and give them only one key goal: price stability. Stable prices blunt inflation and negative consequences that debase the value of fiat currencies.

Chastened by stagflation that proved so hard to defeat, many central banks—but not the Fed—restored the focus on price stability only. They proposed an inflation target that would encourage lending without jeopardizing price levels. The Fed, the Bank of England, and the more recently created European Central Bank have now collectively decided that 2 percent sounds just right. "Although the precise features of inflation targeting differed from country to country, the core framework always articulated an inflation goal as a primary objective of monetary policy," Federal Reserve chairman Jerome Powell said in August 2020 at a policy symposium sponsored by the Federal Reserve Bank of Kansas City.[9] But, unlike other central banks, the Fed always kept a dual mandate where, on top of price stability, the pursuit of maximum employment remained part of its mission.

Inflation targeting did its job for more than two decades. It ushered in a period of extended economic stability, the Great Moderation, from the mid-1980s to the mid- to late 2000s. Minor recessions and the dot-com bubble of 2000–2001 came and went without lasting disruption. Until the global financial crisis of 2008, one lever governed monetary policy: the rate that banks pay to borrow money through each other and via the Federal Reserve. This was one crucial number that the Fed managed and the world watched closely: the federal funds rate. Was the Fed planning to raise it ever so slightly? Lower it? Would the Fed signal its intentions months in advance, so markets would adjust their expectations? These were almost the only questions that mattered to Fed watchers.

The severe recession that started in 2008 forced central banks to rethink the 2 percent target and the monetary policy toolkit. Across all major economies, interest rates were set close to, or even at or just below, zero, and held there for years on end. Despite this ultra-low rate, the major economies were mired in a funk with low growth and inflation below target; so what were central bankers to do?

Initially, they devised a zero interest rate policy. Despite free money and a nifty acronym, ZIRP failed to revive stagnating markets and economies. Some central banks in Europe and Japan tested a negative interest rate policy, or NIRP. Instead of collecting interest on cash reserves residing in central bank coffers, commercial banks paid central banks to hold such reserves. Imposing this added cost was supposed to incentivize banks to generate more loans rather than hoarding cash reserves. But it too fell short.

Instead of adjusting rates into negative territory, the US Fed—and then other central banks—deployed "forward guidance," the commitment to keep policy rates at zero for longer than otherwise. Hinting at the future allows the Fed to adjust interest rate expectations and thus the yield on longer-dated bonds. That's why the Fed kept interest rates at zero for much longer than anyone would have predicted. Used first by the Fed in the early 2000s, forward guidance arms individuals and businesses with information that guides economic decisions. In December 2008, with the stock market in free fall following the collapse of two prominent Wall Street firms, the Fed predicted a scenario "likely to warrant exceptionally low levels of the federal funds rate for some time."[10]

When that was not enough, the Fed's and other central banks' toolkits expanded. "Quantitative easing" and "credit easing" leaped into the headlines. Their application and impact can fill textbooks, but essentially, central banks started buying longer-term government bonds and also private assets to reduce the cost of long-term borrowing in the public and private sectors. By purchasing massive quantities of government bonds (as well as mortgage-backed and other private securities in many countries), the central banks drove down the costs of those bonds for everyone else. Why? To reduce long-term borrowing costs for the government—and for private firms and households borrowing to buy homes and other goods—and to accelerate money circulation in an economy that needed a jolt of energy. Used first to try to push Japan out of its doldrums after its economy tanked during the 1990s, quantitative easing, commonly called QE, furnished a lifeline in the West during the financial crisis. Instead of adjusting the price of money, Japan's central bank elected to adjust the quantity of money in circulation by buying long-term government bonds to push their yield lower.

Quantitative easing helped the West recover from the Great Recession, but only very slowly, and only with the additional help of federal spending by Congress and other legislatures. The real question is whether all that federal spending is a short-term fix that leads to powerful growth, or whether it's a longer-term crutch that cannot bring the economy back to a self-sustaining level as debt levels rise. The recovery from the Great Recession was so slow and so long in coming, that question wasn't definitively answered.

And then came the pandemic. In two years—2020–21—of rock-bottom interest rates, QE, and creating new credit easing and lending tools to backstop not just financial institutions but Main Street itself, the Federal Reserve increased its balance sheet from $4.31 trillion to $8.66 trillion, a whopping increase of over $4 trillion.[11] Its risk appetite has grown increasingly robust. In 2021, the Fed vacuumed up *$80 billion a month* in Treasury securities. Central banks collectively created about *$15 billion per day* of liquidity during the COVID-19 pandemic. Total cumulative purchases exceed $10 trillion. "We've reached this point where QE has become almost the go-to tool for central banks and yet it remains somewhat more experimental than central bankers tend to let on in public and less well understood than the historical monetary tools of monetary policy, and now we've reached this point where it's at an inflection point," says Henry Kerr, economics editor at *The Economist*.[12]

Even to experts, QE resembles a black box. "We know what central banks do on one side of it," Kerr says. "They're buying bonds. We know what comes out the other side, which is the long-term interest rates go down. The evidence on that is fairly clear and the consensus on that is settled. But we don't really know how exactly it does what it does, why long-term interest rates fall." Former Federal Reserve chairman Ben Bernanke summed up the inside take in a memorable way. "The problem with QE," said Bernanke, "is it works in practice but it doesn't work in theory."[13]

Further experimentation emphasized credit easing, the tactic aimed at reducing borrowing costs in the private sector. Central banks reached beyond government bonds into securities from other private issuers. The Fed bought $40 billion a month of residential mortgage-backed securities to ease mortgage rates, and corporate bonds to help corporate borrowers; so did other major central banks. The Bank of Japan went as far as buying public equities.

As governments scrambled to stave off recession during the pandemic, unconventional tools proliferated. Bailouts and backstops rescued banks, non-bank shadow banks, broker dealers, money market funds, commercial paper markets, and households and corporate firms. By some measures, these unprecedented decisions worked exceedingly well: when, in March 2020, the economy threatened to freeze up—with a catastrophic dash for cash in which every bank wanted to hold on to their reserves and call in their loans to all major corporations—the Fed's actions persuaded everyone to halt their panic, and continue to make the normal loans that are the basic fuel of any economy. In that sense, Jerome Powell was continuing the lessons of Ben Bernanke and Janet Yellen: if necessary, apply steroids to show that the lender of last resort, the Federal Reserve, won't abandon an economy in time of need.

Yet there are several unintended consequences of all this precedent smashing. For one, it drew monetary and fiscal policy closer together. The distinction between them became even fuzzier when many mainstream scholars started making the case for printing money to close budget shortfalls under the banner of Modern Monetary Theory (MMT). Discussions of MMT often refer to "helicopter drops" of money. Jerome Powell made clear in public and private that the Fed needed Congress to act—Fed lending wasn't sufficient; federal spending was also essential. And Congress, under both the Trump and Biden administrations, responded with massive outlays: under Trump two acts of stimulus, of $2 trillion and $900 billion in size in 2020; under Biden, a stimulus of $1.9 trillion, followed by an infrastructure plan of about $1 trillion and not-yet-legislated plans of further trillions of social infrastructure spending. A lot of that spending was effectively financed by the Fed via its QE policies, an effective form of MMT.

A related unintended consequence: the convergence of fiscal and monetary goals signals the erosion of central bank independence. History teaches the essential importance of keeping politics out of monetary policy. Yet during the COVID-19 crisis, the direct monetization of fiscal deficits and debts became a de facto norm.

The European Central Bank, launched in 1998 with a mandate to maintain price stability, has scrambled to redefine its purpose in an uncharted environment. "Crisis management has taken the central bank well beyond its strict treaty mandate," the *New York Times* reported in 2010, when Jean-Claude Trichet was the bank's president.[14] "It has become much more difficult for Mr. Trichet to sum up its role with the mantra, 'We have only one needle in our compass and that is price stability.'" Indeed, the *Times* reported that the ECB "has experienced what the US military calls 'mission creep,' shouldering responsibility—for lack of any other federal European institution—for stabilizing the eurozone economy and financial system." From 2014 through 2020, the ECB balance sheet tripled to 60 percent of GDP, according to the Atlantic Council Global QE Tracker.[15]

Instead of sheltering economies from harm, relentless mission and tool creep may eventually endanger them. Innovation that forestalls crises in the short run winds up fueling asset and credit bubbles. We are more vulnerable than before. Financial crises have become more frequent, costly, and virulent in both advanced economies and emerging markets. We may not recognize the tipping point until too late. Negative supply shocks in an era of inventive monetary, fiscal, and credit policies can trigger inflation and even stagflation that debase fiat currencies. The overhang of liquidity created during the COVID-19 crisis has led to asset inflation and now goods and services inflation. Whether this massive asset bubble will turn into a crash is a question of when, not if. It is only a matter of time. And indeed the inflation rate was surging again in 2021–22 to a level not seen since the 1980s.

Debasement used to mean measures like reducing the precious content of coins. Back as far as the time of Roman emperor Nero, governments melted ten coins and reissued them as a package of eleven to give the appearance of increasing wealth. Commensurate price increases squashed that illusion, however. History demonstrates that the fear of debasement can cause the real value of money to decline sharply. In medieval Europe, especially France, base metal coins replaced gold and silver in coins. Henry VIII and Edward VI systematically debased English coins in the mid-sixteenth century when the income from seizing monasteries ran out, according to author Stephen Deng in "The Great Debasement and Its Aftermath." In what is now known as the Great Debasement, silver coins called testons were turned into copper with a thin silver veneer that could easily rub off, with the red showing through. The coins inspired John Heywood to pen a short, sarcastic poetic dialogue:

> *These testons look red: how like you the same?*
> *'Tis a token of grace: they blush for shame.*

After a run of nearly four hundred years, the purity of English sterling slid to 75 percent, then 50 percent, then 33 percent, then 25 percent. Coins issued in 1551 retained just 17 percent of the silver that coins a decade earlier contained.[16] No less a luminary than Sir Isaac Newton, as Warden of the Mint, led the effort to restore the health of British coins.

Advanced nations do not melt down or "clip" coins these days to make more money, because they don't need to. Printing money at a stunning pace is easier and causes more harm. Debasement of fiat currencies is always a temptation. At some point it starts eroding confidence vital to economic growth and prosperity. The mighty US dollar is not aging well. It has dominated all other currencies since the Bretton Woods Conference installed it as the world's global reserve currency following World War II. After a run of seventy-five years, when most nations measured the health of their money by comparing it to the dollar, could modern forms of debasement eventually demote the dollar? In the next five years, probably not. But over the next few decades, the dollar is likely to become tarnished, especially as it's increasingly weaponized for national security goals. Towering public, private, and foreign debt saps growth. Without growth, economies falter. Debt will continue to mount from explicit debt contracts and the implicit tab for addressing unfunded Social Security, health care, and the massive costs associated with climate change.

The United States runs very large fiscal and current account deficits, meaning more dollars exit than enter the US economy. Our imports are far larger than our exports. More dollars today reside outside the United States than inside.[17] Other major economies, by contrast, run current account surpluses. Although the United States enjoys an extraordinary capacity to finance itself more cheaply when borrowing from abroad, given the demand for dollar assets, it is also galloping toward unsustainable public debt and external liabilities. To finance an ever-growing current account deficit, the United States increases its foreign liabilities every year by an amount equal to that external deficit. The United States is already the largest global debtor, to the tune of over 50 percent of GDP, or $13 trillion in foreign liabilities.

At what point will the foreign creditors of the United States decide that they can't finance it at very low interest rates? Powerful forces imperil the dollar over time. Moreover, the United States increasingly uses the dollar as a tool of foreign and national security policy. Trade and financial sanctions punish the country's strategic rivals China, Russia, North Korea, and Iran, among others. Secondary sanctions target countries that do not cooperate with US aims. Targeting incentivizes rivals to rely less or not at all on dollar funding. Indeed, the strategic rivals of the United States are trying to diversify away their foreign reserves from dollar assets in order to rely less on the dollar-funding regime. The draconian financial sanctions imposed on Russia to punish it for the brutal invasion of Ukraine will accelerate the current desire of these four strategic rivals of the United States to move away from a dollar-based global financial system. Even other friends of the United States, like the petrostates of the Middle East, are starting to wonder if they could eventually become the victims of US sanctions if their foreign policy diverges from US policy. The UAE abstained from a UN Security Council resolution condemning Russia for its war in Ukraine. Saudi Arabia pushed back against the Biden administration request to increase its production and exports of oil to keep the rise in energy costs in check. But the increasing weaponization of the US dollar leads both friends and foes to want to diversify away from a dollar-based international financial system. Several leading Russian financial institutions were cut off from the SWIFT system for international financial transactions that links over eleven thousand financial institutions around the world. With calls to fully kick Russia out of the SWIFT system, both US and European voices suggested that the unintended consequences of such actions will push Russia and China to accelerate their plans to dump the US dollar as a global reserve currency. They will start trading goods, services, commodities, and financial assets using the ruble and the renminbi (RMB) rather than relying on the US dollar. Financial wars lead to counter-financial war.

Ordinarily, currency issued by the world's leading global superpower furnishes a reserve currency. The pound sterling prevailed when Britain ruled the waves in the nineteenth century. Power slipped almost seamlessly to the US dollar in the twentieth century when the two world wars exhausted European treasuries. But now?

The twenty-first century appears to favor China. If it becomes the dominant power, then China's trading and financial partners may choose to value their goods and services using the renminbi as a primary unit of account. In tandem with that, the RMB will increasingly furnish a means of payment in global trade, a reserve currency for central banks, and an investment vehicle for private investors. Gradually, the role of the US dollar as the major global reserve currency could start to slip and fade, even faster as the US-China cold war escalates. The Chinese, seeing most of the Russian foreign reserves in dollars, euros, pounds, yen, and so forth frozen during the conflict in Ukraine, will start to accelerate their financial decoupling from a dollar-based international financial system. They have already proposed that Saudi Arabia price oil in RMB. That would make the RMB the means of payment for such trade transactions while boosting the share of the RMB in the Saudi foreign exchange reserves. Of course, China may need to open up its capital account and start running trade deficits to allow foreigners to accumulate RMB assets in significant amounts over time; but even that transformation may take place in due time as China relies less on exports and more on domestic demand to sustain its growth rate.

Indeed, out front in the development of central bank digital currency, the People's Bank of China appears ready to displace the dollar with its own currency. A slow shift could accelerate if fear of a weakening dollar sweeps global investors. Should the Fed end up in a debt trap and become unable or unwilling to tighten monetary policy in the face of rising inflation, the debasement of the US dollar could follow, and inflation would surge further in the United States and dollar-linked economies. Fumbling or sluggish responses by monetary authorities will leave holders of dollars and dollar-denominated assets suddenly poorer, as the value of the dollar weakens.

Even if the US dollar retains global reserve currency status in the short run, over the next two decades its role may very well fade. The Chinese may be more aggressive in creating a digital currency, the e-RMB, and their economic power and influence in Asia and among other emerging market economies may significantly increase. If China becomes a leader in the technologies and industries of the future—starting with AI—it could offer to many emerging markets deals they'd find hard to refuse: e-commerce platforms; digital payment systems platforms; its currency as a means of payment, unit of account, and store of value; its surveillance systems as a way for autocrats to control their restless masses; and its 5G networks, big data, and Internet of Things solution for widespread adoption of new technologies. The role of the dollar could decline if China delivers a competitive economic, trading, investment, technological, monetary, financial, social, and political model.

Chilling implications would follow. Speaking with the *Financial Times,* Sir Jeremy Fleming, who heads Britain's national cyber and security agency, expressed a dire warning. A dominant e-RMB would cede immense power to China. "If wrongly implemented, it gives a hostile state the ability to survey transactions," Fleming said. "It gives them the ability...to be able to exercise control over what is conducted on those digital currencies."[18]

A global currency realignment will start with changing regional currencies. When any given group of nations tries to create a single, optimal currency area, they chase an elusive dream. Differing national priorities and cultures may undermine a regional central bank. The European Monetary Union (EMU) furnishes exhibit A. Can the EMU remain viable, or will myriad pressures cause a breakup, including new security threats at its eastern borders with limited European defense capabilities? We are just two decades into the experiment, and the jury is still out. The EMU was born in 1999 when many European economies decided to give up their national currencies. Overnight, the euro replaced the German mark, the French franc, the Italian lira, and other national currencies (but not the British pound, an omen of Britain's eventual exit from the European Union). The euro has survived a few brushes with collapse so far, and today its economy ranks third in purchasing power parity, behind those of the United States and China.

On close scrutiny, the EMU lacks crucial characteristics of a robust and optimal currency area. Political motives trumped economics at its origin: anchoring a united Germany to Europe was more important than working out the economic details and the optimality of a currency union. For a currency area to succeed, business cycles, overall growth, and productivity rates in its constituent countries should be synchronized. Labor and capital should move freely to help countries adjust when local shocks occur. There must be a way to share fiscal and financial risks.

Successful currency unions also require a shared political framework, so that central bank policies can overrule national authorities without objection, when necessary — and without trampling on democratic legitimacy. Even where liberal democracies prevail, these standards are tough to satisfy. Strong countries worry that any form of risk sharing or a fiscal union may end up with risk transfer and a transfer union, meaning a permanent system by which rich members subsidize their poorer and less productive neighbors. From the start, the EMU has suffered from divergent rates of growth and productivity between rich and poor nations, never mind gaping differences in fiscal policies, budget deficits, and levels of public debt.

During its first two decades, the EMU has suffered repeated disputes between its richer northern states, led by Germany, and its poorer and more indebted southern members. Bailing out Greece in 2015 averted Grexit and the collapse of the EMU, only after significant tensions between member states. But rescuing Greece was relatively cheap. The EMU got off without too much damage. Nevertheless, before the bailout, the prospect of Grexit led to major tremors in European and global financial markets.

Bigger worries lurk now in many parts of Europe. Low growth, low productivity, severe brain drain, high deficits, and massive public debt make Italy the current weak link. Anti-EU and anti-euro populism is on the rise throughout the union. As the European Union's third largest economy, Italy is too big to fail and too big to save. Best efforts by the EU, the IMF, and the ECB cannot muster a bailout sufficient in size if debt exceeding 2.6 trillion euros forces Italy to default. Failure to repay creditors would drive Italy from the EMU or Italexit. Such an ignominious departure could spur other countries to exit voluntarily while the choice is still theirs, in a domino effect that would end the EMU with a whimper. The rest of the world would shudder if EMU were to collapse.

And now that Europe faces new security threats from Russia, and the United States is requesting that European members of NATO implement their long-missed commitments to spend 2 percent of their GDP on defense, Europe is facing another massive fiscal challenge—spending more on defense—without the revenues and financial resources to finance this defense spending. Talk of European-based defense forces is only talk, and Europe depends on the US military umbrella of NATO to stave off the rising Russian threat. Without the US forces in Europe, a Russian attack on the Baltics or any other European state could over-run the European armies faster than the Afghani ones did once the United States pulled out of Afghanistan in 2021.

In the past, a fiat currency could only give way to another sovereign alternative as the global reserve currency—for example, when the dollar replaced the pound. Today, new rivals bring new uncertainties. Innovation has swept a private sector seeking forms of money not subject to central command.

Blockchain technology, a database system shared across a large number of servers, makes it possible to define the ownership of any single element of the data (for example, a unit of a digital currency) without a single institution to validate that ownership, by using cryptographic techniques. This technology has caused a burst of so-called cryptocurrencies with no allegiance to any government or central bank.

A system designed for transparency has an ironically cloudy genesis—in a 2008 paper attributed to Satoshi Nakamoto, a man who may or may not exist (or who may represent a collective of people). The paper's author or authors proposed Bitcoin as a peer-to-peer "electronic payment system based on cryptographic proof instead of trust." Chains of digital signatures create electronic coins and validate transactions with them.

Successive owners transfer coins by digitally signing each one twice, to indelibly mark the previous and the new transaction on a permanent public blockchain.

Despite manic swings in value, the overall market for cryptocurrencies has accelerated enormously. Miami mayor Francis X. Suarez drew wide attention when he declared that he would take a paycheck in cryptocurrency. Mayor-elect Eric Adams in New York City responded in late 2021 by declaring that he would take his first three paychecks in crypto form, never mind the inconvenient fact that New York cannot at present pay salaries in a currency other than dollars.[19] The government of El Salvador officially adopted Bitcoin as a national currency in 2021 in spite of serious advice against it by many institutions, including the IMF, because the country needs a financial bailout given its unsustainable debts. All three declarations underscored the same point: these politicians want to attract the burgeoning business called cryptocurrencies and "decentralized finance" (DeFi) to their cities and countries.

Bullish advocates tout a bright future for crypto and DeFi. In their eyes, crypto currencies can do anything that the dollar, the euro, the pound, or the yen can do — and more. They could manage financial assets without an intermediary that extracts fees. They could pay for groceries, automobiles, or investments. They could allow people to borrow without hefty paperwork. "The concept of renting, the concept of a mortgage, the concept of all this stuff is going to be challenged with this new world because the funding sources are flexible," says LoanSnap founder Karl Jacob. Using BaconCoin, LoanSnap aims to revolutionize home buying by sharing mortgages via the blockchain that can etch every transaction from day one.[20] The first such mortgages changed hands in late 2021. Once inscribed on a blockchain visible to every user, new transactions update the status quo but, in principle, no one can alter or hack what occurred in the past.

The rush to DeFi is premature and ultimately misguided. The rapid rise of Bitcoin, Ethereum, Dogecoin, and thousands of fledgling cryptocurrencies since 2010 exposes our collective wilting faith in the ability of governments to back the money they issue. But elevating crypto to the status of legitimate currencies endorses a dangerous precedent that is most likely to fail miserably.

Fabio Panetta, member of the European Central Bank executive board, gave a sober update in December 2021. "In spite of the substantial sums involved, there is no sign that crypto-assets have performed, or are performing, socially or economically useful functions," Panetta said. "They are not generally used for retail or wholesale payments, they do not fund consumption or investment, and they play no part in combating climate change."[21]

The label "cryptocurrency" is indeed a misnomer. Five features that define a viable currency are missing in the case of blockchain-based alternatives. True currencies function as **a unit of account,** meaning vendors use them to set prices for goods, services, and assets of all sorts. Yet with the value of any particular cryptocurrency fluctuating wildly, vendors simply cannot do so. Even conferences devoted to the topic of crypto avoid setting registration fees in crypto, because an overnight fall in value might wipe out the conference sponsor's profit margins. Debt contracts also require a stable unit of account. Were someone to write a mortgage with principal and interest in bitcoin, a spike in the value of bitcoin would cause the real value of the mortgage to skyrocket. If default then likely occurs, the lender loses money, and the borrower loses her house.

A true currency should also be a **scalable and widely used means of payment.** Bitcoin and Ethereum can handle fewer than a dozen transactions per second, due to the enormous computing resources involved. The Visa network, by contrast, handles fifty thousand transactions per second. The proof-of-work etched into every blockchain transaction may improve its reliability, but it does so at a snail's pace. Another vital attribute makes money a **stable store of value not exposed to dramatic swings in market value.** Deposited savings should accrue interest until withdrawn and they should not be threatened with unpleasant price surprises from day to day. Super volatile cryptocurrencies still don't meet at all that standard. Also, a currency should have a **stable value relative to an index of the price of goods and services.** Otherwise, the purchasing power of that "currency" becomes very unstable and thus an unreliable store of value. With bitcoin rising or falling in value by 10 percent or 20 percent in a matter of days, instability rules it out as a useful currency for exchanging goods and services.

Since the first currency changed hands, value has hinged on providing what economists call a **single numeraire**—shorthand for a benchmark that compares the relative value of all goods and services in a consistent and unified manner. In the Flintstones' world, shells supplied the single numeraire. The relative value of shoes, hats, and foot-powered cars had meaning. In the real world during the twentieth century, the Bretton Woods Conference made the dollar a global benchmark, its price set at one thirty-fifth the price of an ounce of gold. Other currencies measured their value as either a multiple or a fraction of the dollar.

So long as the dollar furnishes a single numeraire, the cost of a pound of sugar in Peoria, Pretoria, or Kuala Lumpur is transparent to consumers using any currency. And within each country with its own currency that currency that is also legal tender is the unit of account and single numeraire for all goods, services and transactions. But in a crypto world of "tokenization," if I need a Pepsi coin to buy a Pepsi-Cola and a Coke coin to buy a Coca-Cola, I cannot calculate their relative value. So in an important sense, the stone-age Flintstones had a more sophisticated monetary system than crypto with shells as the single numeraire. In crypto land, the dollar must serve as a reference. Without it, no one can compare the value of bitcoins, ethers, dogecoins or any other crypto substitute, much less use them to set prices for goods and services.

One of the alleged features of crypto touted by its enthusiasts is that no one can monkey around with the money supply. There is an absolute lid on the issuance of bitcoins: issuance will end after 21 million coins are created or "mined." Is that a protection against inflation, since no government can madly print money?

With no precedent, it's hard to predict what happens when bitcoins reach their limit. Who can enforce a limit? Must we rely on an algorithm? Other issuers give much less assurance. Many cryptocurrencies follow ad hoc rules that put no cap on the supply of coins, exposing value to serious debasement, worse and faster than any fiat currency. Full faith and credit could become a joke. Investors in the crypto space use leverage, up to one hundred times capital on some exchanges, meaning small fluctuations can wipe out positions. As these practices proliferate, a new species of debt may elevate systemic risk.

If nothing restrains the mining of cryptocurrencies, collateral social costs may pile up. Creating cryptocurrency already consumes so much energy that Tesla founder Elon Musk, who briefly embraced bitcoin as payment for his electric cars, reversed policy. The high environmental cost of the data mining that bitcoin demands clashes with the mission of a car company that is weaning automobiles off fossil fuels. Crypto assets are energy hogs, using as much energy as the Netherlands or Argentina. If crypto mining accelerates, they will blunt urgent climate initiatives to slow down global warming.

Cryptocurrencies are subject to other risks that can become systemic. "They are widely used for criminal and terrorist activities, or to hide income from the eyes of the tax authorities," Panetta warns. He also cites a checkered history. "Periods in the past when various forms of private money co-existed in the absence of sovereign money—for example the free banking episodes of past centuries—were marked by recurrent crises."[22]

After Jacksonian populism closed the doors of the second Bank of the United States in 1836, a free-banking era permitted banks to issue their own scrip with scarce restraints. Free banking prevailed until 1864, when Congress asserted authority to regulate banks. "During the debates over the National Banking Act, proponents cited the large number of failures of banks with state charters in the free-banking states and the need to establish a uniform, nationwide currency system," a Philadelphia Fed economic insight recalled in 2016.[23] In short, a world with thousands of privately issued monies was tried in the nineteenth century and it failed miserably, leading to currency chaos and systemic financial crises that caused severe economic recessions. So much for reviving free banking with cryptocurrencies.

We are in a Wild West phase of crypto. One study suggests that 80 percent of initial coin offerings, or ICOs, were scams in the first place that flouted securities laws. "You have scams that routinely make it into the top ten crypto currencies," says Ari Paul, the chief investment officer and cofounder of Blocktower Capital Advisors LP, a blockchain and crypto investment firm. "If you buy a top ten basket of crypto you are buying assets I can tell you will go to zero. They are explicit scams," he told host Kevin Rose on the *Modern Finance* podcast.[24]

One in ten initial coin offerings end with coins losing most of their value. Evidence of widespread market manipulation echoes the most profligate practices by some Wall Street firms: pump-and-dump schemes that manipulate the price upward only to later sell the asset at inflated prices, leaving some retail suckers with massive losses; illegal wash trading that buys and sells securities simultaneously to boost trading volume to pique interest; spoofing with fake transactions; and front running that enters buy and sell orders ahead of clients to rip them off.

Finding DeFi experts requires very little effort these days. They share insights on daily cable business broadcasts, in targeted newsletters, on the web, and in podcasts. YouTube lists videos that promise to unlock the mysteries of cryptofinance. Market reports keep tabs on steep price fluctuations. Attention should certainly be paid to a $1 trillion marketplace built on bold innovation. The modern finance lexicon is full of words that make heads spin, from crypto coins to non-fungible tokens that assign stratospheric prices because they are unique and other investors say they have value. Graphic artist Matt Winkelmann made news in early 2021 when twenty-one of his non-fungible tokens fetched almost $4 million over a single weekend online auction.[25] But now even the NFT bubble is bursting as the market value of most of these pseudo-assets is collapsing.

Whatever its fans, scammers and carnival-barkers proclaim about

DeFi, however, whopping risks abound from this over-hyped financial innovation. Wary investors sail between Scylla and Charybdis, exposed to merciless algorithms and fickle investors. If growth continues apace, volatile price swings will proliferate. In early 2021, the price of a single bitcoin lost half its value, or $30,000, in weeks. A greater percentage drop occurred when by June 2022 Bitcoin fell to below $18,000, a 75 percent drop from its all-time high of almost $69,000 in 2021. Other "shitcoins" fell even more—about 80 percent—in 2022 from their 2021 peaks.

Unlike regulated banks that cater to customers with a weak grasp of their portfolios, purveyors of cryptocurrencies furnish almost no protections. If private keys are forgotten, lost, hacked, or stolen, crypto wealth can vanish with no way to recover it. Because decentralized transactions evade monitoring, the market lures unsavory activities like money laundering, tax evasion, human trafficking, terrorism, criminal financing, and ransomware attacks.

Digital "stablecoins" supposedly pegged one-to-one to the dollar or other fiat currencies are also suspect. If they are backed by risky assets, tumbling market value can trigger runs that rattle the crypto market and far beyond. In 2008, few assets seemed safer than money market securities with net asset value anchored to parity. Yet the run on "safe" assets that were not safe during the global financial crisis created havoc that "broke the buck," meaning net asset value slid below one dollar per share. Cautious observers fear the potential for a similar systemic run on stablecoins. They won't forget May 2022 when a stablecoin TerraUST backed with an algorithm by another cryptocurrency—Luna—broke the buck and lost almost all of its value. So much for calling it a "stable" coin. And other "stablecoin" like the unregulated Tether also came under significant market pressure. This shady new world is very lightly regulated, if at all. Gary Gensler, who heads the SEC, has warned that serious threats in the crypto and DeFi sectors bring to mind the Wild West.

Grave concerns surface in the October 2021 Global Financial Stability Report from the International Monetary Fund: "Many of these entities lack strong operational, governance, and risk practices. Crypto exchanges, for instance, have faced significant disruptions during periods of market turbulence." The report also cites instances of hacking and the theft of customer funds. "As crypto assets become more mainstream," the report warns, "their importance in terms of potential implications for the wider economy is set to increase."[26]

IMF economists cast doubt on insufficient consumer protections and inadequate oversight. Of sixteen thousand tokens listed on various crypto exchanges, close to half have vanished and lost all their value. Many never changed hands, or developers just walked away from their projects. "Some were likely created solely for speculation purposes or even outright fraud. The (pseudo) anonymity of crypto assets also creates data gaps for regulators and can open unwanted doors for money laundering, as well as terrorist financing."[27]

Supporters of crypto dream of a financial system where all financial transactions—including borrowing and lending—occur without intermediaries. Algorithms hitched to blockchain will replace banks and execute smart contracts. Assets will move as smoothly as text messages without friction imposed by third parties. In this ideal world, dreamers forget that DeFi firms have developers and backers that, like banks, seek profits using practices that warrant regulation and supervision, not a Wild West of unregulated chaos. Free-riding DeFi flouts the supervision and regulation that traditional financial institutions face, a practice called regulatory arbitrage. Banks need to do proper AML (Anti Money Laundering) and KYC (Know Your Customer) tracking. Both impose hefty compliance costs. This is unfair competition that also invites financing of illegal activities. Would DeFi survive if properly regulated and subject to the same compliance costs as traditional financial institutions? It's a fair question.

Innovation can be a wonderful thing in any field, including finance. Over decades, innovators have created a dazzling array of private sector financial instruments. Whether any particular innovation advances or undermines stability, however, must be judged on the individual merits. Cryptocurrency is in its infancy. Prevailing wisdom is under attack.

Money is not what it used to be. The question has been asked in earnest by *The Economist:* "Does the World Still Need Banks?" Don't unbuckle your seat belt yet. Even the smoothest ride promises scary twists and turns.[28]

In 2021 Dan Berkovitz of the Commodity Futures Trading Commission (CFTC) stressed the shortcomings of DeFi: it is most certainly illegal, as it flouts securities laws; it lacks investor protections; it preys on regulatory arbitrage against regulated financial institutions because it doesn't pay the compliance and regulatory costs that regulated institutions do. And it doesn't provide the essential services that financial intermediaries provide: "There is no intermediary to monitor markets for fraud and manipulation, prevent money laundering, safeguard deposited funds, ensure counterparty risk performance, or make customers whole when processes fail."[29]

Moreover, decentralization is more myth than reality in crypto land. A small oligopoly of miners — many in remote jurisdictions such as Belarus, China or Russia and outside the reach of US law enforcement — validates most transactions on centralized exchanges. Developers are centralized and crypto designers act as police, prosecutor, and judge when things go wrong. Wealth accumulates unevenly; the Gini coefficient of inequality of Bitcoin is worse than that of North Korea, where Kim Jong-un and his cronies control most income and wealth.

Crypto zealots talk of a world of decentralization where the unbanked are banked, refugees receive digital identities and funds to survive, and the poor have cheaper access to financial services. But most of crypto appears as a greedy coterie of insiders and "whales," investors holding large sums of crypto. Jackson Palmer, the cocreator of Dogecoin — a crypto coin that was founded as a parody but obtained insider success for a while — scathingly remarked in 2021 that "despite claims of 'decentralization,' the cryptocurrency industry is controlled by a powerful cartel of wealthy figures who, with time, have evolved to incorporate many of the same institutions tied to the existing centralized financial system they supposedly set out to replace. The cryptocurrency industry leverages a network of shady business connections, bought influencers and pay-for-play media outlets to perpetuate a cult-like 'get rich quick' funnel designed to extract new money from the financially desperate and naive."[30] Indeed, Dogecoin after a remarkable rally in 2021 lost about 90 percent of its value. A lot of crypto consists of mostly manipulative Ponzi schemes.

If we want to revamp a centralized financial system with safeguards and supervision, we don't need crypto or blockchain. Artificial intelligence, machine learning, big data, 5G, and the Internet of Things can speed transactions, lower costs, and increase reliability. These centralized *fintech* tools and firms collect and process detailed financial data at blistering speeds without any use of blockchain.

Hundreds of firms worldwide have entered the fray with payment systems that handle billions of daily consumer and business-to-business transactions. Companies in the United States and China dominate the industry, but markets have sprouted in other advanced and developing economies. Mobile applications transfer funds and pay bills via Alipay, WeChatPay, M-Pesa, Venmo, PayPal, Square, and other digital providers. Paystack, a Nigerian fintech start-up, sold in December 2020 for $200 million to a US fintech firm.[31]

Working within the boundaries of a widely accepted monetary system, these nimble companies modernize credit allocation, insurance, capital markets services, and even wealth management. They may not deliver the libertarian dream of decentralized finance outside the reach of governments, but they cater to consumers with an expanding array of user-friendly products and services. Investor enthusiasm has spawned a growing list of investment vehicles dedicated to fintech, where bullish observers see lofty growth potential in cashless payments.

Not everyone welcomes newcomers. Banks trapped in outdated technology face massive costs to convert their legacy systems. If customers bolt for fintech options, money will flow out of traditional banks, draining deposits that underpin lending capacity. By luring money away, disintermediation could put banks out of business. Widespread failures would strain a financial system that barely survived the global financial crisis.

A more profound threat to banks may come from the very source of their ability to function. Aware that money has begun departing their jurisdiction for crypto or fintech alternatives, central banks are contemplating the most dramatic innovation yet. "The least noticed disruption on the frontier between technology and finance may end up as the most revolutionary: the creation of government digital currencies, which typically aim to let people deposit funds directly with a central bank, bypassing conventional lenders," *The Economist* reported in May 2021.[32] "Will banks survive the transition to a new monetary system?" the publication asked.[33]

Today only banks have direct accounts with central banks. Individuals and nonfinancial businesses need commercial banks for checks, deposits, wire transfers, and other payments. Imagine a central bank digital currency (CBDC) that gives every individual and business a direct bank account with the central bank. All payments could occur safely, cheaply, securely, and with instant settlement and clearing via the central bank. It would transform payment systems.

The commercial banking business model might shudder, faced with risk on a scale far greater than fintech firms pose. Banks hold cash and cash-equivalent deposits for individuals and firms. They retain a small amount of these deposits in liquid assets and lend the rest in the expectation that depositors will never claim more than a fraction of their assets. This arrangement fuels the fractional reserve banking system. Demand deposits become long-term loans that banks record as assets.

In this scenario, CBDCs create two serious risks to financial stability. The first is disintermediation as depositors move funds from commercial banks to central banks. Survival would mean converting banks into financial institutions that replace low-cost deposits with long-term borrowing at market rates to finance their long-term loans and mortgages, squeezing if not eradicating their profits. Remaining banks would look nothing like they do today. As a telling measure of financial impact, five of the largest US banks alone reached $1.4 trillion in market capitalization in November 2021. If central banks alter the role of banks, investors in the financial sector will pay a stiff price, never mind the consequences for industries built up to service banks. The second systemic risk: for banks that hold on to deposits in normal times, a financial panic could trigger catastrophe. Depositors seeking safety would race to move their bank deposits into their central bank accounts, triggering bank runs.

Less obvious pitfalls lurk. They sound arcane but the consequences could produce convulsive financial results. Suppose a severe recession drives real interest rates below zero. If a bank charges interest on deposits, instead of paying interest, consumers can say thanks very much, we'll store the cash in mattresses and skip the interest payment. Similar logic applies to hefty reserves that commercial banks keep on deposit at central banks. Flexibility limits financial repression.

Suppose, though, that a dominant central bank digital currency emerges, cash and coins are phased out, and nominal interest rates go negative. The central bank might impose an interest charge—a financial repression tax, in effect—on billions of dollars in excess commercial bank deposits. As things currently stand, a commercial bank can convert the reserves to cash that earn a zero rather than a negative return and store them anywhere. But central bank digital currency cannot escape the central bank, removing the brake on financial repression. At a point impossible to predict, very negative rates might entrench a recession instead of easing it. Banks would cut lending activity, businesses would starve, and jobs would vanish.

Monetary and financial innovation cuts two ways. Bold action keeps economies afloat when crises occur. New payment systems speed the movement of capital with less friction. They revitalize tired practices and spur innovators and policy makers to up their game. But crossing the line between running well and running amok is easy to do. We must stay mindful and alert to mission creep by central banks, and to decentralized finance and cryptocurrencies that bring hidden risks.

The playwright and novelist Oscar Wilde described a snob as someone who knows the price of everything but the value of nothing. The description fits eager advocates of mission creep and decentralized finance across the political spectrum. They can quantify QE, but explaining its mechanism and predicting its impact elude the staunchest advocates. Likewise, crypto fans can pinpoint the price of a bitcoin, but its underlying value defies measurement as it has little or no intrinsic value. This looks like a trigger for spiraling liabilities.

Central bank mission creep and instrument creep are fueling asset and credit bubbles. Busts and crashes will go together with debasement of fiat currencies as inflation surges ahead. The role of the US dollar as the major global reserve currency faces growing challenges coming from China and Russia. The world's third major currency, the euro, careens on instability if not collapse in a splintering European Monetary Union. As fiat currencies ebb, the current meteoric rise of crypto alternatives threatens to replace them with speculative Ponzi schemes, with severely unstable systemic effects.

Nothing poses a more clear and present danger to the current banking system than innovation from within. Central bank digital currencies may cut banks out of the payment system that sustains them. Weakness, or even the perception of weakness, may bring banks to their knees. Taken together, some or all of these financial and monetary innovations could prove counterproductive and disastrously so. Instead of promoting stability, they will elevate systemic risk and disruptions to levels we have never seen before.

Expect a major clash. Technologists trumpet the global power of their products: instant access, instant results for anyone who has a smartphone or a laptop. Meanwhile, political leaders are busy campaigning on nationalist themes: closing borders, imposing tariffs, spurning international affairs in order to put America first, or Russia first, or wherever-they-happen-to-live first. Expect chaos and financial instability as fiat currencies get debased, the EMU may eventually implode, the role of the US dollar as the key global reserve currency is challenged, and no clear alternative appears to fiat currencies and the dollar, as cryptocurrencies are neither currencies nor assets. This is a recipe for monetary system chaos and financial instability. This chapter looked at financial technology threats that cross borders with ease. In Chapter 7, we look at the opposite threat. What happens when borders close?

Chapter 7

The End of Globalization?

Opinion columns on trade and globalization in prominent publications often rile readers. When columnists talk of the glories of free trade, readers respond with desperate letters that describe shuttered factories, vanished jobs, communities losing vitality and despairing as production moves from North America and parts of Europe to such regions of the world as China and Asia, where wages are much lower.

No sane economist will dispute that these things happen. They are plain to see in abandoned real estate and unemployment lines filled with workers who used to count on steady paychecks and ample benefits. In one succinct comment, a *New York Times* reader captured the essence of a vexing situation:

> I worked at a manufacturing company when I graduated from engineering. Factory workers my age made 20 percent more than a junior engineer. Factory moved overseas, and I found a new job, moved on. Twenty years later I now make five to ten times my old salary. The factory workers never got similar jobs—and many are working retail at half their previous salary. They were kicked off the economic ladder.[1]

Between six hundred thousand and one million US manufacturing jobs disappeared between 2000 and 2011 due to the "China shock," according to research by economists Gordon Hanson, David Autor, and David Dorn.[2] According to others, overall global trade during that decade displaced nearly 2 million workers. It sounds like a lot. Yet 2 million job losses over a decade represents two hundred thousand jobs per year, a fraction of the annual churn due to technology, the normal rising and falling of firms and industries, and the economic cycle.

Even some left-leaning economists—like Paul Krugman—once vigorously defended free trade and downplayed the adverse impact on domestic employment. Their optimism was premature. Recent research puts a more disruptive spin on trade. Job losses linked to the China shock have exceeded initial estimates. More painful still, those job losses clustered in a crumbling industrial heartland where comparable jobs no longer exist. Critics of globalization saw the bitter fruit of trade policies that favor low cost and productivity over the economic vitality of workers and their communities. Put simply, we traded good jobs with strong wages for cheap imports at big box retailers.

No wonder there is a political backlash. A 2019 *Financial Times* book review put it like this: "Globalization is coming undone. Once thought unstoppable, the forces of liberalisation that spurred many decades of rising cross-border trade are faltering."[3]

"The modern era of globalization is in danger," *FT* editors warned in May 2020, calling globalization a victim of its own success. "The global division of labour—shifting manufacturing jobs out of rich countries and into poorer ones—reduced poverty in the developing world and prices in the rich one. Policymakers, however, did too little to compensate those who lost their jobs in the process, and neglected the sense of pride and ownership people felt in their once thriving communities."[4]

It is easy to leap on the bandwagon against globalization. That economic nationalism bandwagon is one of the things that propelled Donald Trump into the White House. Yet we are at a crossroads. One path favors a course of trade that continues to unite an efficient global marketplace while compensating or retraining workers left behind. Consumers worldwide will continue to enjoy lower prices while employment in emerging markets lifts millions of global citizens out of poverty. The opposite path, call it *deglobalization,* favors protectionist policies aimed at bringing lost jobs back home, aka *reshoring,* and preventing jobs from moving abroad. As appealing as protectionism may sound, when tried before, it toppled the economic ladder for nearly everyone. That is why deglobalization is a megathreat.

Deglobalization geared to preserving twentieth-century factory jobs will backfire, crippling essential trade in much larger markets for services, technology, data, information, capital, investment, and labor. Deglobalization will stymie economic growth, disable the means to cope with massive debts, and grease the rails toward epic inflation and stagflation.

Globalization stalwarts have hard work ahead. "Protectionism has become a growth industry, with numerous nations—including the US—opting for various direct and indirect barriers to trade since the global financial meltdown of September 2008," the *Financial Times* reported way back in July 2009.[5]

The backlash has erupted on multiple fronts. It began in advanced economies where rank-and-file labor groups allied with displaced factory and low-end service workers. A populist movement emerged that fought against unbridled globalization, or *hyperglobalization.* Its constituents played a role in electing Donald Trump in 2016 and in fraying historical bonds that tied the Republican Party to free trade. Fulminations against China and migrants "stealing" American jobs (the "bad hombres" from Mexico and Central America, according to Trump) made globalization an easy target for dime-store patriots.

Similar misgivings, also abetted by prodigious misinformation, spurred voters in the United Kingdom to withdraw from the European Union. Under the Brexit banner, relatively unskilled blue-collar, the underclass, and rural populations opposed European partnerships and agreements that opened trade and allowed free labor migration within the European Union. Brexit finally became official in 2021, during the pandemic. Not long after, as COVID-19 restrictions began to lift and consumer demand surged, Britain found itself short of non-British truck drivers, who faced onerous visa requirements. "You have business models based on your ability to hire workers from other countries," David Henig, an expert on trade policy for the European Center for International Political Economy, told the *New York Times*. "You've suddenly reduced your labor market down to an eighth of the size it previously was. There's a Brexit effect on business models that simply haven't had time to adjust."[6] No wonder that inflation started to surge in the UK in 2021-22 and the specter of recession emerged.

Across continental Europe, populist parties rail against free trade and migration. In France, far-right leader Marine Le Pen has vowed to form a coalition of the left and right to curtail trade and expel migrants. Her dislike of Muslims and Jews is no secret. She lost her presidential bid in 2022 but her nativist populist economic policies remain popular both on the right and the left. Hungarian strongman Victor Orban, first elected in 2010 in a fledgling democracy, makes no mystery of his nativist intentions. In a radio interview he declared it a "moral duty" for his nation to refuse to accept refugees or asylum seekers from outside the EU under a European quota system.[7] He has engineered constitutional changes aimed at keeping him in power at least until 2030.

Globalization has bestowed robust benefits on emerging market economies (EMEs), but that does not satisfy increasingly vocal opponents. Owners of capital in the EMEs, and manufacturing workers in those countries, have chalked up visible gains, but capital owners more than workers. Others—including rural workers—have been left behind. "Income inequality has worsened significantly in some EMEs and, probably more importantly, this deterioration is positively correlated with globalization," authors Yavuz Arslan, Juan Contreras, Nikhil Patel and Chang Shu wrote in "How Has Globalization Affected Emerging Market Economies?"—a paper published by the Bank for International Settlements.[8]

Some fingers point at the so-called Washington Consensus, a doctrine from the late 1980s that had the support of the IMF, the World Bank, and the US Treasury Department (all based in Washington) as a recipe for emerging markets in Latin America. Success hinged on easing capital restraints and import restrictions, privatizing state-owned businesses, liberalizing local economies, and enforcing fiscal discipline and monetary policy aimed at low inflation. Governments of the advanced economies, the G-7 in particular, promoted it as a recipe for affluence, and it won many hearts and minds in the developing world. A 2013 poll commissioned by King's College London asked more than six thousand people worldwide the same question: "Which country or countries, if any, do you think have the right ideas about the economy and jobs that your country's leaders should copy?"[9]

The United States won handily. "More than a third of Brazilians... and over two fifths of Indians and Mexicans said their countries should copy the US," the *Financial Times* reported. "Many South Koreans and South Africans think similarly." But the policies of the Washington Consensus didn't work out neatly in practice. Unfettered capital mobility caused dizzying economic and financial boom-and-bust cycles. In good times money flowed into the EMEs. In bumpy times it flowed out, and severe financial crises and recessions erupted.

Globalization is a mixed blessing at best. "Because of globalization many people now live longer than before and their standard of living is far better," economist Joseph E. Stiglitz observed in his fine book, *Globalization and Its Discontents*. "People in the West may regard low-paying jobs at Nike as exploitation, but for many people in the developing world, working in a factory is a far better option than staying down on the farm and growing rice."[10]

Stiglitz gives a thorough account of the many benefits of globalization, and he does not conceal its faults. "It is clear to almost everyone that something has gone horribly wrong," he writes. Self-serving agendas have backfired. "The critics of globalization accuse Western countries of hypocrisy," says Stigitz. "The critics are right. The Western countries have pushed poor countries to eliminate trade barriers, but kept up their own barriers, preventing developing countries from exporting their agricultural products and so depriving them of desperately needed export income."[11]

Free trade in goods triggered the initial backlash by low- and middle-skilled manufacturing workers in advanced economies. For example, auto industry workers lost their jobs when factories moved to Mexico and other nations with cheaper labor. Disaffection has spilled into a much larger services sector. At the low end, workers in low-wage economies started manning call centers. Increasingly, law firms farm out document reviews. Accountants in Poland can do US tax returns at a fraction of the cost. Technicians anywhere can read medical imagery. And computer programmers all over the world can provide their services to Silicon Valley.

All this economic and sociocultural dislocation led to rising opposition to global population migration. Not only are "we" shipping jobs across our borders, "they" are coming here to take what jobs are left. In fact, there is plenty of evidence that migrants fill menial jobs that Americans and Europeans don't want. History is full of examples of immigrant groups coming to a country, taking menial jobs that natives used to desire but no longer do, and slowly moving up the ladder as yet another group of immigrants enters at the bottom rung. But those facts are no match for the power of rhetoric — it's always tempting for native groups (no matter how recently they arrived) to want to shut the door behind them. Other complaints charge that migrants deplete housing, health care, education, and other public services, never mind ample evidence that immigrants' economic contributions greatly exceed any burden on public finances. Friction often stems from deep-seated cultural, racial, and religious differences that do not sit well with existing majorities.

Capital crosses global borders with less friction than people, goods, or services. Economists applaud the benefits. Foreign direct investment in the EMEs can help create new firms, build factories, attract managerial talent, enhance local technology, and increase jobs and incomes. The fact that capital can cross borders easily is, in this sense, highly beneficial.

Antiglobalization activists decry capitalist motives. They seek curbs on capital mobility in any direction. By their lights, foreign direct investment causes much more harm than good. In advanced countries, it shutters factories and businesses that move to regions where labor is cheaper. In EMEs, skeptics fear exploitation by multinational corporations that abuse workers and strip out natural resources with no thought to long-term impact. In their view, sovereignty and self-respect outweigh low-end jobs that won't last, revenue from nonrenewable resources, and investment capital that can vanish quickly — and often leave financial crises in its wake.

Before the current backlash began to sweep the United States and Europe, resource nationalism was already on the rise. Ten years ago, US authorities blocked a bid by Dubai Ports, based in the United Arab Emirates, an informal US ally, to manage key US ports. In 2005, the United States stopped the purchase of a domestic energy company, UNOCAL, by the China National Overseas Oil Corporation (CNOOC). The Canadian government prevented the sale of a vital potash-producing firm to a foreign bidder. And in something of a wide stretch, French national security concerns halted a bid by a European company for the iconic dairy giant Danone.

Today, rising economic and geopolitical rivalry between the United States and China overshadows all discussions of globalization. The world's two largest economies have erected barriers to trade in goods and services across the board, with ripple effects for every global trading partner. Skirmishes over trade in technology, data, and information form an expanding antiglobalization frontier. Technological decoupling looms as the United States and China scramble to wrest control over artificial intelligence and other industries of the future. China now may enjoy the edge in AI, and it is investing heavily in robotics and automation. The United States is restricting its exports of technology and semiconductors to Chinese tech firms like Huawei and others.

Some restraints that date back to the Trump administration remain in place. The Biden administration has proposed others to offset subsidies that Chinese companies receive from Beijing. China will certainly retaliate, in part by penalizing Chinese firms that launch initial public offerings on US stock exchanges. In a world where strategic rivalries between the United States and its allies on one side and China and its allies—Russia, Iran, North Korea—are mounting, the risk of trade and financial sanctions that exacerbate deglobalization is increasing. North Korea and Iran were already widely sanctioned by the United States and the West, leading them to trade only with informal allies like China, Russia, and a few other rogue nations. Now, with the Russian invasion of Ukraine, the decoupling of Russia from the global economy—that started in 2014 with the Russian takeover of Crimea and the Donbas region of Ukraine—is radically accelerating.

Indeed, the Russian invasion of Ukraine is leading to a rapid decoupling between US and the EU and Russia. Severe trade and financial sanctions have been imposed by NATO members against Russia. Even energy trade—as the EU depended deeply on imports of oil and natural gas from Russia—is gradually on the way down as the EU is comes to terms with the security risks of relying on Russia for a significant share of its energy supply.

But the most serious decoupling and fragmentation of the global economy is ahead of us as the new cold war between China (and its allies) and the United States (and most of the West) accelerates over the next two decades. Expect a gradual but steady balkanization of the global economy as the current geopolitical depression becomes more severe.

Indeed, in April 2022 Janet Yellen, the US Secretary of Treasury, argued that traditional views about the benefits of free trade and global supply chains require updating. "Secure trade" and "friend-shoring" should replace unfettered offshoring in countries that are strategic rivals of the United States. "We cannot allow countries to use their market position in key raw materials, technologies, or products to have the power to disrupt our economy or exercise unwanted geopolitical leverage," she said. "Let's build on and deepen economic integration and the efficiencies it brings—on terms that work better for American workers. And let's do it with the countries we know we can count on. Favoring the "friend-shoring" of supply chains to a large number of trusted countries, so we can continue to securely extend market access, will lower the risks to our economy, as well as to our trusted trade partners."[12]

This is a new twist on globalization. Most trade and investment should be focused among friends and allies and away from strategic rivals. It reflects tensions arising from the new cold war between the US (and its allies) and China, Russia and their allies.

In Europe, concerns about privacy put another brake on globalization. EU countries demand that data on their citizens remain on EU-based servers. Privacy claims mask the real intent of the demand: The underlying motive is pure protectionism aimed at curbing the influence of powerful tech firms in the United States. Europeans want space to create their own high-tech cloud. Actions of this kind threaten vital elements of global trade in technology. This looks to me like deglobalization on steroids.

Globalization is also under assault where wage compensation and labor standards fall short. Expecting poor countries to match the wages or regulations of developed economies is unrealistic. Wages are lower where labor productivity is lower. These kinds of complaints in the United States and Europe are another form of protectionism.

Environmental standards also motivate urgent calls for protectionism. Trade agreements that the United States and Europe sign with emerging markets increasingly push for measures that target climate change. Ambitious greenhouse gas–reduction goals provoke clashes with emerging markets. Emissions will increase in China, India, and other developing countries as their economies grow. Those countries are not keen for the time being to add operating costs. The EU, meanwhile, has proposed a border carbon tax so that European companies can compete on a level playing field with rivals in emerging markets. The US Congress has introduced similar proposals.

Collectively, all these protections hobble globalization. The result is low-balization, slow-balization, and, eventually, deglobalization. The motivations behind these protections are understandable, stemming in part from rage against the widening wealth gap between owners of capital and the vast majority of global citizens. And as always, economic malaise demands a scapegoat. Opponents of globalization have found one, and in the foreseeable climate they will have the upper hand.

Globalization as a concept stretches back to the earliest exchanges of goods between consumers in one village and producers in another. Anglo-Saxons traded across the English Channel during the so-called dark ages, a fact revealed when an amateur English archaeologist located the Sutton Hoo burial ship in a seventh-century Viking grave. "This single burial in a pretty corner of Suffolk embodied a society of remarkable artistic achievement, complex belief systems and far-reaching international connections," according to the British Museum.[13]

Marco Polo did his part for globalization by connecting Italy to China in the thirteenth century. British and Dutch East India merchant vessels took trade across oceans in the seventeenth and eighteenth centuries. However, globalization in its modern sense began around 1820. Europeans, worn down by Napoleonic wars over territory, embraced trade as a civilized way to produce wealth. *Pax Britannica* ensued, emboldened by Adam Smith, David Ricardo, and other brilliant advocates of freewheeling economic development and free trade. Ricardo presented the first formal argument about the benefits of free trade based on producing goods where comparative advantage favors them.

World War I ended robust trade and the first era of globalization. Europeans slid back into their old way of handling international gripes: armed conflict. Millions died over what essentially were land disputes among waning aristocrats. After an armistice ended hostilities, a flu pandemic—the Spanish flu—killed dozens of millions worldwide. Countries spooked by the flu, war-torn economies, and bolshevism in Russia adopted protectionist policies even as a slew of inventions from cars to radios ushered in a modern era of new technological innovations. Powered by these advances, the US economy grew more than 4 percent per year from 1920 to 1929, labeled in history the Roaring Twenties.

Nonetheless, legislators in the United States pushed back against global trade by backing tariffs. The Emergency Tariff Act of 1921 reversed more relaxed policies of the Wilson administration. A year later, the Fordney-McCumber Tariff clamped down even more on cross-border exchanges of goods. France, Spain, Canada, and other countries retaliated. The League of Nations, which the United States had spurned, convened a World Economic Conference in Geneva, Switzerland, in 1927. It aimed to ease tensions but failed. Nations dug in their heels. Tariffs increased.[14]

Eventually, Senator Reed Owen Smoot (R-UT) and Representative Willis Chatman Hawley (R-OR) lobbied for even more protection, something that US citizens soon came to regret. Passed after the 1929 Wall Street Crash rattled nerves, the United States Tariff Act of 1930, aka Smoot-Hawley Tariffs, erected barriers to imported agricultural products. Manufacturers in other sectors clamored for similar legislation.

Ill effects came swiftly. Consumers bristled at higher costs for imports. Gertrude M. Duncan, secretary of the Women's Non-partisan Fair Tariff Committee, urged women to demand an end to tariffs on the clothing and household articles that Smoot-Hawley made more expensive. Meanwhile, American exporters fell on hard times as other countries retaliated and the Great Depression set in. In June 1931, the *El Paso Times* reported, "In the first four months of this year, under the tariff rates of the Smoot-Hawley act, our foreign trade fell off by more than half a billion dollars. Except for a few spurts upward, our exports have been steadily slipping ever since the tariff bill became law a year ago."[15]

Nine decades later, in March 2018, Republican congressman Thomas McClintock from California wouldn't let his colleagues forget a calamitous misstep. "Every country that has cried protectionism has suffered terribly, including ours," he said. "Thomas Jefferson thought high tariffs could fund the government and promote domestic manufacturing. That caused a devastating recession that nearly destroyed our fledgling economy. Herbert Hoover responded to the recession of 1929 with the Smoot-Hawley Tariff Act. It didn't end well."[16] Congress since then has delegated most trade negotiating authority to the president in order to avert another disastrous trade policy mistake, even if formal trade treaties need the supporting vote of the Senate.

Trade restrictions mainly affected movement of goods, but migration and capital mobility slowed also. Some observers argue that trade wars were the principal cause of the Great Depression. I wouldn't go that far. Manufacturing output fell 20 percent and trade among countries fell 60 percent. Yet there were other causes of the Depression, like the lack of appropriate monetary and fiscal stimulus and allowing thousands of financial institutions and firms to go bankrupt. If trade restraints were not to blame alone, they certainly made the Depression deeper and longer than it would have been.

During World War II, the massive transfer of military materials opened doors to new rounds of globalization in peacetime. After 1945 we created a world that gradually liberalized trade. Regulations governing cross-border movement of goods eased. Trade increased steadily as global trade restrictions were lifted during successive rounds of the GATT (General Agreement on Tariff and Trade). The creation of the World Trade Organization (WTO) and regional trade agreements helped set rules by which Europe could begin to integrate. Markets opened progressively. Supply chains stretched around the world at a pace that accelerated after China opened up in 1979 and the Soviet Union and the Iron Curtain collapsed starting in 1989. After centuries of stagnant performance, fledgling economies began to grow, partly thanks to international trade. So did the global economic pie, as basic trade theory predicts about the benefits of freer trade.

The period after 1989 featured hyperglobalization. Most emerging market economies embraced freer trade and capital flows. Cross-border movement in goods, services, capital, investments, labor, technology, data, and information flourished. But the perceived costs of such hyperglobalization started a backlash that accelerated after the global financial crisis. Economist Dani Rodrik and others argue that hyperglobalization, democracy, and national sovereignty create an "inconsistent trilemma." To maintain democracy and sovereignty, hyperglobalization needs to be curtailed. More recently, as the consequence of the COVID-19 crisis and the ensuing disruptions to global supply chains, logistics, and transportation networks, calls for reshoring or friend-shoring of manufacturing and global supply chains have become louder and more popular. Indeed, global pandemics that spread faster because of globalization have first led to draconian restrictions of the movement of people — as during the peak of COVID-19 — when foreign travel became nearly impossible and is still hampered. And now restrictions to the movement of goods are mounting as countries try to achieve the impossible task of greater national autarky in "critical" or "essential" goods.

No one should pretend that free trade by itself guarantees an equitable world where everyone is better off. Greater income and wealth from trade does not distribute evenly. The poor in emerging markets may see gains, but if the gap between the rich and the poor accelerates, they may feel worse off even if they are wealthier. Corporations — including large multinational corporations (MNCs) — use profits and muscle to bend rules in their favor, sometimes in anticompetitive ways. There will always be winners and losers.

Who wins? Manufacturing workers in China, Asia, and other emerging economies where incomes are rising because they have joined the global economy and their exports are growing. Skilled workers in emerging markets who can offer their services anywhere in a digital world. Very skilled workers in advanced economies who stand to gain on the strength of education and specialized experience in high value-added and tech-advanced manufacturing and service sectors. The owners of capital also benefit, especially in export sectors of advanced economies and emerging markets.

Winners also include urban and highly skilled individuals with a cosmopolitan view of society. Their mobility and flexibility give them high value as borders vanish. If trade increases the size of the overall economic pie, globalist elites — the top 1 percent of all owners of financial assets — will get even richer. And don't forget consumers. We will all pay less for cheaper goods and services.

Workers in the financial sector will reap disproportionate financial benefits. Capital mobility and financial globalization bestow ample benefits for banks and other financial institutions and investors. Rewards at the top will be lavish if not stunning. Those lower down might receive modest rewards.

Who loses when globalization prevails? Low- and medium-skill manufacturing and industrial workers in advanced economies. When cheaper goods are produced elsewhere their wages will fall. Many manufacturing jobs will vanish forever. Jettisoned workers will suffer even after adjusting for the lower cost of goods. They face transitional unemployment and a downward income spiral moving from high-paid jobs in manufacturing to lower-paid jobs in low-value-added service sectors (the "hamburger-flipping" jobs). Globalization can pose a threat, meantime, to anyone who feels their national, ethnic, cultural, or religious identity might suffer. Rural, low-skilled workers most fear this loss of status.

Globalization and trade have hurt low-skilled blue-collar workers in advanced economies. A similar fate will increasingly hurt low- and semi-skilled white collar service workers where virtual access can substitute for physical presence. With a few months of training and no language barriers to worry about, virtual counterparts in emerging markets can fill many service jobs remotely. Middle-class security offers no refuge from competition. Call centers come to mind first, but accountants, lawyers, and even doctors may increasingly face virtual competition. Rivals in China and Asia have proliferated. Even if jobs are secure, job candidates will multiply, easing pressure on employers to raise pay. Indeed, with 2.5 billion citizens in China and India, dubbed Chindians, and many more in other emerging markets joining the global labor force, workers in advanced economies need to beware. Your paycheck and benefits are at risk.

Lawmakers have occasionally tried to assist workers who lose jobs for reasons stemming from trade. In 1962 Congress created the Trade Adjustment Assistance Program, the first in a series of programs including the Trade Adjustment Assistance (TAA) Reauthorization Act of 2015. Aimed at unskilled and low-skilled workers who lose jobs because of trade, TAA programs don't get much respect from skeptics. "Trade Burial Assistance" is what cynics call it. There is simply no easy way to replace jobs lost to trade.

Proponents of basic trade theory have a naive answer to this controversy. They argue that when a rich country trades freely with a poor country, each one will pursue its comparative advantage. The poorer country might become a manufacturing giant while the richer country becomes a services giant; in the poor country, wages will go higher, while in the rich country, skilled workers' wages will go higher but those of unskilled workers will fall together with their jobs. Data does show net increases in overall output across importing and exporting economies generally. Incomes overall grow. Competition lowers prices. Consumers can buy cheaper imported goods and thus their purchasing power increases. This effect resembles a tax deduction that most people would applaud at any income level. But try telling all this to the people who lose their jobs in the richer country, and struggle to find new jobs at similar salaries.

In principle the answer to this problem should not be to restrict trade. The answer is to enact policies that are more generous for the people who suffer: we need to compensate those who are left behind in order to make everyone better off with freer trade. Instead, we've been amassing wealth for the winners, and expanding inequality to unprecedented levels. Globalization redirects wealth, but obstacles to equity are political and social. It's a problem of extracting and redistributing benefits from an economic pie increasing in size. That's not socialism, as critics fear. It's capitalism aimed at maximizing returns to owners of productive assets. They can improve their lot by agreeing to assist workers displaced by globalization. Partisan preconceptions block a system of social welfare that provides income, a benefits safety net, skills training, and vital goods and services to those left behind.

Conflict between labor and capital has gone on since the early days of mass production in factories. Following the first industrial revolution, activist workers pressed for minimum wages, unions, pensions, and health care. Karl Marx and Friedrich Engels urged workers to rise up and demand the wealth created by their own work efforts. Resistant authorities complied, if only to prevent disruptions and civil strife. In Western market economies these steps have supported democracy and free markets. As enlightened bourgeois classes realized, building a social safety net and a welfare state for workers prevents upheaval and revolutions. Meanwhile, in countries where workers remained persistently oppressed, socialist revolutions took place. China and Russia experimented for much of the twentieth century with communism that made almost no one better off and ultimately failed.

Everything changed when former communists unlocked their economies and embraced global free markets, though much more so in China than Russia. "Almost overnight, China became the world's factory. Between 1990 and 2015, the country's share of global manufacturing exports rose from 2.8 percent to 18.5 percent," wrote economist Gordon Hanson in "Can Trade Work for Workers?"[17]

Successful development of its comparative advantage in labor-intensive, light-manufacturing sectors produced the China shock. In less than the span of a generation, China vaulted from an impoverished, third-world nation to the world's second largest economy. Besides shrewd planning and hard work, unfair trade practices aided China's rapid progress. They led to resentment and eventually trade restrictions. The Trump administration listed a litany of alleged Chinese trade violations. The litany includes currency manipulation that kept China's currency weak, a ploy that bestowed a competitive advantage on exports as trade surpluses mounted: "For many years, China has pursued industrial policies and unfair trade practices—including dumping, discriminatory non-tariff barriers, forced technology transfer, overcapacity, and industrial subsidies—that champion Chinese firms and make it impossible for many United States firms to compete on a level playing field."[18]

Overall, trade flourished from 1945 until the start of this century, fostering a world of relative peace and prosperity. Countries that welcomed trade flourished. Those that remained in relative isolation stagnated. Look at North and South Korea. When the Korean War ended in 1953, both countries were poor, but the North had a larger industrial base and natural resources. South Korea started trading. Today its economy is robust, and affluence abounds. North Korean citizens remain mired in poverty, subject to food scarcity and famine.

Careful examination of data contradicts assertions that workers in China, India, or Vietnam have stolen most jobs in advanced economies. Contrary to this widely held belief, the vast majority of jobs that have vanished fell victim to technology, not to globalization.

The McKinsey Global Institute (MGI) exposes the myth that trade accounts for the loss of most manufacturing jobs:

> Reality: Changes in the composition of demand and ongoing productivity increases are the main reasons for the decline in the number of such jobs in mature economies. The share of manufacturing in these countries' total employment is bound to decline further, from 12 percent today to less than 10 percent in 2030, according to our analysis. MGI finds that trade or offshoring are responsible for the loss of around 20 percent of the 5.8 million US manufacturing jobs eliminated between 2000 and 2010.[19]

There is something seductive in calls to go back to an idyllic time when plenty of good, solid manufacturing jobs offered high wages and benefits in advanced economies. But it just cannot happen again.

A more realistic narrative likens trade to technology. Suppose a new invention allows manufacturers to produce a new toaster, a microwave, or a coffee machine with one fifth of the labor and capital? Those new devices sell for $10 instead of the $50 that they used to cost. Every consumer who buys one enjoys a benefit worth $40. What do you suppose will happen next? Four-fifths of the workers in the industry that produced toasters, coffee machines, and microwaves will lose their jobs. Households need only one toaster, so a lower price won't change the demand for toasters by a factor of five or even two. Demand is relatively fixed. Those jobs won't come back, at least not the way people remember them.

Factories once employed nearly 25 percent of the US workforce. Now it's below 10 percent. Apart from mobilizing English Luddites who smashed mechanized looms in the early nineteenth century in hopes of preserving their jobs, technology seldom stirs a turbulent backlash. People don't say, "Let's not produce a better toaster in California because it will cost jobs." Change resulting from better technology is almost always accepted as positive progress. Change resulting from trade: that's different.

Economists often tell a variant of the tale about an entrepreneur who introduces a good—say a toaster—costing far less than alternatives. He credits the lower price to new technology. Happy consumers flock to his toaster. They stop buying expensive toasters and call him a genius who has increased the purchasing power of their income. Then he reveals that he did not invent a new process. He bought the cheap toasters in China. So this was his great revolution. This was a fake miracle, people say. And he is bashed because the Chinese are taking away jobs.

The two outcomes are identical, but people don't see them that way. When people lose their jobs because of technology they might try to slow its adoption but they can't stop progress. We don't blame technology; we usually applaud it. We celebrate Moore's law, the principle that computer speed and capacity double every two years.

We humans don't double our own capacity every two years. Algorithms have supplanted jobs from supermarket checkers and highway toll takers to travel agents to bank tellers. Who's next? There will be others. But in the past, when technology displaced workers, it used to create new opportunities. Buggy whip workers became auto workers. People have worried about technology killing jobs ever since the industrial revolution, two hundred years ago. In those two centuries, technology has rocketed forward and, yes, destroyed many jobs. But employment rates have remained strong, notwithstanding crises like the Depression or the beginning of the COVID-19 pandemic.

We think of trade as a zero-sum game, as if someone wins while someone else loses. Instead of applause for a process that streamlines production, maximizes output, and lowers costs, we often face a backlash focused on job displacements. That's where we are today, perched on a precarious precipice—instead of improving social safety nets, many countries are shutting their borders and erecting tariffs.

Globalization has flaws, to be sure. Wealthy and powerful corporate players exercise influence and often get what they want to advance their interests, even as protesters decry the World Trade Organization and prevent the United States from forming vital commercial alliances in Asia under the Trans-Pacific Partnership. "These elites will not explicitly tell you, 'We don't care about you anymore,'" Harvard economist Dani Rodrik told *Promarket,* an online publication of the Booth School of Business at the University of Chicago. "They'll tell you, 'Look, we can't afford to care about you because we're competing in a global economy and therefore we have to make these choices, we have to outsource and we have to move, we have to look for low-tax environments because we can't afford not to.' They'll complain that they have no choice."[20]

Indeed, as Rodrik and other critics of globalization have argued, trade agreements bear the self-serving fingerprints of politically connected financial firms, multinational corporations, and pharmaceutical companies. They bend international rules governing global investment and property rights. They exploit accounting adjustments that assign income to the lowest tax jurisdictions. They praise global trade as a good thing. Their actions suppress competition and hoard power and profits mainly for the benefit of capital owners. Their actions multiply job losses and exacerbate inequality.

Displacement and rising inequality need urgent attention by policy makers in civilized societies, for self-preservation if not for nobler reasons. But before we succumb to impulses that elevate the cause of deglobalization, prudent attention should weigh its economic, political, and social consequences.

Tariffs sound painless, but they actually cause disproportionate injury to consumers with low incomes. Raising tariffs on consumer goods to protect domestic producers ends up taxing shoppers, who pay more at cash registers. Eventually, trading rivals respond in like fashion. A protectionist policy ends up by depleting every consumer's bank account. The rich suffer very little while the poor get poorer.

The rise in inequality is only partially due to trade; more powerful forces—to be discussed in Chapter 8—are also at fault. Deglobalization would close the door on the chance to raise living standards worldwide to an acceptable level. Restricting trade would reduce global output, shrinking the number of jobs that displaced workers could fill. The global economic pie would get smaller.

A physical representation of global supply chains built over three decades might dazzle observers. They form a robust and intricate web connecting millions of end users to component production facilities across the world where efficiencies are greatest. Deglobalization would disrupt these networks, spurning efficiencies and catering instead to demand for jobs, often where bloated cost structures might impair competition in global markets.

Geopolitics weigh heavily when the world's two largest economies go head-to-head. "US-China Feud Is Accelerating the Biggest Shift in Trade Since the Cold War, Away from Globalization," a *South China Morning Post* headline reported in July 2019.[21] "After decades in which globalisation seemed to be an unstoppable force, the trade war is accelerating a complete transformation of global trade towards a more fragmented model." Fragmentation had its day, before the industrial revolution demonstrated the decisive advantage of efficient production. But decoupling the United States from China is now under way, and it will cause significant economic damage to both sides. And the decoupling between Russia and the West is now on steroids with the Russian invasion of Ukraine. Geopolitically driven balkanization of the global economy is ahead of us and a further nail in the coffin of globalization.

Deglobalization unleashes other dangerous currents. When most people think about trade, they are likely to picture giant containers carried on ocean freighters. Focusing on trade in goods misses a much larger question. Tangible goods make up only a fraction of economic activity subject to trade in a digital world. What about services, labor, data, technology, and information? All are vital to economic growth. That's where most value resides these days. If trade in goods pushes policy toward balkanization, what price will we pay for trade restraints on intangibles?

When we go beyond the realm of goods, the urge to deglobalize makes everything curiouser and curiouser, as Alice in Wonderland might say. Case in point: technology. We worry about TikTok collecting data about our teenagers and how the Chinese will use it or whether Grindr, a gay dating app owned by a Chinese media company, opens a door to blackmailing users. That makes partial sense. But now the Chinese complain that every Chinese driver with a Tesla is unwittingly giving information on where she goes and what he does. Will these data end up in the hands of the NSA? Probably not, I'd say, but you can't rule it out any more than you can say unequivocally that China won't try to influence malleable teenage minds or blackmail some people if it has access to their private data. In a world where data will become an asset as valuable if not more valuable than traditional goods and services, data protectionism lurks. As restrictions multiply, they will clog trading in goods and services.

Where do trade restrictions begin and end? This is actually one of the biggest threats to globalization. Restricting trade in technology will eventually affect all trade. Today the US government says we don't want 5G technology from Huawei for our telecom systems because it has a back door for the Chinese government to keep tabs on Americans. We're also urging Europeans and other allies to avoid that 5G. But tomorrow, guess what? Every consumer product will have a 5G chip. First you track it in the production system, and then to operate anything in the Internet of Things it must have a 5G chip. Access only begins with smartphones. Eventually, every home appliance—a toaster, a microwave, a coffee machine—will have a 5G chip, will be a potential listening device, and might furnish information—to what purpose I can't say. Will ubiquitous technology force us to eventually impose restrictions on everything?

If you think services cannot be traded, then you are trapped in antiquated thinking. It's no longer as if services require someone to travel elsewhere to get them. Toss out that notion. Economist Richard Baldwin borrows an analogy from the TV series *Star Trek*. An accountant in Warsaw or Bangkok earns a fraction of what his or her counterpart in the United States earns. What if you could beam that foreign accountant for a day into Manhattan? Thanks to digital technology, you can.

Baldwin calls this the *globotics revolution,* the merger of globalization and robotics. Given the progress of technology, many more services are now tradable. "Telemigrants" in countries with low wages can perform the same jobs as millions of higher-paid service workers in advanced economies. When accountants in the United States join the ranks of factory workers who watched their jobs go abroad, should we impose trade restrictions on foreign accountants? On insurance agents? On money managers and lawyers? Or computer programmers? Or call center service workers?

Initially, workers in poor economies will compete with service workers in advanced economies. Over time, robots or *globots* will replace service workers everywhere. They take no lunch breaks, bathroom breaks, vacations, and at least in the foreseeable future they won't demand raises. Hence, Baldwin predicts a "globotics upheaval" ending in a violent confrontation between humans and the machines replacing them.

The consequences of global trade and technology shift relative economic power. Disruptions mobilize antiglobalization advocates. But let's not be too hasty, even where China is concerned. "Mutual efforts to exclude one another's technologies from national supply chains would break the global innovation ecosystem," former US Treasury secretary Henry Paulson warned in a *Financial Times* column.[22]

Instead of shutting down forces that have propelled centuries of global progress, the right solution is to forge a peaceful coexistence for trade, automation, and people, with policies that seriously support those left behind. As any policy maker can attest, however, anything resembling the optimal result is far easier said than done.

However well intentioned, deglobalization fights the wrong battle. No one says it more succinctly than my colleague Gordon Hanson: "Encouraging optimism about the reshoring of jobs would only lead to more disappointment, and might further fuel the backlash against free trade and globalization."[23]

An excessive backlash to trade and globalization is a megathreat to the high-tech world in which we live. We will be lucky if, after three decades of hyperglobalization, we don't slip into a radical deglobalization. A *slowbalization* outcome—while not ideal and still quite costly—looks preferable. In a *slowbalized* world, the US and China would operate competing trading and investment systems. Most nations will align with one. Some may try to stay on good terms with both rivals. Decoupling on technology, data, information, and some sensitive services (say apps that collect sensitive information) and goods (say microchips) would be quite significant. Low-end trade in goods would remain in place. Restrictions might hamper investment in tech and sensitive sectors, but foreign direct investment would continue. Labor mobility—even in the academic world—would face new hurdles but not outright bans. We will see reshoring and friend-shoring at the expense of full on-shoring. Resource nationalism would surface but not to a radical extent. Workers left behind will depend on social welfare programs and retraining in lieu of protecting jobs that no longer make economic sense. Regional trade would displace global pacts. To be sure, slowbalization would curb competition and productivity, adding stagflationary pressures. But catastrophic results comparable to the Great Depression would be avoided.

As Chapter 8 will show, trade is not the biggest factor to fear. It is artificial intelligence and automation that might soon eclipse not only globalization, but Homo sapiens too, as a megathreat to our common prosperity.

Chapter 8

The AI Threat

I have argued that technological progress does not, in the aggregate, destroy jobs. But what happens when that technology is actually intelligent? As science fiction and reality merge in the realm of artificial intelligence, machine learning, robotics, and automation, brace for a cruel twist on the hopes and dreams of inventors ever since the first "mechanical assistants." No matter what work you do, artificial intelligence might eventually do it better. Will modern Luddites, for the first time since the original Luddites, finally be correct? The possibility is very real that a tiny top echelon will win while everybody else loses their jobs, their incomes, and their dignity. Mary Shelley's Frankenstein pales next to this lurking megathreat.

Until very recently the burden of proof stymied believers in the transformative power of artificial intelligence, or *AI*. A so-called AI winter prevailed during the 1980s and 1990s, as progress was painfully slow and seemed to support skeptics who maintained that computers could never match, much less exceed, the je ne sais quoi of human intellectual prowess. Machines improved at doing repetitive things, but deep thinking appeared to remain an exclusively human dimension.

Debate still persists, but the gap between organic and artificial intelligence has decidedly narrowed. Algorithms often ask humans if we are robots before granting access to sensitive websites. By some accounts the gap will soon vanish. More pressure these days compels skeptics to name tasks that computers can *never do*—from bricklaying to neurosurgery. But even with bricklaying, why couldn't a robot handle it, as there are already AI and 3D technologies printing prefab homes that can build walls far faster than any bricklayer?

Every boost in computing speed and capacity shortens the list.

An extreme scenario features the marriage of super intelligent humans with computers that surpass human intelligence, and with robots that have superhuman mechanical abilities. Beyond that point, the world becomes unrecognizable. In effect, we would face a whole new hybrid human species with superior brains and brawn that could displace Homo sapiens, just as we displaced Neanderthal hominids.

If you think your job is safe, think again. Along with desirable boosts in productivity, AI packs unwanted personal and systemic disruption. Before machines get more intelligent than humans, effectively taking control of major portions of technology itself, and technological growth becomes uncontrollable and irreversible, a moment that experts call the singularity, vanishing jobs will strain consumer demand. New jobs may come along to replace them, as in the past, but not if tailored algorithms can fill those jobs as well. Raising productivity sounds great as the economic pie grows fast until rising inequality and shrinking consumer demand puts more people out of work. When the spiral accelerates, economies hit hard times.

For now, the race is on to deploy artificial intelligence without limit. "This technology will be applied in pretty much every industry out there that has any kind of data—anything from genes to images to language," AI entrepreneur Richard Socher, the founder of MetaMind, told *The Economist* in 2016. "AI will be everywhere." Salesforce, a public company that helps other companies reach customers, got the message and acquired MetaMind.[1]

Here's one recent example of technology that reduces costs and eliminates jobs, one that could be directed by AI. Early in 2021, the *New York Post* reported that a 1,407-square-foot gray house with white trim and a front porch on a quarter-acre lot went up for sale in Calverton, New York.

As the first 3D-printed house to obtain approval for sale on Long Island, it made news.[2] Equipment that prints houses and office buildings resembles a giant hot glue gun on a mechanical arm. Guided by a computer, it dispenses layers of liquid cement in lines to create walls, leaving space for windows and doors. Constructing the frame in nine days required just two workers to monitor the equipment. It cut in half the cost for a conventional house.

In July 2021, the Netherlands' Queen Maxima watched a robot cut a ribbon to open a footbridge that spans a canal in the heart of Amsterdam and had been built using a 3D printer.

Touting the bridge's aesthetic appeal, a spokesman predicted much more to come. "It's not about making things cheaper and more efficient for us," Tim Geurtjens said, "it's about giving architects and designers a new tool—a new very cool tool—in which they can rethink the design of their architecture and their designs."[3] But now consider the power of AI connected to this scale of 3D printing. When will a computer propose designs without a bridge architect? An architect spends years learning her craft by studying engineering and design. A computer could acquire as much structural knowledge in less than a day.

Do not suppose that creativity requires people. The elusive spark of human ingenuity faces digital competition. To beat world chess champion Garry Kasparov multiple times in 1997, IBM Deep Blue devised inventive strategies. Yet that was just an opening gambit compared to Deep Mind, a self-teaching algorithm. In 2016, a Deep Mind computer christened AlphaGo mastered a game with more possible moves than there are atoms in the universe. "It studies games that humans have played, it knows the rules and then it comes up with creative moves," *Wired* editor in chief Nicholas Thompson told PBS *Frontline*.[4] In a much-touted contest, AlphaGo outplayed the reigning world Go champion Lee Sedol in four out of five tries.

Game two marked a watershed moment for AI. The thirty-seventh placement of a piece on the Go board "was a move that humans could not fathom, but yet it ended up being brilliant and woke people up to say,

'Wow, after thousands of years of playing, we never thought about making a move like that,'" AI scientist Kai-Fu Lee told *Frontline*. Another expert observer suggested, in a sobering coda, that the victory for AI wasn't so much about a computer beating a human as one form of intelligence beating another. In this battle of brains, neither side enjoys special status.

"You can get into semantics about what does reasoning mean, but clearly the AI system was reasoning at that point," says *New York Times* journalist Craig Smith, who now hosts the podcast *Eye on AI*.[5]

A year later, AlphaGo Zero bested AlphaGo by learning the rules of the game and then generating billions of data points in just three days. Deep learning has progressed with mind-bending speed. In 2020, Deep Mind's AlphaFold2 revolutionized the field of biology by solving "the protein-folding problem" that had stumped medical researchers for five decades. Besides probing massive volumes of molecular data on protein structures, AlphaFold deployed "transformers," an innovative neural network that Google Brain scientists unveiled in a 2017 paper. Resolving the protein-folding problem opens the door to significant new bio-medical breakthroughs.

AI-generated artistic initiatives have earned applause. "We have taught a computer to write musical scores," Gustavo Diaz-Jerez, a software consultant and pianist, told the BBC in 2017. "Now we can produce modern classical music at the touch of a button." Apart from a rule that playing the music cannot require more than five fingers on each of two hands, compositions proceed with very little guidance — and the London Symphony Orchestra has performed several of them.[6] It may only be a matter of time until AI-generated songs make it to the top of the Billboard Hot 100 chart or when an AI-generated novel reaches the *New York Times* bestseller list.

Technology has already channeled Pablo Picasso. A century ago he painted over an image that was hidden until now. "The nude portrait of a crouching woman has been brought to life by an artificial intelligence–powered software trained to paint like the legendary artist," NBC News reported in October 2021.[7]

Don't rule out machines that care. "Xpeng Unveils Smart Robot Pony for Children, Taking It a Step Closer to Its Vision of the Future of Mobility," the *South China Morning Post* reported in September 2021. "The company said the smart pony, called Little White Dragon, is equipped with power modules, motion control, intelligent navigation and intelligent emotional interaction capabilities."[8]

Forbes book reviewer Calum Chace saw robotic empathy in *A World Without Work,* by Daniel Susskind. "We cannot be confident," Chace wrote, "that jobs requiring affective capabilities will always be reserved for humans: machines can already tell if you are happy, surprised, or depressed. Or gay. Some AI systems can tell these things by your facial expressions, and others by how you walk, or dance, or type."[9] So even nursing jobs for the elderly—previously thought as being available only to humans—may be soon replaced by emotionally intelligent nursing robots.

How many middle-class, white-collar jobs hinge on random access at the right moments to information and skills acquired and stored over the course of a career? The McKinsey Institute, a research arm of the global management consulting firm, concluded in 2016 that compared to the industrial revolution, AI is transforming society "ten times faster and at 300 times the scale, or roughly 3,000 times the impact."[10]

Researchers Carl Benedikt Frey and Michael Osborne at Oxford University looked into potential job disruption by computers in 702 occupations. Their study, published in 2013, determined that 47 percent of jobs in America were highly vulnerable to substitution by computer capital in the near future. During the Great Depression, 25 percent of Americans were out of work.[11]

Unlike board games that adhere to strict rules, the television game show *Jeopardy!* features puns, slang, red herrings, vernacular, mischievous wordplay, and obscure associations to elicit factual knowledge on topics from pop culture to the esoteric. No human competitor outperformed erstwhile computer programmer and trivia whiz Ken Jennings, who won *Jeopardy!* seventy-four times, a legendary streak. Under intense pressure, with the speed of a Google search, he named, for instance, the leader whose brother is believed to be the first known European to have died in the Americas and the disease that prompted US surgeon general Walter Wyman to establish a hospital in Hawaii in 1901 (answers: "Who is Leif Erikson?" and "What is leprosy?").

Jennings, though, was no match for AI. By his own account in a 2013 TED Talk, IBM's Watson defeated him handily. He commiserated with Detroit factory workers who became obsolete when robots took their jobs. "I'm not an economist," Jennings said. "All I know is how it felt to be the guy put out of work and it was freaking demoralizing. It was terrible," he recalled. "Here's the one thing that I was ever good at and all it took was IBM pouring tens of millions of dollars and its smartest people and thousands of processors working in parallel and they could do the same thing. They could do it a little bit faster and a little better on national TV and I'm sorry Ken, we don't need you anymore." He began to wonder, Where would digital outsourcing of jobs stop? "I felt like a quiz show contestant was now the first job that had become obsolete under this new regime of thinking computers and it hasn't been the last."[12]

The philosopher Friedrich Nietzsche envisioned upheaval a century before personal computers arrived. "Every step forward," he warned in *The Genealogy of Morals*, "is made at the cost of mental and physical pain to someone."

Robotics and AI firms say you'll have to wait quite some time before you can own anything remotely similar to Rosey the Robot from *The Jetsons*, the *Washington Post* reported in March 2021. Rosey worked for the cartoon family residing in a future with flying cars and homes elevated to cloud level. "Rosey cooks. She cleans. And she still finds time to play ball with Elroy. Rosey is the ideal maid. Respectful. Even tempered. Does exactly what she's told. She's the computer-driven Jill of all trades." What's more, Rosey gives sass when suitable. "Beneath the aluminum alloy core beats a battery-powered heart of pure gold."[13]

We'll get there. "The biggest problem is safety," the former chairman of Boston Dynamics, Marc Raibert, told the *Post*. The company has developed agile robots that resemble animals. "The more complicated the robot, the more safety concerns. If you have a robot in close proximity to a person, and anything that goes wrong, that's a risk to that person," Raibert said.[14]

Decades ago, long before there were any actual robots, the science fiction writer Isaac Asimov proposed three laws to keep us safe from machines we create. Widely quoted since, he first enumerated them in a 1942 short story titled "Runaround." One, a robot may not injure a human being or, through inaction, allow a human being to come to harm. Two, a robot must obey orders given it by human beings except where such orders would conflict with the First Law. Three, a robot must protect its own existence as long as such protection does not conflict with the First or Second Law.

These laws may not be enough. Writing in the Spring 2016 *Harvard Journal of Law and Technology,* Matthew Scherer weighed inherent conflict when safety competes with completing a task. "Much of the modern scholarship regarding the catastrophic risks associated with AI focuses on systems that seek to maximize a utility function, even when such maximization could pose an existential risk to humanity."[15] In other words, robots may pose a threat by doing what they are supposed to do.

What can go wrong on the job? Plenty. A twenty-two-year-old worker died in a Volkswagen plant in Germany, crushed against a metal plate while setting up a stationary robot in 2015. The same year, a robot arm killed a woman in a Michigan auto plant. A self-driven Uber vehicle killed a woman in 2018 while its back-up safety driver was streaming an episode of *The Voice*.[16] Authorities let Uber off the hook and charged the back-up driver with negligent homicide.

Killer robots are not the only hitch. People still do some jobs better. Walmart sacked inventory robots in 2020 because "humans can scan products more simply and more efficiently than bulky six-foot-tall machines," according to the *Washington Post*.[17]

An employer can't tell a computer to suck it up and work harder.

"Flippy, the burger-flipping robot that threatens to supplant short-order cooks, has taken its first extended break," *USA Today* reported.[18] Flippy, billed as the world's first autonomous robotic kitchen assistant, wasn't to blame. It seems that publicity surrounding her deployment in 2018 in Pasadena, California, created too much demand. Flippy could not keep up. The CaliBurger chain retired Flippy 1.0 and hired more people.

CaliBurger has since deployed Flippy 2.0 in Fort Myers, Florida.[19] There is a hefty appetite for wider use in the fast-food industry where employee turnover can exceed 50 percent a year at a cost of $3.4 billion in recruiting and training.

Despite some large hurdles, the smart money bets on artificial intelligence. Consumers do not sound surprised. A study by the Pew Research Center in 2017 concluded that three-fourths of Americans find it at least "somewhat realistic" that robots and computers will eventually handle most jobs that people do now.

In Japan, convenience store operator FamilyMart has embraced AI, partly in response to the country's worker shortage. The company intends to open one thousand fully automated shops by the end of 2024. An unmanned FamilyMart outlet will stock around three thousand items, the same selection available in shops where people work. A trial store about a third the usual size used fifty cameras to monitor activity and handle payment.[20]

Algorithms are rewriting the art of selling. "Retail Set to Overtake Banking in AI Spending," the *Wall Street Journal* reported in 2021. The website Pinterest assists retailers that use the site to sell their goods. "Everything you can think of in almost every part of retail is being powered by AI," Jeremy King, Pinterest's senior vice president of engineering, told the *Journal*. King is also a former executive vice president and chief technology officer at Walmart; he currently sits on the board of Wayfair, which sells furniture and home goods online, and which uses AI to match shoppers with items they might want.[21]

Since 2017, a German e-commerce retailer named Otto has applied AI technology used in particle physics experiments at the CERN laboratory.

"It analyses around 3 billion past transactions and 200 variables (such as past sales, searches on Otto's site and weather information) to predict what customers will buy a week before they order," *The Economist* reported.[22]

Home Depot, a brick-and-mortar retailer, taps machine learning to restock shelves. Experts predict that global spending on AI by retailers alone will exceed $200 billion in 2025, a big jump from $85 billion in 2021.[23] "You cannot really operate anymore without having the heavy investment in machine learning," Fiona Tan, Wayfair's head of customer and supplier technology, told the *Journal*.

Rudimentary automatons have existed since ancient Greece and Rome ruled the world. The earliest inventors used springs and coils to make mechanical devices mimic movements by humans or animals.[24]

Meaningful devices that help humans perform tasks proliferated with the industrial revolution in the late eighteenth century. The prospects of machines doing work soon spawned conflict, most famously with the Luddites, who smashed knitting looms. Mill owner William Horsfall paid the ultimate price for automating work. He was shot dead in 1812 while heading home from the Huddersfield town center.[25]

Economist David Ricardo recognized the handwriting on the wall by 1821, thinking seriously about the "influence of machinery on the interests of the different classes of society." In 1839, Thomas Carlyle (who famously called economics "the dismal science") fretted about the "demon of mechanism" and its prospects for "oversetting whole multitudes of workmen."[26] Around the same time, Karl Marx took aim. "Capitalist production," he warned, "develops technology, and the combining together of various processes into a social whole, only by sapping the original sources of all wealth—the soil and the laborer."[27]

In 1930, John Maynard Keynes contemplated "Economic Possibilities for Our Grandchildren":

We are being afflicted with a new disease of which some readers may not yet have heard the name, but of which they will hear a great deal in the years to come—namely, *technological unemployment*. This means unemployment due to our discovery of means of economising the use of labour outrunning the pace at which we can find new uses for labour.[28]

Keynes foresaw only "a temporary phase of maladjustment." He was largely correct, at least until now. "All this means in the long run that mankind is solving its economic problem," he wrote. "I would predict that the standard of life in progressive countries one hundred years hence will be between four and eight times as high as it is to-day. There would be nothing surprising in this even in the light of our present knowledge. It would not be foolish to contemplate the possibility of far greater progress still." He also predicted that technological innovation would lead to a sharp fall in the workweek so that workers could spend most of their time enjoying leisure and artistic and creative activities.

World War II accelerated the pace for automation. Assembly lines built war materiel, newfangled radar tracked aircraft, and researchers at Bletchley Park, England, used advanced mathematics to break secret German naval codes that revealed the whereabouts of deadly submarines. The brilliant and tragic Alan Turing led the code-breaking initiative. His Enigma machine shortened the war and saved countless lives.

After the war, Turing wrote a paper entitled "Computing Machinery and Intelligence." Instead of asking whether machines can think, he wondered whether computer responses might seem human by replicating the external manifestations of human thought processes. "This is the premise of Turing's 'imitation game,' where a computer attempts to convince a human interrogator that it is, in fact, human rather than machine," according to Matthew Scherer in the Spring 2016 *Harvard Journal of Law and Technology*.[29]

Turing imagined a place for artificial intelligence two decades before the term was coined. According to his biographer, Andrew Hodges, "[Turing] supposed it possible to equip the machine with 'television cameras, microphones, loudspeakers, wheels and *handling servo mechanisms* as well as some sort of *electronic brain.'"* Turing proposed, moreover, "that it should 'roam the countryside' so that it 'should have a chance of finding things out for itself.'"[30] We are now not far from satisfying the Turing Test, when a human cannot tell if she is interacting with a machine.

No institution caught on faster than the Pentagon. "New Navy Device Learns by Doing," the *New York Times* reported in July 1958. "The Navy said the perceptron would be the first non-living mechanism 'capable of receiving, recognizing and identifying its surroundings without any human training or control.'" In 1962, the first commercial robot took its place on an automotive assembly line.[31] President John F. Kennedy nixed a press conference on the subject of robots and labor and took no action to form a Federal Automation Commission, but he did give a speech about the need to address problems arising from automation.

Anthropomorphic computers got an eerie boost when HAL 9000 commandeered a mission to Jupiter in Stanley Kubrick's 1968 film, *2001: A Space Odyssey.* Suddenly, humans were dominated by a computer instead of vice versa. HAL's intentions were suspect. "I know I've made some very poor decisions recently," a deadpan HAL confessed to astronauts aboard the spaceship, "but I can give you my complete assurance that my work will be back to normal. I've still got the greatest enthusiasm and confidence in the mission. And I want to help you." He added a dire warning: "This mission," HAL announced, "is too important for me to allow you to jeopardize it." For any artificial intelligence, completing a mission is paramount.

In the years after the film, computers began to alter the nature of work as robots proliferated on shop floors. In 1980, the *New York Times* published an op-ed by Harley Shaiken, a labor activist. Its title: "A Robot Is After Your Job."[32] Shaiken was blunt: "The introduction of revolutionary new technologies such as robots—versatile computer-controlled mechanical arms—raise two painful possibilities: sizeable losses of jobs and a deteriorated quality of working life." He advocated an ethos that competed with unfettered capitalism. "The goal, after all, should be a technology that benefits people—not one that destroys them."

Harvard economist Wassily Leontief amplified a grim message in a 1982 special issue of *Scientific American* magazine. Leontief spelled out issues that have intensified ever since:

> There are signs today, however, that past experience cannot serve as a reliable guide for the future of technological change. With the advent of solid-state electronics, machines that have been displacing human muscle from the production of goods are being succeeded by machines that take over the functions of the human nervous system not only in production but in the service industries as well... The relation between man and machine is being radically transformed... Computers are now taking on the jobs of white-collar workers, performing first simple and then increasingly complex mental tasks. Human labor from time immemorial played the role of principal factor of production. There are reasons to believe human labor will not retain this status in the future.[33]

Leontief wryly compared humans to horses displaced when the industrial revolution supplied automated horsepower. Artificial intelligence is on track to displace human brainpower in the same way, challenging policy makers to keep up. Yet not until October 2016 did the Obama administration release a report entitled "Preparing for the Future of Artificial Intelligence."[34] Both a primer on artificial intelligence and a prescription for interactions between humans and machines, it relied on evidence suggesting that the negative affect of automation would hurt low-wage jobs most.

The artificial intelligence genie is out of the bottle. Its powers are growing, fueled by human nature and free markets. "No matter what monks in their Himalayan caves or philosophers in their ivory towers say, for the capitalist juggernaut, happiness is pleasure. Period," writes Yuval Harari, the author of *Homo Deus,* a book that posits the marriage of Homo sapiens with artificial intelligence—and super intelligent offspring. By his lights, scientific research and economic activity seek happiness by "producing better pain killers, new ice-cream flavours, more comfortable mattresses, and more addictive games for our smart phones, so that we will not suffer a single boring moment while waiting for the bus."[35]

Demographic challenges spur AI to do more. "As China's working population falls, factories turn to machines to pick up the slack," the *South China Morning Post* reported in 2021.[36] Don't look for a person on the shop floor at Midea, a leading maker of home appliances, in Foshan, China. "Human beings have been physically removed from this assembly line, replaced by robots and digital-savvy technicians and engineers operating at a distance." Once machines get the hang of decisions that remaining people make, those jobs will vanish too.

Efficient competition can bend rules in unsavory ways. "As pricing mechanisms shift to computer pricing algorithms, so too will the types of collusion," authors Ariel Ezrachi and Maurice Stucke contend in the *University of Illinois Law Review*. "We are shifting from the world where executives expressly collude in smoke-filled hotel rooms to a world where pricing algorithms continually monitor and adjust to each other's prices and market data."[37] Surrender scruples or face unpleasant consequences.

Uneasy lies the head that built the algorithm. Is AI a friend or foe? Will self-learning algorithms replace more human roles, including programmers, than industries of the future can create?

In their book, *The Second Machine Age,* authors Erik Brynjolfsson and Andrew McAfee dismiss the fear that the job market will vanish. They anticipate jobs no one has yet thought of thanks to staggering technological progress.[38] Who foresaw jobs in electronics, data processing, or telecommunications when agricultural and manufacturing jobs began to disappear?

It's a fair question, but replacing brainpower is different from replacing muscle power. Good jobs that emerged from the decline of manufacturing and rise of services required brains, not brawn. "Knowledge worker" was the category that everyone wanted to join. But now we have lost our monopoly on knowledge. Artificial intelligence can handle desirable jobs better and faster than human brains can handle them. There will be jobs for people, but who will want them?

"The problem is not the number of jobs but the quality and accessibility of those jobs," says MIT economist David Autor, a prominent expert on the future of work. He reminds a TED audience that automated teller machines (ATMs) slashed the need for bank tellers.[39] The result? Banks built more branches and put would-be tellers to more productive use.

Authors Daniel Susskind and Martin Ford embrace dystopian views in their respective books. They expect AI and robots to fill most jobs. "As we move through the twenty-first century, the demand for the work of human beings is likely to wither away, gradually,"[40] Daniel Susskind warns in *A World Without Work*. Likewise, Martin Ford in *Rise of the Robots* worries about the threat of a jobless future.

Let's pause for a moment and look harder at the argument that this time, technological progress will be different. That this is the revolution that will leave us with few and/or worse jobs, unlike all past revolutions. What is different this time?

Industrial revolutions increase productivity. The first revolution introduced steam power. The second revolution launched mass manufacturing. The third revolution harnessed electricity. The first three industrial revolutions ended many jobs but created more new ones, after some turmoil. None permanently displaced humans. Incomes rose as manufacturing jobs lured superfluous farm workers to move to cities. When manufacturing jobs vanished, the service sector started hiring.

Today, however, there are fewer places for human workers to go. High-tech firms, the last bastion of fruitful careers, employ far fewer workers than industrial giants in past generations. Facebook—now Meta—is a good example. In late 2021, Meta's market cap (the combined value of all of its shares) was $942 billion, making it the world's seventh most valuable company. But it employed roughly 60,000 workers. Contrast that with Ford Motor Company: its market cap was $77 billion, but it employed 186,000 workers. Silicon Valley is full of extreme wealth and fast-growing companies, but the tech sector employs far fewer people than older sectors.

And what will happen to Uber drivers and truck drivers worldwide when automobiles drive themselves? Millions of jobs will disappear.

Technology has revolutionized work across the board. Robotic baristas and chefs can displace humans. Recipes are step-by-step instructions on how to cook meals—algorithms, in effect. Express checkout stations replace workers in brick-and-mortar retail stores. Today, e-commerce warehouses rely on robots to move inventory around. Tomorrow, robots and drones will deliver goods to their destinations.

Traditional education capped the typical classroom size at a few dozen students. Nowadays one teacher can reach millions of viewers. Why go to community colleges when top universities come into your home? The experience is not the same, and the outcomes are not identical—as study from home during the COVID-19 crisis showed. But the cost differential is massive, and over time the quality of online education and training will massively improve.

Financial services barely resemble those of a generation ago. Fierce competition has automated tens of thousands of back-office and customer-facing jobs. Computers handle payment services, credit allocation, insurance, capital market support and even asset management. Leading firms advertise algorithm-based guidance that diversifies and adjusts portfolios faster than humans.

Accounting and legal professionals are looking over their shoulders at electronic job candidates that read and process mountains of documents in seconds. After a pandemic boost, telemedicine has accustomed patients to online health assessments. Computers can instantly recall tens of thousands of similar symptoms and diagnoses. Mounting evidence that they discover health problems as reliably as humans moves medicine closer to automating the services of radiologists, nurses, and even physicians. Roles that require human empathy are not exempt. In Japan, hospitals and health care facilities deploy robots to cope with an aging population and a shortage of caregivers.

"If you think being a 'professional' makes your job safe, think again," warned former US labor secretary Robert Reich in an article that the World Economic Forum published. "The two sectors of the economy harboring the most professionals—health care and education—are under increasing pressure to cut costs. And expert machines are poised to take over."[41]

Researchers Daron Acemoglu at MIT and Pascual Restrepo at Boston University have measured the impact of robotics as it has been introduced in various industries. They found that one additional robot per thousand workers reduces employment by two tenths of one percent, and wages by half a percent.[42] If that sounds trivial, consider the trend. Jobs and incomes are supposed to increase over time. If automation reverses the trend, how do we progress?

MIT's Autor foresees plenty of jobs for highly skilled and very low-skilled workers. Corporate strategists, neurosurgeons, and health care aides need not make way yet for computers. The vast middle, however, looks problematic. Those jobs "carry out well-defined and codified procedures that increasingly can be done by machines." Dilberts everywhere, watch out.

Algorithms that learn on their own can do many more jobs once thought exempt from mechanization. Anyone who monitors data, whether doctors, lawyers, teachers, or forest rangers, must compete with mind-boggling computing power that scans and remembers vast amounts of data, and then might propose unconventional responses.

All this is why the AI revolution may be the first one that destroys overall jobs and wages. Complacency this time—the assumption that once again, the Luddites will be wrong—looks like a fatal mistake. AI encroaches on more jobs than in prior revolutions. It affects jobs across many industries, and it affects knowledge workers just as much as blue-collar workers.

Machine learning has accomplished one of the long-term hurdles holding back AI: natural-language processing. By allowing machines to scan vast corpuses of texts and do their own pattern analyses, AIs have learned how to translate between languages with remarkable success, and how to generate new texts with remarkable authenticity. The subtle grasp of language crosses one of the last obstacles en route to satisfying the Turing Test. "Distinguishing AI-generated text, images and audio from human generated will become extremely difficult," says Mustafa Suleyman, a cofounder of DeepMind and till recently head of AI policy at Google, as the "transformers" revolution accelerates the power of AI.[43] As a consequence, a large number of white-collar jobs using advanced levels of cognition will become obsolete. Humans won't know that their counterparts are machines.

When I met Demis Hassabis—the other cofounder of DeepMind— he compared the coming singularity to super intelligence that resembles ten thousand Einsteins solving any problem of science, medicine, technology, biology, or knowledge at the same time and in parallel. If that is the future, how can any human compete?

Indeed, AI initially replaced routine jobs. Then it started to replace cognitive jobs that repeat sequences of steps that a machine can master. Now AI is gradually able to perform even creative jobs. So for workers, including those in the creative industries, there is nowhere to hide.

All this is vaulting us even closer to artificial general intelligence, or AGI, where super intelligent machines leave humans in the dust. Author Ray Kurzweil and other visionaries predict a pivotal moment that will disrupt everything we know. An intelligence explosion will occur when computers develop motivation to learn on their own at warp speed without human direction. There are no limits to how fast or how much they can learn and what new connections they will find. This is what singularity looks like. Human brains will resemble vacuum tubes in the era of printed circuits, severely limited in capacity.

I asked Demis Hassabis whether ideas once relegated to science fiction look real. He predicts that we are only five major technological innovations and about twenty years away from the singularity.

Unless humans merge with computers, writer Yuval Harari warns, Homo sapiens are finished. They will become obsolete just like Homo erectus, Homo habilus, and other early humans that have long since vanished. Enter Homo deus, says Harari, which is smarter, stronger, and immortal so long as knowledge can move from one machine to the next iteration.

Oxford University philosopher Nick Bostrom, the author of *Superintelligence,* ranks artificial intelligence next to giant asteroid strikes and nuclear war as an existential threat to humanity. The late mathematician Stephen Hawking worried that AI "could spell the end of the human race." That is why he suggested that humans should move to other planets—as the machine will take over not only all jobs but also the human race. Tesla founder Elon Musk welcomes AI that controls electric cars his company makes, but putting AI in ultimate charge worries him. "It's fine if you've got Marcus Aurelius as the emperor," Musk told *The Economist,* "but not so good if you have Caligula."[44]

No one knows how long it will take for severe structural technological unemployment to make most workers irrelevant. But even the interim looks rocky, prone to negative demand shocks. All signs indicate that AI alternatives will drive down wages and salaries, and that downward drive affects a problem that is already festering.

As people earn less, inequality will grow. Technological innovation is capital intensive, high-skill biased and labor saving. If you own the machine or are in the top 5 percent of the human capital distribution, AI will make you richer and more productive. If you are a low- or even medium-skilled blue- or white-collar worker, AI will eventually reduce your wages and make your job obsolete. The trend is already visible in advanced economies where social stability depends on the universal opportunity to achieve success. Data compiled by the Central Intelligence Agency reveal that income inequality in the United States roughly matches levels in Argentina and Turkey.[45]

Daniel Susskind notes that wealth inequality in the United States is racing out of control. From 1981 to 2017, "the income share of the top 0.1 percent increased more than three and a half times from its already disproportionately high level, and the share of the top 0.01 percent rose more than fivefold." Susskind also cites research into inequality by the scholar Anthony Atkinson, who determined that the top 10 percent of earners saw their wages rise faster than the bottom 10 percent worldwide. Over four decades, Susskind reminds us, CEO incomes in the United States vaulted from 28 times that of an average worker to more than 376 times in 2000.[46]

Inequality also afflicts the world's second largest economy. The Chinese government is worried about the growing imbalance between rich and poor. "China's Media Stars Caught in Harsh Spotlight of Inequality Drive," *Nikkei Asia* reported in September 2021. "The country's tech titans have come under the watchful eye of authorities for practices deemed monopolistic or that run contrary to the common good. Now, even some of China's most popular stars find themselves in the unforgiving glare of the campaign."[47]

When the wealthy get wealthier and workers get less, economies suffer from a consumption problem: there isn't enough of it. Growth eventually may fall as low-income households spend almost everything they have, while the wealthy tend to save more. "As jobs and incomes are relentlessly automated away," author Martin Ford warns in *Rise of the Robots*, "the bulk of consumers may eventually come to lack the income and purchasing power necessary to drive the demand that is critical to sustained economic growth."[48]

Although there's no evidence it actually occurred, the colorful exchange attributed to Ford chairman Henry Ford and United Auto Workers president Walter Reuther helps illustrate the dilemma. The two men were mulling the advent of automation. Ford asked Reuther how robots will pay union dues. Reuther replied, how will Ford get them to buy his cars? That's how AI may cause capitalism to eventually self-destruct. A neo-Marxian view of underconsumption spurred by rising inequality that technology exacerbates.

Stepping back to the connections between our megathreats, this is where the debt burden and AI collide. In a world increasingly driven by AI the economic pie might become huge for those with highly developed skills that cannot be automated and those who own the means of production.

"Karl Marx was right," entrepreneur Jerry Kaplan told a tech-savvy audience at Google. "The struggle between capital and labor is a losing proposition for workers. What that means is that the benefits of automation naturally accrue to those who can invest in the new systems.'[49]

Massive debt disproportionately burdens the people left behind, who live off shrinking paychecks or with public assistance. Less developed countries are highly vulnerable. Those with capital can generate incomes and manage debt. It doesn't get ahead of them. But for most workers left behind by the rising machines, a bigger economic pie does not resolve the growing debt problem; it only gets worse.

As a human, I root for people. As an economist I must ask what is the most efficient use of resources? How can we assure the long-term continuation of progress and take care of workers? Priorities conflict.

Over the next decades there will be winners in parts of Europe, China, and North America. Many other countries will become losers, swept under by technological unemployment and drowning in debt they cannot service much less ever repay. Polarization will pit the rich against the poor.

Enter the new *precariat*, educated and semi-skilled workers who lose careers to AI and end up in gig work with unstable income and no benefits. They will go from job to job with no future, falling through a fraying safety net. Then what happens? As incomes fall, they may try to borrow more. Debt loads increase as income gaps widen. An ugly situation that currently looks intractable gets worse with no sure remedy in sight.

Education geared to a world with increased automation might salvage some incomes, but a shrinking job market limits potential. Unfortunately, more education is no panacea to the onslaught of AI. Returns on education were higher when a modest upgrade in skills could lead to a better job and more income. When entry-level jobs require advanced degrees, however, upgrades short of that won't change the picture. Not everyone has enough talent and inclination to program computers,

explore databases, improve AI, write successful novels, or become entrepreneurs. When AI displaces skilled work, the returns from education
become smaller.

If people cannot work, then what? The answer looks like a political
minefield: it's time to tax the winners. A tiny contingent will reap the
lucrative rewards that AI bestows. Taxing robots as if they were human
sounds appealing but really amounts to almost the same thing: taxing the
owners of the machines.

If we adjust taxation for this brave new world the next question centers on redistribution that is vital to sustaining demand for the goods that
robots produce. One option surfaced during the 2020 presidential campaign in the United States: universal basic income (UBI) that lets consumers consume. Besides replacing lost income, proposals include more
robust public services under the banner of universal basic provision
(UBP). Twists abound, including community service in exchange for UBI.
We could give each individual a share of ownership of all firms. Then
they would receive capital returns even if their labor incomes are challenged. If you think about it, this is a form of socialism where every worker
owns the means of production. It is not hard to envision a scenario where
people who demonize these choices today as socialist will clamor for them
when algorithms perform brain surgery and prepare fast food.

Any of these options will lead to pitched political battles. If we squabble long enough, computers may get to decide how to divide the economic pie. By then, let's hope they have empathy.

"The most important question in twenty-first-century economics,"
says Yuval Harari, "may well be to do with all the superfluous people.
What will conscious humans do once we have highly intelligent
non-conscious algorithms that can do almost everything better?"[50] In
some dystopian scenarios, "superfluous" people disappear. UBI lets them
play video games all day and use drugs that eventually precipitate "deaths
of despair." Drug overdoses caused more than one hundred thousand
deaths in the United States in 2021. Alternatively, young men may become
sexually inactive *incels* who don't reproduce themselves and thus

disappear. Our dystopian future may conflate Orwell's Big Brother, Huxley's Brave New World and the Hunger Games.

We are racing toward destiny. Human nature propels us forward. I won't sugarcoat a story about super intelligent artificial offspring. I do not foresee a happy future where new jobs replace the jobs that automation snatches. This revolution looks terminal. The flowering of artificial intelligence might alter human life beyond recognition.

Earth may be lucky to reach the intelligence explosion of the singularity. Will a deadly pandemic finish us before the transition to machines is complete? Will climate change destroy the planet before rational machines come to the rescue? Will we suffocate under a mountain of debt? Or will the United States and China destroy the world in a military conflict as competition to control the industries of the future becomes extreme? Indeed who controls AI may become the dominant world superpower. This geopolitical rivalry forms the megathreat we turn to next.

Chapter 9

The New Cold War

If you want to gauge the scale of China's geopolitical ambition, visit Tiananmen Square in Beijing. As big as eighty-three American football fields, it is vast not only in size but also in history. On one side, the Forbidden City evokes six centuries of emperors who lived there in divine seclusion. Across the square, the Great Hall of the People celebrates the revolution that launched the Chinese Communist Party to power in 1949. The plaza itself recalls the 1989 uprising that ended in a government massacre of peaceful protesters, settling any question of who's in charge.

In 2015 the Berggruen Institute invited several dozen Western business and academic leaders to meet the Chinese president, Xi Jinping. We convened at the Great Hall, with its sweeping marble steps and grandiose columns. A majestic lobby dedicated to the people resembled a royal palace. We sat down in a large auditorium where hundreds of party functionaries often applaud their leaders on cue.

Xi Jinping appeared when we were silent and still. The message was obvious. Like an emperor, *he was granting us an audience.* Tall and self-confident, this son of a party leader who fell from favor during the Cultural Revolution held total command of the Middle Kingdom.

His remarks took a turn rooted in European history. He talked specifically about the Thucydides Trap, a concept that refers to the friction between two ancient Greek city-states, a dominant Sparta and a rising Athens. Thucydides, the ancient historian, argued that their competition for influence and power sparked the Peloponnesian Wars during the latter half of the fifth century BCE. Xi argued that the rise of China would be peaceful and one should not worry that the emergence of China would lead to a modern Thucydides Trap.

Does the rise of a new power, threatening an established power, always lead to war? Harvard professor Graham Allison tested that ancient thesis in his book, *Destined for War: Can America and China Escape Thucydides's Trap?*[1] He looked at sixteen confrontations between rising and dominant powers since the 1500s. In twelve of them, wars erupted. They engulfed Portugal and Spain, France and the Habsburg Empire, the Habsburg and the Ottoman Empires, France and England, among others—until two world wars and the prospects of nuclear annihilation sobered us up. The Cold War is one of the four exceptional cases that ended peacefully, mostly because the rising Soviet Union became a declining power, eventually collapsing from within.

Another exception is the British Empire. The United States eclipsed the United Kingdom without a fight, in part because changing control posed no threat to the English language or its political and economic regime; and the United Kingdom needed the US support in both world wars. Those two exceptions do not provide much encouragement for the United States and China.

On balance, Thucydides got it right. When rising and existing powers chafe, wars usually and eventually occur. Professor Allison dubbed this predicament the Thucydides Trap for good reason.

Xi Jinping, whose daughter attended Harvard, referred repeatedly to the Thucydides Trap in his remarks. China and the United States can both flourish, he reassured us. China is on its way to becoming the world's dominant power, but don't worry. Rivals need not shed blood. We can cooperate and compete without going to war, he implicitly suggested.

I left that meeting impressed by Xi but not ready to relinquish an ancient Chinese lesson: *study the past,* Confucius advised, *if you would divine the future.*

Even setting aside the worst-case military scenario, bruising economic and geopolitical rivalry endangers us all. Once China wields the world's biggest economic club, as most experts predict it will before 2030, squabbles over offshoring and protectionism will sound trivial. The United States may lose leadership in the technologies of the future that increasingly link everything from toasters to aircraft carriers. An emerging new cold war is already becoming colder and will disrupt supply chains and rearrange alliances. Disruptions will unsettle markets. Tie-ups will make post-pandemic scarcity seem like abundance. Prices may rise as the US economy stalls, the twin hallmarks of stagflation. Crises may rattle manufacturing, banking, and housing not once in a while but with numbing frequency.

Brace yourself. As a new cold war between the United States and China reshapes global economic and geopolitical reality, an authoritarian China may dictate new rules. And in this cold war each side will rely on its allies to confront the other power. The United States has its NATO allies in Europe as well as allies in Asia, such as Japan, South Korea, Australia, and increasingly now an India that fears the rise of China. China on its side has a number of de facto allies: Russia, Iran, and North Korea—as well as Pakistan and other nations—all revisionist powers that are trying to challenge the economic, financial and geopolitical global order that the United States and the West created after World War II. So a broader cold war between the West and China (and its allies) is rapidly brewing, with the brutal Russian invasion of Ukraine being one of the first military salvos of a cold war that is likely to become hot at some point in the next two decades. Indeed, Xi and Russian president Vladimir Putin met in early 2022—right before the Russian invasion of Ukraine—to form an implicit alliance between their two countries. They declared that their strategic partnership has "no limits."

Who could have foreseen this vigorous competition when President Nixon visited China in 1971? The two countries shared little apart from a desire to flourish. The United States, a liberal democracy less than two hundred years old, led the world in almost every economic measure. The dollar supplied the world with a stable currency everyone could rely on. The United States had problems, to be sure, but no one in the free world questioned its hegemonic global leadership.

In China, a fledgling Communist regime struggled to feed a vast and growing population. China's civilization dates back to the Qin dynasty, two centuries BCE. Its Great Wall took nearly two hundred years to complete. The Grand Canal, a waterway built over twelve centuries using technology no more advanced than shovels, stretches two thousand kilometers, about the distance from Bangor, Maine, to Denver, Colorado. China invented papermaking, movable type printing, gunpowder, the compass, alcohol, and the mechanical clock,[2] but Nixon touched down in a country where industry barely existed in the rubble of failed economic policies and a cultural revolution that had made Western education a crime.

American expectations for the historic visit centered on improved exports to a country with a billion people. "Grains and Soybeans Advance on News of Nixon's China Trip," the *New York Times* reported.[3] In its analysis, the *Times* concluded that "Mr. Nixon's immediate objective is to make his trip to China a genuine turning point in American diplomacy and not just a stunt for political and propaganda effect."[4] Strategically more important, the opening to China also helped the United States isolate the Soviet Union, a factor that helped bring the Cold War to its successful conclusion two decades later.

Sensing history in the making, local newspapers made space for international coverage. "The visit unquestionably will serve a two-fold purpose," wrote editors at the *Greenfield Recorder* in Greenfield, Massachusetts. "Business for the U.S., and propaganda for the Chinese. It remains to be seen which becomes foremost and whether Nixon will gain the results he desires." The editorial added a memorable caveat. Should "Red China" extend its global influence, it might mean "responsibility for precipitating the world into military and economic chaos."[5]

Prevailing wisdom did not stifle the late economist and Hoover Institution fellow Harry Rowen. "When will China become a democracy?" he asked in 1996. "The answer is around the year 2015. This prediction is based on China's steady and impressive economic growth which in turn fits the pattern of the way in which freedom has grown in Asia and elsewhere in the world."[6] This prediction proved to be wrong.

As the eighties unfolded, a gigantic and cheap labor force lured American companies to China. The previous decade of strikes and stagflation lent irresistible appeal to low-cost production and complacent workers who could not walk out. Goods made in China started reaching retail shelves worldwide and China became a powerful manufacturing exporter. The Chamber of Commerce and other American industry groups lobbied for accommodating trade arrangements. Eager for new markets, the United States bestowed most-favored-nation status on China, subject to annual renewals.

China grew fast but the United States also grew robustly in the 1980s, easing any jitters that China might become a formidable adversary. Meanwhile, Chinese students flocked to US colleges, universities, and graduate schools to study science and business. They returned home with American technology and voracious appetites for free enterprise and a more market-oriented economy.

The Chinese Communist Party under Chairman Deng Xiaoping encouraged private markets without relinquishing its iron grasp on power. Free enterprise zones proliferated. Yet the party did not view the West as a model to emulate. Partisan democracy saddled with economic stagnation looked to Chinese policy makers very much like the precipice that doomed the impoverished Soviet Union. "If there is one thing the CCP can be relied on never to produce," observed historian Niall Ferguson, "it is a Chinese Mikhail Gorbachev."[7] In 1989, amid pro-democracy protests in Tiananmen Square, the party unleashed the military. There is no official death toll, but the numbers were certainly in the hundreds, if not thousands. It marked the end of any hopes for an elected government and a gradual transition to democracy.

The crackdown stoked division in Washington, DC. Secretary of State James A. Baker III, speaking for the administration of Republican president George H. W. Bush, cautioned against punishing China, proposing a balance between human rights and the strategic value of courting China. Senate majority leader George J. Mitchell, a Democrat, sought sanctions to punish "organized murder—terror by a government against its own people."[8]

Two years later, President George H. W. Bush rebuffed critics like Mitchell by renewing China's most-favored-nation status. It would, he said, "help create a climate for democratic change."[9]

Access to global consumers sparked a robust leap forward for China in the nineties. Exports soared. Products made in China proliferated. Most-favored-nation status became permanent under President Clinton. Chinese GDP grew nearly fourfold and narrowed the US lead by doubling in size, to 12 percent of the US economy. The American consensus continued to believe that China would gradually evolve toward a liberal democracy and free market economy, notwithstanding all evidence to the contrary.

Two months after terrorists flew planes into the World Trade Center, China became a full-fledged member of the global trading community. Hopes ran high. "I believe that as this century unfolds and people look back on this day, they will conclude that in admitting China to the W.T.O. we took a decisive step in shaping a global economic and commercial system," the American trade representative, Robert B. Zoellick, said.[10]

Over a billion hungry Chinese consumers beckoned. American officials expressed confidence that growing trade commitments would swing open doors to lucrative markets for American farmers, retailers, manufacturers, and bankers. The new century began on that positive note. There were frictions over human rights and intellectual property rights, but none looked insurmountable compared to the potential for commercial gain.

The United States and China entered the twenty-first century still far from rivals. Democratic free markets generated unmatched wealth. Developing nations with the notable exception of China signed on to the Washington Consensus, a term for macroeconomic policy that emulates

American-style free markets and governance. Then the West stumbled into a global financial crisis. Western institutions looked weak and vulnerable while their political systems became increasingly polarized and partisan. Real estate prices collapsed. The banking system shuddered. Stock market values vanished and economies stalled. China started to believe that its model of benevolent technocratic autocracy and state capitalism was superior to poorly regulated market economies and dysfunctional liberal democracies.

As Western institutions scrambled to stay viable, China offset a drop in exports by making infrastructure and property investment a priority. Borrowing ballooned and real estate prices climbed as Chinese families embraced private homeownership. New cities materialized in record time, connected by high-speed rail and more miles of expressway than the United States can claim. Old cities modernized without delay. Graham Allison likes to recall the emblematic saga of repairs to a two-lane bridge in his hometown of Cambridge, Massachusetts. After four years and repeated delays, repairs cost three times over the original budget. In 2015, says Allison, China renovated the four-lane Sanyuan Bridge in Beijing in forty-three hours.

A single economic data point illuminates the growing rivalry between the United States and China in the first decade of the twenty-first century: China's output more than tripled, taking it to 41 percent of the US GDP. In sixty years under Communist rule, one of the world's poorest nations had transformed itself into a dynamic, middle-income country. Average life expectancy doubled. Primary and secondary school enrollment increased more than tenfold. Unemployment plummeted. "There is no doubt in my mind that material conditions for the overwhelming majority of people in China have improved phenomenally and in an unprecedented manner at an unprecedented speed and magnitude in the thirty years after 1980," said author and Columbia University economics professor Jeffrey Sachs.[11] Indeed China had—since its economic opening—almost three decades of 10 percent GDP growth.

While the unopposed Chinese Communist Party chalked up stunning gains, US and Western democracies often succumbed to partisan paralysis. In developing countries, struggling people marveled at China's progress and scoffed at the West. Democracy, in their eyes, took a back seat to growth. "'Give me liberty or give me death' is all well and good if you can afford it," the economist Dambisa Moyo told a TED audience. "But if you're living on less than one dollar a day, you're far too busy trying to survive and to provide for your family than to spend your time going around trying to proclaim and defend democracy."[12]

China basked in a growing reputation when Xi Jinping rose to power in 2013, allegedly free of corruption charges that stained other candidates for the top job. His wife, a famous singer in China, Peng Liyuan, helped burnish his populist appeal.

Once in charge, Xi moved quickly to cement his power. He eliminated political rivals and reshaped the country's economic model. A zealous anticorruption campaign sent thousands of party members to prison and to reeducation camps. He touted the vitality of Marxism. "There are people who believe that communism is an unattainable hope but facts have repeatedly told us that Marx and Engel's analysis is not outdated," Xi said. "Capitalism is bound to die out."[13]

He condemned the growing wealth inequality that accompanied China's newfound prosperity. Billionaire Jack Ma, who founded Alibaba, China's version of Amazon.com, disappeared from public view. Others from the business and entertainment worlds have had their wings clipped. And Xi's grip on power has expanded into a cult of personality, with a limitless future. In 2017, the party's central committee suspended term limits, preparing the way for Xi to stay in power well beyond 2022.

"A prominent leftist commentator in China has denounced 'big capitalists' and entertainment industry 'sissy-boy stars,'" the *Financial Times* reported in November 2021. "Leading public figures are disappearing from view. Others are racing to declare their fealty — and pledge billions of dollars — to the policy priorities of an all-powerful supreme leader who has life-tenure."[14]

While the United States frittered away trillions of dollars on Middle

Eastern conflicts and eventually withdrew from both Iraq and Afghanistan, a major debacle in the latter case, China invested in high technology and infrastructure projects at home and abroad. Experts put the tab at $180 billion just to develop 5G capacity in 2014 and 2015.[15] As a result, says Asia Society director and former Australian prime minister Kevin Rudd, a fluent Mandarin speaker, China enjoys undisputed leadership in many of those categories. The CIA's *World Fact Book* adds others: mining and ore processing, iron, steel, aluminum, and other metals; coal; machine building; armaments; textiles and apparel; petroleum; cement; chemicals; fertilizer; consumer products (including footwear, toys, and electronics); food processing; transportation equipment, including automobiles, railcars and locomotives, ships, and aircraft; telecommunications equipment; commercial space launch vehicles; and satellites.[16]

Extending its footprint, China launched the ambitious Belt and Road Initiative (BRI) that made China the primary financier for vital infrastructure and development efforts in dozens of low- and middle-income countries across Asia, the Middle East, Latin America and Africa. Chinese bankers wielded power where Western lenders feared to tread. Loans were extended to build roads, railroads, power-generating facilities, and much more across Asia and Africa. Researchers commissioned by the College of William and Mary looked at more than thirteen thousand BRI projects worth $843 billion across 165 countries. Over an eighteen-year period through 2017, BRI outspent the United States and other major powers on international development by two to one.[17] In many cases, if the host countries cannot repay China's generous loans, China will gain direct control of the ports and other assets it is funding.

A milestone in 2017 provoked controversy over the trading advantages China has enjoyed as a developing nation. "China Overtakes US as No. 1 in Buying Power, but Still Clings to Developing Status," the *South China Morning Post* reported.[18] The statistic known as GDP, gross domestic product (or output), adds the value of all goods and services a country produces. The United States leads in that category. Purchasing power parity (PPP), on the other hand, measures national wealth using the relative cost of equivalent goods and services. On that score, China edged past the United States in 2017, to $19.6 trillion. Yet China's National Bureau of Statistics insisted that the number one ranking in PPP-based GDP should not alter China's status as the world's largest developing country. Developing status allows China to only partially abide by the open trade rules of the World Trade Organization.

As wealthy countries deepened ties with their top trading partner, poor countries eyed China with awe. It took a global pandemic to tarnish China's image. Obfuscations and denials surrounding the origins of COVID-19 in Wuhan spawned frustration and anger. But unlike ravaged economies everywhere else, China eked out growth in 2020, further expanding its strength and influence.

As the pandemic gradually recedes, two global rivals now compete on a nearly equal footing—with some profound distinctions. A mature US economy faced overwhelming numbers of COVID-19 cases and deaths, massive and increasing inequality, ever-larger deficits and debts, never mind corrosive polarization in the political sphere. China also faces a debt crisis and growing inequality, but it has no political polarization and it has established relatively more control over the pandemic (even if its Zero COVID policy was seriously challenged in 2022 by the spread of the Omicron variant of COVID-19). And it continues to outpace the United States in annual growth.

In 2019, China counted 100 million people with wealth exceeding $110,000, surpassing the United States for the first time. Because its population is four times bigger, a fraction of US per capita GDP will vault China well past the United States in total income. When China matches the per capita GDP of Japan, around three-fifths the level in the United States today, it will be 2.3 times wealthier than it is today.[19] More wealth will position China to bankroll its lofty ambitions.

The Western consensus—that China's joining the global trading and financial system will cause it to slowly, slowly, embrace a market economy and become less authoritarian—has been flat-out wrong. China had other ideas. "Though Beijing talks about 'market allocation' efficiency, it isn't guided by what mainstream economists would call market principles," says Kevin Rudd. "The Chinese economy is instead a system of state capitalism in which the arbiter is an uncontestable political authority."[20]

China has become more authoritarian in the last decade, not less. Seasoned China watcher John J. Mearsheimer gave the original plan a fitting epitaph in the November/December 2021 issue of *Foreign Affairs*. "Engagement may have been the worst strategic blunder any country has made in recent history," wrote Mearsheimer, the author of *The Great Delusion: Liberal Dreams and International Realities*. "There is no comparable example of a great power actively fostering the rise of a peer competitor. And it is now too late to do much about it."[21]

During a Hoover Institution webinar, former national security advisor to President Trump and retired Lieutenant General H. R. McMaster shared a similar assessment. "We clung to this assumption that China, having been welcomed into the international order, would play by the rules," McMaster said. "As it prospered it would liberalize its economy and liberalize its form of government, and of course that didn't happen."[22]

While the West nurtured false hopes, China bided its time and hid its growing strength, as former Communist Party chairman Deng Xiaoping had advised. Westerners failed to reckon with the deep-seated anger over injuries inflicted during China's "century of humiliation" from 1839 until the establishment of the People's Republic of China in 1949.[23] It began with the two Opium Wars of the mid-nineteenth century, when Britain and France defeated the Qing Dynasty, taking control of territories and forcing trade concessions. It continued with the Boxer Rebellion and the defeat of the Imperial Army by an eight-nation alliance including the United States, Japan, Russia, and multiple European states. It ended with China's defeat in World War II, after a brutal Japanese invasion and occupation. Western analysts underestimated the enduring imprint of that century on Chinese culture. Now that China has risen it wants to be recognized as a great power in Asia and globally, not just in the economic realm.

To be fair, we had cause for optimism. In Europe, capitalism triumphed over socialism. In Asia, the most successful economies that were once authoritarian—Korea, Thailand, Taiwan, and Indonesia among others—had liberalized and became democracies. Even Singapore followed this path, if in a more constrained way. Maybe these are not perfect democracies up to American or European standards, but they are reasonable democracies. It was understandable that many people thought that as China reached middle-income status, it would eventually follow the same path. First open up economically, then politically.

Instead, China has tightened controls. One-party rule forecloses policy debates. China can attack crippling issues like wealth inequality and climate change by fiat. Xi Jinping says Chinese children waste too much time playing video games. By decree, he stops it. He decides there is too much investment in private tutoring that tilts scales toward those with wealth. He stops it, and for good measure he raises taxes to promote economic equality. If big tech firms have accumulated too much power, the government goes after them. To address climate change, it shuts coal mines.

Yet repression imposes a cost that is hard to measure. An authoritarian state can slash red tape, but can it make space for the freedoms that sustain innovation and growth?

While Chairman Hu Jintao led China from 2003 to 2013, each March I attended a development forum in Beijing, where we met senior officials over the course of three days. In 2012, I mentioned the upcoming trip to a friend at the Guggenheim Museum in charge of Asian art. She urged me to meet the prominent artist and dissident Ai Wei Wei, who was under house arrest after release from prison for the crime of advocating social justice and freedom of expression. I visited him at his home on the outskirts of Beijing. We chatted for two hours about the world, about China, and other shared interests.

I took a selfie with Ai Wei Wei, and I posted it on my Twitter account. I gave some thought to an earlier conversation with sources at Weibo, the Chinese version of Twitter. They found my tweets interesting and asked if they could repost them automatically for their audience. I said fine. I had no Weibo account so they created one for me. As soon as I posted my selfie with Ai Wei Wei, my Weibo account reposted it. All I wrote was that we had an interesting exchange about art and culture.

I knew that Ai Wei Wei played a cat-and-mouse game on Weibo. He would open an account and in minutes the censors would shut it down. So I kept my comments generic. I carefully avoided any suggestion that we discussed topics that might raise official eyebrows. It didn't matter. A half hour later, my Weibo account vanished. That's how the Great Firewall works.

Never mind dissidents. Routine interactions expose the party's iron grip orders. I used to visit China and arrange meetings with no problem. It was possible to talk with academics and policy makers in an open way. China now feels much more closed. Everyone is circumspect. They feel uncomfortable because friendship with Westerners today can invite trouble.

Now when I call, my contacts hesitate. When we do talk, candor is out; caution is in. China's former finance minister speaks fluent English. When we first met we spoke freely. Recently, before COVID-19, we sat on opposite sides of a table and he used an interpreter. Even speaking English is risky. It's a small detail but, in my view, a telling one. China is not moving toward us; it's moving away.

As 2021 ended, the *Financial Times* reported that any hint of democracy is on its heels. "A sudden frenzy of political activity over the past two weeks has many people wondering if China is entering a new political era, one that embraces elements of Maoist political campaigns as the Communist party continues to take a more domineering role under President Xi Jinping."[24]

Before 1990, no one feared that China would ever rival—much less surpass—the United States. We welcomed mutual cooperation along with the kind of competition that any economics textbook will say is good for consumers. We knew China might rise with a different political system, but that was okay. So long as it remained moderately authoritarian at home while nurturing a private sector, observers cheered its entry into the global economy. A massive marketplace outweighed evidence of dumping, intellectual property theft, and unfair trading practices. China had plenty of work just to haul itself up by its bootstraps. Urgent domestic needs relegated geopolitical ambitions to a lower priority than robust trading relationships, or so the West believed.

China's progress surprised the experts. Critics point to unfair trade practices, which are part of the explanation. China credits its success to lessons it learned from the West on what *not* to do. Its political system can set and achieve goals without dissent. China embraces socialism but in name only; technocratic authoritarian state capitalism is a more apt description. Whatever name they bestow, to the Chinese it beats dysfunctional democracy and self-serving global financial institutions by a country mile.

Despite early promises to stay in its lane, China increasingly competes with the West. It has launched its own versions of the World Bank and the International Monetary Fund. It has kept American Big Tech firms out of the country, while nurturing homegrown giants. It has built new islands in the South China Sea and claimed territories that the West insists are in international waters. Yet Xi continues to proclaim that a rising power does not make aggression inevitable. Unlike the United States and its allies, China has not fought a war since 1979, apart from border skirmishes.

Indeed, China has ample incentive to foster peace. Shipping lanes must stay open for its trading power to thrive. Confrontation would jeopardize the trade that fuels the Chinese economy. Along with Asian partners, it has signed the Regional Comprehensive Economic Partnership, a free trade agreement. It is lobbying for membership in the Comprehensive and Progressive Agreement for Trans-Pacific Partnership, successor to a vital trade agreement that the United States helped negotiate before President Trump pulled out and Biden decided not to attempt to resuscitate.

The increasing fear in Washington is that China is planning to supplant the United States as the new economic and military superpower, first in Asia and then globally. On the economic side the alarm bells rang in the United States in 2015 when China presented its new industrial policy plan named Made in China 2025; this plan aims to use vast subsidies and financial incentives to move China away from low valued-added and labor-intensive manufacturing to leadership in the key industries of the future: information technologies (including AI, the Internet of Things, smart appliances, semiconductors), robotics (including automation and machine learning), green energy and green vehicles (including EVs and autonomous vehicles), aerospace equipment, ocean engineering and high-tech ships, railway equipment, power equipment, new materials, biotech, medicine and medical devices, and agriculture machinery. On top of that, in 2017 China presented its "New Generation Artificial Intelligence Plan" that aims to make China the world leader in AI by 2030.

China is also building a powerful military. It has added nuclear warheads to its arsenal, improved delivery capabilities, and expanded a blue water navy. It is all defensive, they say, but that's what the United States says about its own military. Their message: We are a great power; respect us. We're not coming for you—unless you try to contain us.

Concern about China's geopolitical ambitions spurred a strategic pivot to Asia by the Obama administration. It turned attention away from Europe and toward the region of the world where the most pressing economic opportunities *and* military threats reside today. The Trump administration turned up the heat with rhetoric that plays well at campaign rallies. Its national security strategy labeled China "a strategic competitor" and (along with Russia) a "revisionist power," challenging the global order in force since World War II. The Trump administration named China and Russia as the greatest threats to US national defense. It claimed that China "seeks Indo-Pacific regional hegemony in the near-term" and "global preeminence in the future." This was not just a slogan for campaign rallies. It has become the new Washington consensus. All of this amounts to formal acknowledgment that a new cold war has started.

The new cold war leads now in only one direction, toward major disruptions in global supply and demand. For the first time in nearly a century, the United States faces a formidable adversary who controls vital natural and industrial resources. I do not expect a Hollywood ending. "The era of Western domination was a 200-year aberration," Singapore diplomat Kishore Mahbubani told an audience at Harvard's Kennedy School of Government in early 2021. "It's coming to an end."[25]

I'm of the view—like many other analysts—that a cold war will get colder with more competition and confrontation, and less cooperation. It might remain a cold war without a hot war. We'll be rivals in a divided world with tensions—but just tensions. "It may not yet be Cold War 2.0," says Kevin Rudd, a careful analyst who avoids provocative language, "but it is starting to look like Cold War 1.5."[26]

But cold war with China looks very different from cold war with the Soviet Union. Because trade between the United States and the USSR never exceeded a few billion dollars a year, cold war meant a military standoff with tanks on borders and missiles pointed at each other. "Today," CNN anchor Fareed Zakaria reported, "the United States and China trade that much in a matter of days. The Soviet Union barely existed on the economic map of the free world."[27]

The closed Soviet Union relied mainly on commodities. China operates a diverse industrial base and leads the world in many sectors. Its diplomacy is far more sophisticated. Although it is building its military capability in visible ways, the front lines of the new cold war lie mainly on economic and technological turf.

Cold War II, as some have dubbed the current scenario, features de-integration, or decoupling between the two rivals and their respective partners. This decoupling has already started in trade, technology, investments, movements of capital and labor, data, and information.

A headline in the *South China Morning Post* came right to the point in September 2021. "US-China Decoupling: If It Comes Down to a US Bloc vs China Bloc, Who Stands to Gain the Most?" It might have asked, Who will lose the most? Americans may worry that supply chains will break down, leaving retail shelves bare. A Beijing adviser feared that "loss of access to hi-tech goods from US would equate to having an abundance of rice but no delectable foods."[28]

Yu Yongding, a prominent economist and a former adviser to China's central bank, told the *South China Morning Post* that he expects decoupling to have a "huge" impact on China. Research by Capital Economics, an independent macro research firm, concluded that gradual decoupling should favor the West. Countries in the Chinese bloc have a slightly larger population but far less economic muscle than the Western bloc with 68 percent of the world's GDP.[29] "China has a large number of countries in its camp, but most are small in economic terms," says Capital Economics. "China still relies far more on the West for both final demand and inputs."

That's the good news. Yet focusing on trade in consumer goods alone clouds the bigger picture. Decoupling would disrupt trading in goods, technology, and services. It would restrain movement of capital investment, mobility of labor, students, and scientists, even the transfer of data, the lifeblood of the information age.

"China Drafts Tough Rules to Stop Data from Leaving Its Borders as Beijing Tightens Grip on Information," the *South China Morning Post* reported in October 2021. The Cyberspace Administration of China wants to review all business-processing data before it exits the country.[30] The United States is also imposing restrictions on Chinese ownership of apps that can collect data of US citizens. Since data is the new oil, the crucial driver of big business, this is the beginning of a much wider form of protectionism and trade restrictions.

Tariffs and restrictions imposed by both countries during the Trump administration have accelerated decoupling. A more fragmented economy will increasingly divide the world into two competing economic systems, one dominated by the West, one by China.

If decoupling forces poor and semi-authoritarian nations to choose a side, they may prefer China's geopolitical framework, robust growth, and less expensive technology. The Chinese will try to snare market dominance with preferential trade agreements and access to investment capital. Its cheaper 5G technology will vault developing countries forward. It will furnish top-notch IoT (Internet of Things), AI, and telecom solutions. China will advise clients to replace dollars with renminbi as their reserve currency. Chinese lenders will gain influence. Surveillance technology and tactical weapons will help these client states squash domestic dissent.

Chinese leaders know that rising wages will bring an end to its production cost advantages. That's one reason why China wants to become the world's leader in artificial intelligence by 2030. Former Google chairman Eric Schmidt keeps a wary eye on progress that may leave the United States in the dust. "The Chinese government has four times more engineers," Schmidt told *Bloomberg* in a 2021 video titled "China's Race for AI Supremacy."[31] "They're putting massive amounts of money into AI transformations and digitization. The rapidly improving power of computer systems has the potential to touch every facet of the twenty-first-century economy and the Chinese Communist Party has stated it wanted to drive that advance."

Some observers declare the tech arms race already over. According to Nicholas Chaillan, the Pentagon's first chief software officer, "we have no competing fighting chance against China in 15 to 20 years. Right now, it's already a done deal; it is already over in my opinion."[32]

New cooperation and development agreements between China and its clients will forge partnerships that increasingly isolate mature industrial economies. Informal alliances already link China with Russia, Iran, and North Korea. They have begun participating in military exercises. China and Russia recently sent ten warships on a narrow path of international water between the Japanese main islands of Hokkaido and Honshu—a path that Japan intentionally allowed to exist so that US warships could travel it freely during the original Cold War.[33] And the Russian invasion of Ukraine in 2022 cemented the de facto alliance between China and Russia as Putin and Xi met before the start of the invasion to formally seal the new economic and geopolitical alliance between the two countries. With China having Taiwan in its sights the Chinese have de facto rubber stamped the attempted Russian takeover of Ukraine. Welcome to Cold War II if you were still in doubt that such a cold war is brewing.

Traditional US allies that trade with China are facing a challenging future. They'll get caught on the horns of decoupling. In 2020, China displaced the United States as the European Union's largest trading partner in goods.[34] What happens when one side demands that Europe stiff the other? The United States has already pressured European states to ban Huawei's 5G wireless network, arguing that it is a security risk, as the Chinese government might monitor its traffic. Some countries have agreed to that demand, but many others have not.

In Europe, the United States holds the ultimate trump card. NATO allies only spend $200 billion collectively on defense. The United States spends $700 billion. The NATO states cannot defend themselves against a massive attack (for instance, by Russia), as the recent Russian invasion of Ukraine has woken up the peaceful European to concerns about the further imperial ambitions of the Russian bear. Suppose the United States agrees to maintain troops that keep Russia at bay but that means the Europeans cannot do business as usual with China? They must decouple. They must support a Western counterbalance to China at great cost to their economies. Indeed, in a 2021 interview with the *FT* the head of NATO argued that "countering the security threat from the rise of China will be an important part of NATO's future rationale . . . marking a significant rethink of the western group objectives that reflects the US's geostrategic pivot to Asia."[35]

The Chinese will warn Europeans that if they go with the United States, then they must gradually exit China. That means fewer car sales and business deals. Less foreign direct investment and manufacturing in China. Full decoupling will be brutally expensive.

As it will be for China. Yet it looks like China can manage. In 2021 it embarked on the Fourteenth Five-Year Plan, which can be read as preparation for decoupling. The goal is economic "self-reliance" and "indigenous innovation," made feasible by a domestic market with 1.3 billion consumers.

During the Trump administration, tough talk produced tariffs that mainly hurt Americans at cash registers. The Biden administration, though more inclined to favor diplomacy, also views China through the lens of competition and rivalry. Describing the relationship, US-China trade representative Katherine Tai minced no words. "For too long, China's lack of adherence to global trading norms has undercut the prosperity of Americans and others around the world," Tai said. "In recent years, Beijing has doubled down on its state-centered economic system. It is increasingly clear that China's plans do not include meaningful reforms to address the concerns that have been shared by the United States and many other countries."[36]

Unlike most issues nowadays in Washington, DC, there is bipartisan cooperation when it comes to China policy. In June 2021, the Senate voted to level the playing field by passing the $250 billion United States Innovation and Competition Act, a bill aimed at bolstering American leadership and production in advanced technology. The legislation incorporated an earlier bill that was cosponsored by Senate Majority Leader Chuck Schumer, a Democrat from New York, and Senator Todd Young, a Republican from Indiana. The legislation was also approved by the House in early 2022.

The second cold war looks so different from its predecessor at the start, and we should not expect it to end in the same way, either, with our adversary folding up its tent. Writing in *Foreign Affairs* in 2019, two current advisors to President Biden proposed an alternative. "Rather than relying on assumptions about China's trajectory, American strategy should be durable whatever the future brings for the Chinese system," wrote Kurt Campbell, the former board chairman and cofounder of the Center for a New American Security, and National Security Advisor Jake Sullivan. "It should seek to achieve not a definitive end state akin to the Cold War's ultimate conclusion but a steady state of clear-eyed coexistence on terms favorable to U.S. interests and values."[37]

In an earlier article for *Foreign Affairs,* Campbell and coauthor Ely Rattner issued a blunt warning. "Washington now faces its most dynamic and formidable competitor in modern history."³⁸ Both now advise President Biden, who wasted no words when a reporter asked about Xi Jinping. "Let's get something straight," Biden said. "We know each other well, we're not old friends. It's just pure business."³⁹

If the rivalry escalates, can a cold war with China get hot? Expert opinions span a range from maybe to yes, while everyone quickly adds that they hope not.

In formal speeches, leaders sometimes try to lower the temperature. "The time we live in is full of challenges and full of hope," Xi Jinping has declared. "Where should the future of humanity be headed? China's answer is to call on the people of all countries to work together, respond to the call of the times, strengthen global governance, pursue innovation-driven development, and advance the building of a community with a shared future for mankind."⁴⁰ But at other times Xi sounds much more bellicose. In July of 2021 he stated that those who will try to prevent China's rise will have their "heads bashed bloody against a Great Wall of steel," a statement consistent with the so-called Wolf Warrior diplomacy, the aggressive style of diplomacy adopted by many Chinese diplomats in recent years. (The name is taken from a Chinese film, *Wolf Warrior 2*, which had a tagline, "Whoever attacks China will be killed no matter how far the target is.") Nationalism and xenophobia are certainly on the rise in China.

For his part, President Biden touts the merits of "relentless diplomacy." Recent phone calls and diplomatic exchanges have explored the potential for dialogue, according to press reports. But the national security strategy of Biden is not really different from that of Trump. If anything, the frictions are increasing as Biden, unlike Trump, cares about human rights and democracy in Hong Kong, Tibet, Taiwan, and Xinjiang. And the Biden administration has threatened new tariffs against China, given the domestic subsidies of the continued industrial policies of China.

Shortly before Joe Biden was inaugurated, Chen Yixin, a close confidant of Xi, declared that "the rise of the East and the decline of the West has become [a global] trend and changes the international landscape in our favor." China believes that the United States and the West will continue to decline over time.[41]

Former Australian prime minister Kevin Rudd, who led efforts to reinforce Australia's ties with China, is superbly positioned to analyze the Sino-American balance. In "The Avoidable War," published by the Asia Society that Rudd heads, he acknowledges a grim fact. "Prior to the current crisis, the postwar liberal international order was already beginning to fragment."

There have been provocations by both sides. Mao Zedong is back in favor in China, celebrated "for having boldly gone to war against the Americans in Korea, fighting them to a truce." Americans frightened by China have taken to denouncing Richard Nixon "for creating a Frankenstein."[42] A *Financial Times* headline in 2021 highlighted "the Maoist echoes of Xi's power play."[43]

Rudd sounds less fearful of war arising from carefully plotted strategic reasons than from mishaps involving planes, warships, or careless politicians. Rudd and others remind readers that an event of minor global significance, the assassination of Archduke Ferdinand, ignited World War I.

The status of the waters around China invites a catastrophic miscalculation. Besides China, six countries stake overlapping claims to parts of those waters: Brunei, Indonesia, Malaysia, the Philippines, Taiwan, and Vietnam. Beijing asserts "historical maritime rights" within a "nine-dash line" that encroaches on its neighbors. China did not like a 2016 decision by the Permanent Court of Arbitration that ruled against its claims. A "gray zone" strategy deploys fishing and coast guard vessels to establish de facto claims that spite the court. If a navigational confrontation ends with one of those ships sinking, it could lead to catastrophe.

Besides exchanging fighting words, strategists on both sides conduct war games. The United States sends ships through water that China calls territorial. Alarmed that we lack the imagination to foresee events that will spiral into conflict, retired Admiral James Stavridis coauthored a novel with Elliot Ackerman that posits a full-scale war between the United States and China in 2034.[44] For its part, China has claimed and militarized islands in the South China Sea despite assertions of peaceful intent, taunting Japan. Its planes regularly buzz Taiwanese airspace, risking a military incident.

China's intentions now reach to outer space. A hypersonic Long March rocket circled the earth in a recent test. "Such a system could, if deployed, circumvent US missile defences," the *Financial Times* reported. China, naturally, called it a routine space launch with no military objectives.[45]

Current leaders of both nations emphasize cooperation and mutual respect while lining up allies. Xi Jinping touted a successful video meeting with Vladimir Putin and the Treaty of Good Neighborliness and Friendly Cooperation with Russia. "The China-Russia comprehensive strategic partnership of coordination for a new era boasts strong momentum and broad prospects," Xi declared.[46]

Actions by the United States, meanwhile, prompted *Foreign Affairs* to publish an article under the title "America Is Turning Asia into a Powder Keg." The article lists US initiatives designed to parry China's growing naval presence: encouraging Japan to develop hypersonic weapons; boosting arms sales to the Philippines despite human rights abuses; equipping Australia with nuclear submarines; building a new radar system in Palau; and generally expanding a Western footprint across the Indo-Pacific region. The United States is beefing up the Quad — a strategic forum to counter China — that includes the United States, India, Australia, and Japan. NATO may become a tool to contain the rising power of China. What the United States and the West perceive as defensive — to limit the aggressive rise of China in Asia — China perceives as an attempt to contain its rise and its legitimate defense needs in Asia.

In response, China is building ties with revisionist powers that want to displace the United States and Western global order. Russia is bent on re-creating the former Soviet sphere of influence, a goal that puts every neighboring country in its sights, starting with the brutal Russian invasion of Ukraine in 2022. Shiite Iran opposes the United States, Israel, and several Sunni Arab countries competing for hegemony on the Persian Gulf. War may eventually prevail if a revised nuclear deal with Iran fails or is rejected after 2024 by a new Republican administration. Israel, which sees a nuclear Iran as an existential threat to its survival, is likely to strike Iran if Iran continues its current path of nuclear escalation. North Korea, a failed state by every measure except its nuclear arsenal, poses a clear and present danger to Japan, Korea, and the United States. It is likely to continue missile launches and other provocations that will at some point precipitate an outright military confrontation. Other countries slipping into the Chinese orbit of influence include Pakistan and Cambodia, the former an unstable nuclear power in a constant rivalry with a nuclear India that has serious territorial disputes with China.

The principal flashpoint in Asia is Taiwan. A cover story in *The Economist* called it "the most dangerous place on earth" because China has made its objective clear.[47] It intends to annex an island with 23 million people, a freely elected government, and a vibrant economy that supplies the world with, among other vital goods, microchips. In October 2021, People's Liberation Army jet fighters buzzed Taiwanese airspace dozens of times.

China has reiterated its determination to reclaim territory. The Taiwanese have no interest in bending to the will of the mainland. Although no formal defense alliance exits, President Biden has clearly signaled support for Taiwan, where a contingent of Marines trains its military. The European Union has dispatched representatives to Taiwan, underscoring friendship.

The United States has maintained some strategic ambiguity on whether it would fully defend Taiwan in case of a Chinese attack. To prevent or make very costly an attempted invasion of Taiwan, the United States is likely to beef up its supply of military equipment to the island, as it belatedly did for Ukraine. But what if China—instead of trying to invade Taiwan—imposes a naval blockade on the island? Would the

United States try to break the blockade? Or will the United States blink and effectively allow China to strangle Taiwan and take it over? And how would that outcome affect the already weakened credibility of the United States in defending its other allies in Asia, especially after the Afghanistan debacle and the decision not to militarily defend Ukraine against the Russian invasion? After all, Taiwan, like Ukraine, is not a formal member of NATO or a formal ally of the United States. Will the United States go to war with China to protect Taiwan or would it only—like in the case of Ukraine—provide it with weapons to defend itself? No one knows the answer to such questions. Yet Xi wants to make history as the leader who reunited the mainland with Taiwan. That's why a potential war with China is a looming megathreat.

The direction of the US-China rivalry will depend in part on growth trends in the next decade. If the United States remains vigorous by reinventing its economy, as it has in the past, it may be able to partially preserve the status quo in Asia and Taiwan. If China continues to grow and the United States stumbles, the United States will see its strategic advantages vanish and China will become more assertive and aggressive. Continuing investment in its military arsenal will empower China to try to act with impunity. If the United States were to back down in a confrontation, doing so would imperil its leadership.

Or China might stumble. Not everyone believes that that country is a juggernaut. A Communist Party intent on retaining power at all costs may suppress incentives that propel economic growth. A widespread crackdown against the high-tech industry and its titans—like Jack Ma—together with a campaign against conspicuous consumption and inequality has depressed the confidence of the private business sector. By clamping down on the tutoring industry and requiring all tutoring materials to be government approved, China took a step away from intellectual freedom and removed a means for the middle class to perpetuate itself. When the party goes to those kinds of lengths to suppress potential rivals, it stifles a lot more than just dissent.

The legacy of the one-child policy, imposed early in the Communist regime to ease demand for scarce food, has come back to haunt employers. The workforce is aging at an accelerated pace. Some observers say that China will grow old before it grows rich in a sustainable way. As in advanced economies, fewer young workers are supporting more and more workers in retirement. The sheer numbers of retired workers pose a dilemma for policy makers that will challenge the regime.

China faces several other challenges. A deadly border skirmish with India in the frozen Himalayan foothills put its Asian neighbors on notice. The regime's harsh suppression of its Muslim Uyghur population and the crackdown against democracy in Hong Kong have been condemned by many nations.

And after years of uninterrupted increases in prices for residential real estate, reality has intervened. Prices began to falter in recent years. Buildings and ghost towns remain unoccupied. Evergrande, the world's most indebted real estate company, teetered on the verge of bankruptcy, and many other property firms are in a similar predicament. Foreign lenders may suffer losses. This is part of a larger issue that could rattle China if defaults begin to spiral. Private and public debt in China was already more than three times its GDP in 2019 before the COVID-19 crisis led to a further surge of this debt load. A debt crisis would divert state resources from its strategic objectives and would hurt China's reputation abroad. The Zero Covid policy further depressed growth in 2022.

Unfortunately, China's problems may become our problems. Xi Jinping must deliver prosperity and reduce inequality. If he cannot, then he may look for other ways to rally his people. Stoking xenophobia and nationalism, and adding territory, especially Taiwan, would burnish his legacy at home. Even if weaker, China may become more aggressive toward Taiwan.

There are two extreme views of China's future in the popular press: China's going to dominate the world or China's going to collapse. I don't agree with either of them. People have predicted a hard landing for China for decades, and they have been proven wrong every time. China is still growing at about 4-5 percent, more than twice the rate of growth by the

United States (except for 2021). China *will* become the largest economy in the world, there's no doubt about that—it's only a question of when. As China transitions from low income to middle income and from there possibly to high income and thus avoids the "middle income trap," it will become increasingly innovative in technology. China is economically dynamic, especially in industries for the future. We may not like their state capitalist model but guess what: it has worked so far even if at the cost of creating some economic inefficiencies.

Americans must adjust their mindset. China is on track to become the world's dominant power. We must find ways to thrive without remaining number one. Escaping the Thucydides Trap will be welcome, but avoiding that trap does not guarantee a happy conclusion. The rivalry between two great powers is here to stay.

The nine megathreats we have discussed so far focus mainly on human decisions that govern debt levels and policy directions. In theory, we could collectively wake up and begin to address them in hopes that changed behavior would make a difference. The final megathreat is more familiar and yet more confounding. It stems from many decades of human activity aimed at promoting prosperity but destroying our ecosystem in the process. Global climate change is no surprise. In fact, we may tire of hearing about it. Weariness magnifies the peril. Resolving this megathreat requires international cooperation among great powers that the current geopolitical rivalry between the US and China thwarts. We must stop looking at climate change as an isolated problem. Instead we must ask what if it has passed the tipping point already? And what horrific consequences lurk when climate change interlocks with other megathreats?

Chapter 10

An Uninhabitable Planet?

Unless you live on high ground in cool latitudes with plenty of drinking water and rich farmland, get ready to move. If good luck has landed you in the right place, expect lots of new company dispersed by global warming, both human and microbial.

Debating the causes of climate change wastes valuable time. "It is unequivocal that human influence has warmed the atmosphere, ocean and land. Widespread and rapid changes in the atmosphere, ocean, cryosphere and biosphere have occurred," the International Panel on Climate Change reported in August 2021. "Global warming of 1.5 degrees C and 2 degrees C will be exceeded during the 21st century unless deep reductions in carbon dioxide and other greenhouse gas (GHG) emissions occur in the coming decades."[1] Less than a year later in the spring of 2022, new scientific research suggested that the world was increasingly at risk of experiencing global warming of 1.5 degrees C within the next five years.

We can ignore bulletins or we can do something. The track record so far is a sorry one. Scientists warned President Lyndon Johnson about atmospheric carbon accumulation in a 1965 report.[2] Since then we have mostly dithered. Meanwhile, dangers keep mounting.

The search for solutions increasingly engages economists along with climate scientists. Besides devising measures to sustain life on earth, someone must say how we can afford them. No one exemplifies this convergence more than Nobel laureate William Nordhaus, an economist and former colleague of mine at Yale University. He accepted his prize in 2018 by giving a lecture with the title "Climate Change: The Ultimate Challenge for Economics." He is cautious if not skeptical about our prospects. "Technological change raised humans out of Stone Age living standards," Nordhaus told his audience. "Climate change threatens, in the most extreme scenarios, to return us economically whence we came."

Nordhaus calls global warming "the most significant of all environmental externalities," a term that describes costs not borne by those who impose them. "It menaces our planet and looms over our future like a Colossus. It is particularly pernicious because it involves so many activities of daily life, affects the entire planet, does so for decades and even centuries, and, most of all, because none of us acting individually can do anything to slow the changes."[3]

In their alarming book *Climate Shock: The Economic Consequences of a Hotter Planet,* authors Gernot Wagner and Martin Weitzman predict "the potential for planet-as-we-know-it altering changes." They frame the challenge correctly: "First and foremost climate change is a risk management problem, a catastrophic risk management problem on a planetary scale."[4]

This disaster should catch no one by surprise. Reports on climate change fill books, documentaries, podcasts, newspapers, magazines, social media, films and television talk shows. Why then so little meaningful action? So many science fiction films portray alien threats that erase differences among people who are united in defense of humanity. Climate change should generate the same global response, but so far, it hasn't. That sad fact demolishes my former faith in shared responses to existential crises. I was too optimistic. This megathreat has a paralyzing price tag.

"The math is punishing," writes author Elizabeth Kolbert in *Under a White Sky: The Nature of the Future.* Her previous book on climate change, *The Sixth Extinction,* garnered a well-deserved Pulitzer Prize. Keeping average temperatures within targets means massive dislocation, she warns. "This would entail, for starters, revamping agricultural systems, transforming manufacturing, scrapping gasoline and diesel powered vehicles and replacing most of the world's power plants."

The International Energy Agency calls coal the single largest source of global carbon emissions. Declining use in 2020 looked like a promising development. "But 2021 dashed those hopes," the Agency reported. Instead, global coal demand resumed a path toward a new all-time high.[5]

In the space program, extraterrestrial failure is not an option. Sadly, that mantra does not extend to climate change on earth's surface. It looks like we are choosing to fail. "Just as with the alarm in the morning," Climate Outreach founder George Marshall told the BBC, "when you hear the alarm sound what you do is you hit the snooze button."[6]

There are at least a few faint signs of hope. A report released in October 2021 by the UN High-Level Climate Champions, Climate Action Tracker, ClimateWorks Foundation, Bezos Earth Fund, and World Resources Institute noted significant progress on the environmental front. Electricity from wind and solar sources grew at an annual rate of 15 percent over the previous five years and both are now more cost effective than ever in most places than power from coal. Electric vehicles approached nearly 5 percent of global light duty vehicle sales in 2020, capping five years in a row of 50 percent compound annual growth.

These and other commitments to restrain global warming fall far short, though, on every key measure watched by the Climate Action Tracker. "Yet the hard truth is that despite these bright spots, none of the 40 indicators are making progress at the pace necessary for the world to cut greenhouse gas emissions in half by 2030 and fully decarbonize by mid-century, which are both necessary to limit global temperature rise to 1.5 degrees Centigrade."[7]

Deadly consequences stare us in the face. As water warms, it expands. Never mind the melting polar icecaps—because oceans cover two thirds of the earth's surface, we have a massive challenge. Wherever oceans meet shoreline, water is gaining ground, and yet that is where huge populations of people and other creatures tend to congregate. Facts gathered by the National Oceanic and Atmospheric Administration (NOAA) find that four in ten US residents live in densely populated coastal areas vulnerable to flooding, shoreline erosion, and severe storms. Of the world's ten largest cities, the UN Atlas of the Oceans reports that eight sit on or near precarious coastlines.

Rising air temperature affects the ice sheets that cover Greenland and Antarctica. They are melting faster than ever. Greenland alone lost 34 billion tons of ice per year between 1992 and 2001. By 2016, ice was becoming seawater at the rate of 247 billion tons per year, more than a sevenfold increase.

"Earth is now losing 1.2 trillion tons of ice each year. And it's going to get worse," the *Washington Post* reported in January 2021, citing a report by the American Association for the Advancement of Science (AAAS). As ice becomes seawater, oceans claim yet more land.

"We're the guinea pigs," Windell Curole told *National Geographic* magazine. A Cajun resident of Louisiana's Gulf Coast for more than five decades, Mr. Curole has watched Gulf waters claim his high school girlfriend's house, his grandfather's former hunting camp, and a local cemetery. "We live in a place of almost land, almost water," he said.[8]

Like his neighbors, Mr. Curole has stayed dry by moving inland. It's not ideal. No one should be dislodged this way. Yet the water's edge threatens thousands of coastal communities worldwide. "Tuvalu, a small country in the South Pacific, has already begun formulating evacuation plans," *National Geographic* reported in "The Big Thaw."

Rising saltwater seas push deeper into freshwater deltas, altering local ecologies. It can seep through porous rock into underground aquifers vital to drinking water and crop irrigation. "In the Nile Delta, where many of Egypt's crops are cultivated," according to *National Geographic*, "widespread erosion and saltwater intrusion would be disastrous since the country contains little other arable land."[9]

Other developing countries face crippling exposures, according to Columbia University's Earth Institute. "In Guyana, Maldives, Belize, and Suriname, 100 percent of the urban population lives at an elevation lower than 10 meters above sea level, and 81 percent of the urban populations of Thailand and Bahrain live at this low elevation," the Institute found.[10] Even temporary flood disruptions could shut down national economic development and growth, to say nothing of flooding that makes cities uninhabitable.

The headlines are grim. "From China to Europe, Being Ill Prepared for Floods Will Leave Us Soaked in Regret" and "Malaysia Floods Are Asia's Latest Sign to Act on Climate Change," the *South China Morning Post* reported in January 2022.[11] "Floods do not discriminate by country or region," the newspaper warned. "However, it is almost certain they will affect developing countries more than developed ones given their lack of long-term investment in fighting climate change and increasingly severe flooding."

Americans watched Hurricane Katrina swamp New Orleans, but that disaster was only a prelude. The climate clock is ticking for every city at the ocean's edge. None is more vulnerable than Miami, Florida, partially situated on a barrier reef less than seven feet above sea level. Sunny-day floods occur routinely nowadays when ocean water backs up into drainage systems.

"In every generation there's going to be a big cause.... Today we have climate change," warned former Miami mayor Philip Levine. The estimated taxable value of Miami real estate at risk exceeds $20 billion. To protect that investment Miami will have to dig deeper than its public budgets can afford. It budgeted a mere $95 million toward "resilience and public works" in 2020, a category that covers flood prevention, affordable housing, and traffic.[12]

In Florida alone, seawater will displace 1.5 million state residents by the time COVID babies hit middle age, in 2060. Non-residential properties at risk include 334 public schools, 82 low-income housing complexes, 68 hospitals, 37 nursing homes, 171 assisted living facilities, 1,025 churches, synagogues, and mosques, 341 hazardous materials sites including 5 superfund sites, 2 nuclear reactors, 3 prisons, 74 airports, 115 solid waste disposal sites, 277 shopping centers, and 19,684 historic structures.

From Miami to Galveston, San Diego to Juneau, Boston to Jacksonville, time is running out for urban dwellers. Vast property lies in the path of rising seas. "We found that there are over two and a half million commercial and residential properties at risk of chronic inundation by the end of the century. Those are valued today at over $1 trillion," warns Kristina Dahl, a senior climate scientist at the Union of Concerned Scientists.[13]

The Center for Earth Science Information Network, which operates under the aegis of Columbia University, assesses risks stemming from rising seas. More than 10 percent of the world's population lives in urban or quasi-urban areas less than ten meters—thirty-six feet—above sea level. New York City sits thirty-six feet above sea level, a margin that afforded scant protection from Hurricane Sandy in 2012. When the storm ended, floodwaters filled subways and basements throughout lower Manhattan, Flushing, and elsewhere. Subway repairs took nine years to complete. The damage to the subways after just that one storm: $5 billion.[14]

Worldwide, China has the largest population residing in coastal areas. Sea rise could displace 130 million of its citizens. In India, 55 million people could see their homes permanently submerged in a few decades, followed by Bangladesh, where 41 million people live near sea level.

Tourists vacationing in Thailand, Indonesia, and Sri Lanka the day after Christmas 2004 got an awful glimpse of the future. Triggered by an earthquake that measured 9.1 on the Richter scale, the deadliest tsunami in history ended 230,000 lives in an instant, under waves one hundred feet high.[15] There is indeed now scientific research showing a link between global climate change and more severe hurricanes, typhoons, and earthquakes that lead to tsunamis.[16]

The ravages of climate change extend far inland. China is home to a fifth of humanity but a mere 7 percent of the world's fresh water. The population is growing, but the vital water supply is shrinking. "Thousands of rivers have disappeared, while industrialization and pollution have spoiled much of the water that remains," *Bloomberg* reported in

December 2021. "By some estimates, 80% to 90% of China's groundwater and half of its river water is too dirty to drink; more than half of its groundwater and one-quarter of its river water cannot even be used for industry or farming."[17] A desperate need for fresh water adds a vital priority to China's global ambitions.

Regions with fewer resources than China must handle disruptive climate change in creative ways. "Rising temperatures will negatively affect the agriculture sector in Africa," warns Patu Ndango, who started CLSV Foundation, a Cameroon-based company that transforms waste into crop fertilizer. More frequent dry spells and floods make planting seasons less predictable. If farmers sow and rain is delayed, blistering heat can dry seeds out before they germinate. Regions where food is already scarce face even grimmer prospects if rains don't provide timely irrigation. In parched conditions, says Ms. Ndango, rain often falls too fast for the land to absorb. Instead of nurturing crops, it floods residential areas.[18]

Increasing scientific evidence links global climate change and more frequent and extreme weather events: droughts, fires, desertification, and more frequent and virulent floods, hurricanes, and typhoons. Thus, the damage from global climate change is increasingly present today rather than in the distant future.[19]

Across the United States, global warming will upend daily life. Because the atmosphere and oceans are getting warmer, scorching heat and violent storms occur more often in more places. A lethal tornado ripped through Kentucky in December 2021, pulverizing a town and taking lives. "That's hard to think about—you go to bed, and your entire family is gone the next day," Ronnie Ward, a member of the Bowling Green Police Department, told the Associated Press. "They usually tell people to get in a bathtub and cover up with a mattress, but that probably would've made little difference here: some homes were destroyed so completely the tornado ripped all the way through the floor, exposing the earth below."[20]

In summer 2021, thermometers soared in the Pacific Northwest, where a mild climate usually prevails and few residents own air conditioners. More than one hundred people died during a June heat wave that triggered a drought across much of the region. A record high temperature in Salem, Oregon, hit 117 degrees Fahrenheit, beating the previous high by nine degrees.[21] The heat caused drought conditions that made the region ground zero for massive wildfires that swept western states. Heat waves all over the US had already started in the spring time rather than summer in 2022.

Fires and floods loom ahead. Fifty years from now, coasts may be flooded, much of the south may be too hot for people to want to live there, and a good part of the US population may have to relocate to the upper Midwest or Canada, the only region that will continue to be viable economically. The timeline of coastal relocations could shorten if either of two ice sheets in Greenland and Antarctica were to snap and slip into the ocean. Sea levels could rise dramatically in a matter of months.

Nations are failing because of global climate change. Forests become deserts, water supplies collapse, and agriculture becomes too unreliable to support crops, livestock, and communities. Students of history will recognize the early signs of chaos when people battled over food and water supplies. *Global Crisis: War, Climate Change and Catastrophe in the Seventeenth Century,* by the prolific historian Geoffrey Parker, documents this behavior and its awful consequences.[22]

When warfare raged over control of arable land, kings, tsars, emperors, and petty despots fought each other. Civil wars ripped societies apart. It has happened in Syria and across the Middle East and most of the African continent in the last twenty years, where a number of failed states have emerged. It will only get worse as climates deteriorate.

Arab-Israeli conflicts over decades are due in no small part to quarrels over who controls water sources in the Golan Heights. Those sources bring water to the Galilee valley and then all the way to Israel. People forget that before the Syrian civil war there was a drought in 2006–7 that led to the collapse of agriculture.[23] Until that collapse, Sunni, Shia, Alawites, and Kurds did not like each other but they managed an uneasy peace, since there was food for everybody. When food became scarce, violent conflicts erupted. That was the beginning of the Syrian civil war. The same thing is now happening in sub-Saharan Africa.

The megathreat of climate change is already upon us. We should expect to see conflict and grinding poverty push migration to a scale never seen before. Hundreds of millions of hungry people will want to move because economies are failing.

Africa comprises fifty-four nations. The roster includes some relatively healthy countries, such as Botswana, Namibia, Rwanda, and Ghana, but it also includes very fragile and near failed states such as the Democratic Republic of Congo, Somalia, Central African Republic, and South Sudan, and others on the brink. Many Africans are faring better today than their parents and grandparents. Visible progress features pockets of entrepreneurship and wealth. Nevertheless, Africa resembles an environmental time bomb. Its population will double to two billion by the end of this century. It is already a challenge to feed the existing population, never mind quenching their thirst. Many communities rely on water sources miles away by foot. If those sources begin to dry up, what will happen?

"Climate change deprives 70 percent of Somalis of safe water," the Somali news service *Hiiran Online* reported in March 2021. "Reduced rainfall and severe water shortages are also killing livestock, causing crop failures, and diminishing household incomes, leaving children in these families with fewer daily meals and less nutritious food," *Hiiran* reported.[24]

Global climate change is making equatorial regions uninhabitable. The land is becoming drier every year, bleached by relentless sun. Water is too scarce to support irrigation. People are leaving farms and moving to cities, where they become poor marginal workers—if they can find jobs. The rest try to head for healthy economies. Africans and South Americans face the same challenges. In both hemispheres, we should expect massive migration away from the equator.

In a Sunday magazine feature titled "The Great Climate Migration," the *New York Times* reported on conditions in Central America: "Many semiarid parts of Guatemala will soon be more like a desert. Rainfall is expected to decrease by 60 percent in some parts of the country, and the amount of water replenishing streams and keeping soil moist will drop by as much as 83 percent."[25]

Facing "a relentless confluence of drought, flood, bankruptcy and starvation," the last farmers have abandoned a once fertile region where coffee plantations and healthy forests used to flourish.

By 2022, massive and unprecedented droughts afflicted India and Pakistan, East Africa, Mexico and large sections of the West of the United States. Global crop failures and rising food prices put millions at risk of starvation from Africa all the way to the Indian sub-continent.

Wealthy countries are dispensing cash to contain climate-related stress. European countries are paying the Turkish government billions of euros to stop migrants from heading northward. Yet borders are porous, particularly in Greece. The Turkish island of Lesbos is five miles off the coast of Greece. Cross that stretch and you are a refugee. Wider stretches of water have claimed hundreds of lives.

Because of its proximity to the Middle East and Africa, Europe faces the largest tide of refugees of any temperate-zone destination in the world. It has stirred resentment toward those vulnerable travelers. A former prime minister of Singapore, speaking about migration, said that vast bodies of water and unpredictable typhoons in Asia impede refugee travel to Australia or Japan. By contrast, the Mediterranean is shallow, distances are smaller, and storms are milder than in Asia or via a Caribbean route to the United States.

Libya, a failed state, collects money from European countries to stem the flow of immigrants from sub-Saharan Africa who are heading north. Or look at Egypt, where 100 million people are mostly young and unemployed. Many support the Muslim Brotherhood, a group at odds with the military regime that seized power from a duly elected Muslim Brotherhood president in 2013. Ruling authorities must decide whether to subsidize restive young people or give them a boat to sail to Europe. Many young Egyptians have embarked already.

Climate refugees may mushroom to hundreds of millions if not billions in the most extreme scenarios, where global temperatures rise between 3 and 4 degrees C.

As *The Economist* reported in a 2021 cover story titled "A 3°C World Has No Safe Place":

> If temperatures rise by 3°C above pre-industrial levels in the coming decades—as they might even if everyone manages to honor today's firm pledges—large parts of the tropics risk becoming too hot for outdoor work. Coral reefs and livelihoods that depend on them will vanish and the Amazon rainforest will become a ghost of itself. Severe harvest failures will become commonplace. Ice sheets in Antarctica and Greenland will shrink past the point of no return, promising sea rises measured not in millimeters, as today's are, but in meters.[26]

So here we are with rising temperatures and sea levels pushing us closer to environmental debacle, and with very little political progress to counteract it. In 2015, at the Paris environmental talks, the world's richest economies promised to take actions to limit greenhouse gas emissions so that temperatures would rise less than 2 degrees C. Yet very little was done in practice to achieve that goal. Many scientists worry that we are too late to preserve the world we knew. Reports worldwide now echo a blunt warning from the International Panel on Climate Change: "Many changes due to past and future greenhouse gas emissions are irreversible for centuries to millennia, especially changes in the ocean, ice sheets and global sea level."[27]

Voluntary agreements that lack penalties for missing targets offer scant hope against a challenge of this magnitude. Global free riding (inaction while other countries act on climate change) erases incentives for any nation to invest precious resources. Say, for example, taxpayers in one nation shoulder massive and costly efforts to reduce GHG emissions. They're screwed if other nations fail to act. Their money goes to waste, with negligible impact on greenhouse gasses. The dysfunction dooms everyone.

Generational free riding inflames our potential conflicts. Mathematical models of the costs of global climate change often use assumptions that shift the economic burdens onto future generations. These distortions lead to policies that minimize GHG reductions today in the magical belief that new technologies and increasing wealth will solve the problem later. Dress that assessment up any way you want, but it still means that too few legislators and policy makers today have the courage to speak boldly about current sacrifice. It is no surprise that young generations care about climate change that will impose frightful consequences when leaders of today are long gone.

The interests of rich countries often clash with those in emerging markets and with developing poor countries. Lofty pledges promise to reduce emissions by 50 percent for the United States and 55 percent for Europe by 2030, but actual policies in rich countries cannot meet such ambitious goals.

With advanced economies at peak GHG output, a brake on global warming will depend in part on a developing world that is out of step with environmental goals. "If energy transitions and clean energy investment do not quickly pick up speed in emerging and developing economies, the world will face a major fault line in efforts to address climate change and reach other sustainable development goals," the International Energy Agency warned in a 2021 special report. "This is because the bulk of the growth in global emissions in the coming decades is set to come from emerging and developing economies as they grow, industrialise and urbanise."[28] In other words, it was okay for the United States and other rich countries to pass through a period of massive emissions, until they became wealthy enough to have the resources to start to curb them. Should that luxury be denied to India, China, and other states that lag behind in economic development?

More than half of power generation added in the developing world from 2018 to 2020 was "climate misaligned," according to the journal *iScience.* "We find that approximately half the generation executed in those years is too carbon-intensive to align with keeping Earth's average temperature from exceeding 1.5°C above pre-industrial levels, largely because of the prevalence of new natural-gas–fired power plants."[29]

Emerging markets including China and India, the world's two most populous countries, expect to increase emissions for the next decade. Any reductions must wait until after 2030. These countries correctly blame global climate change on advanced economies. Asking emerging markets to clip their growth when still relatively poor penalizes them for a problem that rich countries created. No wonder they bristle at restraints to their current and future growth when the United States and Europe created this mess over the past two centuries.

Sounds bad? Just wait—it gets worse, due to crossover effects. Global climate change appears to unleash frequent and virulent pandemics. After the Spanish flu of 1918–19 we didn't experience any major global pandemic until the Asian flu of 1958, a much milder version of the Spanish flu. Since 1980, by contrast, we have been hit by HIV, SARS, MERS, bird flu, swine flu, Ebola, Zika, and now COVID-19 and its multiple variants. Why? One hypothesis blames the destruction of animal ecosystems on climate change. Thus, bats, pangolins, and other animals carrying dangerous pathogens live in closer proximity with livestock and humans, making transmission of zoonotic diseases nearly inevitable.

An investigation by Harvard University's Center for Climate, Health and the Global Environment has focused on this linkage. "With fewer places to live and fewer food sources to feed on, animals find food and shelter where people are, and that can lead to disease spread," says Dr. Aaron Bernstein, who directs the center. "Climate change has already made conditions more favorable to the spread of some infectious diseases, including Lyme disease, waterborne diseases such as Vibrio parahaemolyticus which causes vomiting and diarrhea, and mosquito-borne diseases such as malaria and dengue fever."[30]

A team of researchers at the World Bank, the University of Oxford, and the France International Institute for Applied Systems Analysis concurs. "When pandemic and extreme weather events combine and interact within an economy, they generate non-linear effects that can amplify losses significantly," they reported in *ScienceDirect*, a peer-reviewed journal. "Indeed, the total impacts can be larger than the sum of the individual shocks." They determined that simultaneous shocks to firms' production and household demand "can increase unemployment, reduce wages, and reduce household welfare." Long-lasting negative socioeconomic effects can impede growth and hamper recovery.[31]

Melting icecaps and glaciers will release more than water, according to *Scientific American*. "As the global climate continues to warm, many questions remain about the periglacial environment. Among them: as water infiltration increases, will permafrost thaw more rapidly? And, if so, what long-frozen organisms might 'wake up'?"[32] Authors Kimberley Miner, Arwyn Edwards, and Charles Miller give ample cause for alarm. "Organisms that co-evolved within now-extinct ecosystems from the Cenozoic to the Pleistocene may also emerge and interact with our modern environment in entirely novel ways," they reported. Scientists have traced an anthrax outbreak in Siberia to permafrost thaw. Melting ice may also have freed Orthopoxvirus, a pathogen that causes skin lesions. "As the Arctic continues to transform, one thing is clear: as climate change warms this microbial repository during the 21st century, the full range of consequences is yet to be told." Moreover, the melting of the permafrost will release massive amounts of methane "with a 100 year global warming potential 28-34 times that of CO_2."[33]

Okay then, how much will it cost to stop global warming? Of course, we cannot let the earth burn up, but can we find the money to preserve the environment without choking economic growth?

The Natural Resources Defense Council (NRDC) assessed the economic effects of climate change in four areas: hurricane damage, real estate losses, energy costs, and water costs. Leaving other areas aside, it estimated that just these four will impose a $1.9 trillion price tag *every year* by the end of this century. That amount, the NRDC warns, is the low end of cost estimates.

"All the available methods for protection against sea-level rise are problematic and expensive," the NRDC concluded. "It is difficult to imagine any of them being used on a large enough scale to shelter all low-lying US coastal lands that are at risk under the business-as-usual case."[34]

The main fix would be "mitigation," meaning a course that achieves net zero GHG emissions as soon as possible. Given current technologies, this draconian solution implies zero or negative growth for most of the world for decades to come. We got an unwelcome taste of that in 2020 when the COVID-19 pandemic stalled earthbound activity, delivering the worst recession in six decades. But net emissions fell by only 8 percent globally. And even that partially good news for climate change delivered terrible news for jobs, incomes, and for the level of debt retirement that depends on a growing economy.

William Nordhaus describes the bottom line this way: "Economists have focused on strategies to slow climate change. The most promising is mitigation, or reducing emissions of CO_2 and other GHGs. Unfortunately, this approach is expensive. Studies indicate that it will cost in the range of 2 to 6 percent of world income (roughly, $2 trillion to $6 trillion annually at today's level of income) to attain international climate targets, even if mitigation is undertaken in an efficient manner."[35]

Successful mitigation means persuading developing nations to keep the rise in temperatures below 2 degrees C. Unless rich countries pony up far more to much poorer economies — and so far they have not delivered even on their existing meager promises of $100 billion of subsidies — mitigation looks impossible. Even meeting current commitments might not stop a rise of 3 degrees C by 2100, which triggers Armageddon. As *The Economist* reported after reviewing the scientific evidence, "Three degrees of global warming is quite plausible and truly disastrous."[36]

The second option is "adaptation": accept that the temperatures may increase by 2.5 to 3 degrees C or even more and then try to limit the damage. But adaptation on a massive scale would be extremely expensive and unaffordable, even for wealthy countries.

Hurricane Sandy in 2012 caused $62 billion of damages to New York

City and the region nearby. It triggered cries for preventative measures. One proposal featured a six-mile string of man-made islands with retractable gates. Closing the gates would protect the city from storm surges the next time.

This one quixotic proposal would cost $119 billion and take twenty-five years to build. Worse, the whole plan, when ready, might be obsolete. It would protect New York from storms but not rising sea levels. Under some scenarios, sea levels could rise between four and nine feet by the end of this century. But even if the plan made great sense, who would pay for it? Mind you, this is the cost for only one city.

Despite a lot of talk about adaptation, no one is really seriously considering its unaffordable cost. A UN study estimates that if mitigation goals are breached, the cost of adaptation in developing countries alone could be $500 billion per year by 2050.[37] Who knows what the estimate would be by 2100? Many poor developing countries with cities at risk are already heavily indebted. How will they afford such costs?

Between mitigation and adaptation, the most sober cost estimates sound mind-boggling. Speaking in Glasgow at the November 2021 United Nations Climate Change Conference known as COP26, the US secretary of the treasury Janet Yellen stated: "Some have put the global figure between $100 and $150 trillion over the next three decades."[38] How will such huge resources—about $3 to $5 trillion a year—be mobilized between the public and private sector? It looks like mission impossible.

To ease unfairness in combating climate change, rich countries have proposed carrots for developing countries. The 2015 Paris Agreement recommended annual transfers of $100 billion to the developing world, spare change relative to what is needed. Although these transfers look like too little too late, only a fraction of that sum has actually changed hands so far.

A third option, solar geoengineering, features a friendlier price tag. It has roots in the 1991 eruption of Mount Pinatubo in the Philippines. That eruption sent a column of ash and smoke twenty-eight miles into the atmosphere. Once aloft, these aerosols, as scientists call them, deflected significant heat from the sun. Global cooling followed, lowering temperatures by 0.7 degrees C in some areas, nearly erasing a 0.8 degree increase in average global temperature since the industrial revolution began.

Maybe mimicking this volcanic effect can delay or even stop climate change, hopeful advocates say. Release particles in the high atmosphere to slow or reverse global warming. It sounds feasible and, better yet, much more affordable than mitigation or adaptation. But there are many reasons for doubt. This untested technology may have serious side effects. Critics have urged a global ban. Instead of solving climate change, they argue, it merely distracts attention from the primary cause: too much carbon entering the atmosphere.

"At best it's a Band-Aid or perhaps a pain killer that quite literally masks the underlying problem of carbon pollution," says economist and *Climate Shock* coauthor Gernot Wagner.[39] If implemented it would not prevent ocean acidification that is killing fish and bleaching corals. Artificial shade might harm global agriculture that needs sunlight. Solar power production would suffer under a white sky. And longer-term consequences are totally unknown.[40] Without a breathtaking technological breakthrough, geoengineering resembles a freak-science solution to global warming. "If the prospect of injecting millions of tons of tiny artificially engineered particles into the planet's stratosphere to create a sun shield of sorts doesn't scare you," says Wagner, "you haven't been paying attention." There is now even some scientific research that suggests that geoengineering may increase the risk of malaria for one billion people globally.[41]

Hope springs eternal on the greenhouse gas battlefront, but alternatives like nuclear fusion look like pipe dreams for now, even if some research progress has been made on this front. Slightly more realistic alternatives like clean hydrogen cost far too much to produce on a scale that would make a dent in climate change. They also require fossil fuels as part of their creation, defeating the purpose of reducing their use. Current nuclear fission technology may be another option, but it stirs political battles over safety.

Two closely related solutions have generated interest in scientific circles: carbon capture and storage (CCS) and its variant, direct air capture (DAC). Both technologies would require stratospheric investment to make them feasible. Vacuuming up vast amounts of airborne carbon looks like another mission impossible. Capping the rise in global average temperature increases to 1.5 degrees C, "a whopping 17 billion tons of carbon dioxide would need to be removed annually," says a report by the United Nations.[42] In 2019, human activity pumped 43.1 billion tons of CO_2 into the air.[43]

Aggressive decarbonization requires phasing out fossil fuels—such as coal, oil, and natural gas—and replacing them with green renewable energy such as solar, wind, biomass, hydro, and a variety of other small but promising alternatives. The International Energy Agency (IEA) warned in May 2021 that to reach the goal of net zero emissions in 2050, the world must immediately halt investment in fossil fuel supply projects and table plans for unabated coal plants that do not mitigate carbon dioxide emissions.[44]

Progress in the last decade has not been fast enough to slow global warming to any significant extent. The share of total energy consumption coming from fossil fuels went from 80.3 percent in 2009 to 80.2 percent in 2019. The share of modern renewables went from 8.7 percent to 11.2 percent—a snail's pace when we need to sprint.[45]

Much more can be achieved in the next few decades given the sharp fall in the cost of producing solar and wind power. But the idea that we will fully phase out fossil fuels in the next few decades is totally far-fetched. Moreover, solar and wind power require scientific breakthroughs and massive investment in energy storage—that is still too costly—to smooth cyclical and seasonal fluctuations.

Market-based solutions alone won't cut it. Companies commonly voice sympathy with environmental goals. Ford Motor Company, on the front line of fossil fuel consumption, has published a sustainability report every year since 2000. Ford claims credit as "the only full line U.S. automaker committed to doing its part to reduce CO_2 emissions in line with the Paris Climate Agreement and working with California for stronger vehicle greenhouse gas standards."[46]

Overall, however, the private sector lacks the resources, the will, or both to cause real change. The Edison Electric Institute represents investor-owned electric companies that provide power to 220 million Americans in fifty states and the District of Columbia. It lobbies for government intervention. "The costs of, and regulatory and economic barriers to, the use of CCS must be addressed in any federal action or legislation to reduce GHGs."[47]

The effort to win hearts and minds could boomerang. We are phasing out fossil fuels, steadily reducing our ability to extract and process them. If overall energy production lags behind demand, however, we may see an oil shock reminiscent of the 1970s, the trigger for stagflation. We appear headed that way. In 2021, U.S. retail energy prices posted the biggest jump since 2008, the U.S. Energy Information Administration disclosed in March 2022.[48]

Energy prices in the Goldman Sachs Commodities Index soared almost 60 percent in 2021 as supply lagged behind demand.[49] Pressure on institutional investors from eco-minded shareholders has slashed investment in new fossil fuel projects by 40 percent, according to one estimate.[50] Production of renewables has increased but not fast enough. Surging energy demand after the end of the COVID-19 recession drove price increases and even energy shortfalls in China, India and the United Kingdom.

A green transition also requires copper, aluminum, lithium, and other vital raw materials. Mining and processing them requires energy that fossil fuels produce. If current policies raise the price for fossil fuels we may end up with "greenflation." Simply put: There is no free lunch in the transition to green energy.

Sanctions and supply interruptions following the Russian invasion of Ukraine spiked oil and natural gas prices. Rising tabs to drive cars and heat homes sidelined policy plans to develop renewable energy. Even the Biden administration, seriously committed to the climate crisis, changed tack. It begged Gulf states to increase oil and gas production. It accelerated negotiations with Iran on a nuclear deal so as to increase Iranian oil exports. It even pressed the pariah populist regime of Venezuela to ramp up oil production. Discussions weighed the merits of easing environmental restraints on the domestic production of energy, including shale gas and oil. Biden barely mentioned climate change in his first State of the Union address in 2022 as gasoline prices surged at the pump. His plans for a Build Back Better infrastructure plan—that included $500 billion for climate change–related projects—stalled at the legislative level. So the goal of cutting GHG emissions in the US in half by the end of the decade looks dead on arrival.

Everyone must bear the cost of progressive energy policies. To accelerate a transition toward renewable energy, carbon taxes must replace historical subsidies for fossil fuel producers. That of course spells yet higher prices for gas and oil.

Ending fossil fuel subsidies won't be easy. They are large and widespread. An IMF study estimates that "global fossil fuel subsidies amount to around $6 trillion in 2020—this is 6.8 percent of global GDP. More than 70 percent reflects undercharging for environmental costs."[50] Reducing, let alone eliminating, such subsidies is politically very arduous.

Economists agree on the efficiency of carbon taxes to end fossil fuel addiction, yet politically, such taxes stir worldwide opposition. In 2018, France passed a hike in the tax on diesel and gasoline to support the country's transition to green energy. It spurred a massive grassroots political revolt among motorists, the "yellow vests" revolt. Introducing new carbon taxes while energy prices are high and rising looks like political suicide to politicians who want to keep their jobs. In early 2022 extreme violence erupted in Kazakhstan as the government doubled the price of fuels. Only a brutal crackdown by that authoritarian government kept the regime in place, for better or for worse. All over the world in 2022 governments started to cut energy taxes rather than raising them to deal with the popular anger about rising energy costs.

If enacted, carbon taxes that accelerate the switch from fossil fuels to renewables may hurt. A rate of $35 a ton on CO_2 emissions in 2030 would double the price for coal and boost prices for electricity and gasoline by 10 and 25 percent, respectively, the IMF estimates.[51] That's the good news. Taxing carbon at $35 a ton would not stem global climate change, says Nordhaus. "I have worked on models that suggest a current carbon price in the range of $40 per ton of CO_2, rising over time," he says. "This policy would lead to eventual warming of around 3°C above preindustrial levels."

A serious effort to keep increases below 2 degrees C means a carbon tax rate closer to $200 per ton of CO_2 emitted.[52] Few countries impose a national carbon tax. Notably, the United States has no national policy. California and other states tax carbon emissions and must battle in courts to maintain those unpopular taxes. The global average carbon tax in 2022 is $2 per ton. How can anyone expect a 100-fold increase to $200 to achieve the upper limit of 2 degrees C of the Paris Agreement?

Miraculous developments might someday lower the cost of mitigation—if it's not too little too late. Hardheaded realism by scientists and economists casts doubt on such hopes. "While some miraculous technological breakthroughs might conceivably be discovered that can reduce the costs [of mitigation] dramatically, experts do not see them arriving in the near future," says Nordhaus. "New technologies—particularly for energy systems that have massive investments in capital such as power plants, structures, roads, airports, and factories—take many decades to develop and deploy."[53]

The message has reached cost-conscious asset managers who tout adherence to environmental and social goals in their investments under the environmental, social, and governance (ESG) banner. Noble intentions look counterproductive to Tariq Fancy, the former chief investment officer for sustainable investing at BlackRock, the world's largest asset manager. In a November 2021 column published by *The Economist*, he declared that greenwashing and greenwishing waste valuable time.[54] "The utopian storyline around ESG actually undermines the case for government to play a role. Misleading public-relations activities foist the idea that sustainable investing, stakeholder capitalism and voluntary compliance are the answers." Share prices and marketing budgets at ESG-focused companies increase but so do carbon emissions. "The PR is especially noxious," Mr. Fancy wrote, "because you can't fix a market failure with marketing."

He rejects faith in markets to correct a catastrophic environmental imbalance:

"The short-term incentives of business do not always align with the long-term public interest. The deluge of non-binding commitments made by companies usually hail from their communications departments, not operations teams. Although markets have a role to play, they cannot work by themselves. As a result, little ESG work meaningfully affects actual capital-allocation decisions, a prerequisite for corporate promises to have any chance at reducing real-world emissions."[55]

The results of the 2021 COP26 meeting at Glasgow confirmed what skeptics fear. In spite of impassioned speeches and signed commitments to stop global climate change, there has been scant real progress toward the Paris Agreement goal of a 1.5 degree C cap on average temperature increases. Given current policies and actions the world is headed instead toward an average increase in temperature of 2.7 degrees C.

Country after country presents lofty goals that are not backed by the whole range of actions that would achieve meaningful emission goals. Since Tokyo and then Paris, the pattern has been of a string of broken promises. Glasgow will highly likely be the same.

The term "singularity" usually describes the moment when artificial intelligence surpasses human intelligence, and (to pessimists) it's game over for Homo sapiens. Yet a version of singularity can apply to climate change. That's when we pass the point of no return.

"There are known unknowns aplenty," write authors Wagner and Weitzman in *Climate Shock*. "Unknown unknowns may yet dominate and tipping points and other nasty surprises seem to lurk around every corner. Some of them may put warming itself on overdrive."[56]

In the worst case, primordial conditions will reappear. Soils will fry. Deserts will expand. Fires will incinerate communities. Hurricanes will increase in number and frequency. Tornadoes will strike far and wide. Collapsing supply chains will cause negative shocks to spiral. Wealth will evaporate. Migration will reach monumental scale. Those who see no megathreat in climate change today will wonder why we did nothing when we had the chance to act.

The answers will be the same as always. We listened to the wrong people. The deniers exploited marginal uncertainties in the scientific community. We ignored grim facts. We didn't believe our eyes. And, most ironic, we didn't have the resources to act. It cost too much.

PART III

CAN THIS DISASTER BE AVERTED?

Chapter 11

Dark Destiny

This book explores economic, financial, political, geopolitical, technological, health, and environmental megathreats hurtling toward us. Sound policies might partially or fully avert one or more of them, but collectively, calamity seems near certain. The most plausible solutions are complex, costly, and fraught with political and geopolitical friction. We probably won't achieve them.

The March 2021 report "Global Trends 2040: A More Contested World" by the US National Intelligence Council describes five scenarios on how the world will evolve over the next two decades.[1] Most of the five scenarios are quite disturbing, with such names as "Tragedy and Mobilization," "A World Adrift," and "Separate Silos." Only one, "Renaissance of Democracies," sounds optimistic.

Strip away the nuances and two scenarios highlight the outcomes that matter most. In one scenario, one or several megathreats materialize, and civilization backslides toward severe instability and chaos. That's dystopia. In the other, good judgment and sound policies across the board manage to partly deflect each of the megathreats. We stumble, but we don't collapse. I call this a "utopian" version even if it is far from ideal.

Let's consider dystopia first. We'll look at the "utopian" alternative in Chapter 12. What does dystopia look like? Start with the observation that megathreats are structural. Income and wealth inequality, massive private and public debts, financial instability, climate change, global pandemics, artificial intelligence, and geopolitical rivalries have deep roots in worldwide systems and cultures. We cannot attack their causes without risking unintended consequences. For instance, instituting a significantly progressive tax policy in one country to tackle inequality could lead the wealthiest citizens to relocate to lower tax jurisdictions or depress capital spending. Signing a major treaty between the United States and China to renounce AI in weapons systems could lead other nations to develop their own cyberweapons. Stimulating growth via unconventional policies leads to bubbles and more unsustainable debt accumulation. Cleaning the environment and reducing global climate is very expensive and may reduce growth and increase public debts.

Even if solutions were fairly obvious, the tenacity required to achieve them is unprecedented. Like a cancer that ravages bodies, megathreats will wreak havoc on the global infrastructure and current world order. Expect many dark days, my friends.

Asteroids smash into the earth with spectacular effect. Megathreats, on the other hand, unfold while decision-makers watch and dither, arguing about their importance and their likelihood. (In the timely film *Don't Look Up*, senior policy-makers equivocate while a massive and destructive asteroid hurtles towards earth.) Workers and unions lose the power to preserve a middle class. Tax policy and regulations help powerful corporations and business interests bend polices to favor capital over labor. "Deaths of despair" in hollowed-out communities plague an unskilled and semiskilled underclass with few jobs, savings or hope. Personal wealth garners political influence. Financial institutions grow too big to fail. Tech companies gain vast power over consumers and other firms, with few restraints. Algorithms replace a human workforce and may eventually make Homo sapiens obsolete. Coastal cities flood. Farmland gradually dries out in drought. The criminal justice system locks up millions of poor Americans and minorities with no plan for helping them return productively to society. Inequality frays the social fabric and breeds populism. These are all relatively slow-moving crises that are unlikely to generate the massive, coordinated response of an asteroid-like threat.

International cooperation is vital yet elusive, if not hopeless. Think global climate change, pandemics, cyberwarfare, global financial crises, conflict between the United States and China and Russia, Iran, and North Korea. Deglobalization, global financial crises, mass migration, and ethical uses of artificial intelligence sound very different to authorities in rich and poor countries, or even among leading economic and geopolitical rivals.

Perils hide in plain sight. A widening gulf between haves and have-nots signals the proximity and severity of megathreats. Trade and globalization produce economic winners and losers in advanced economies and emerging markets. Production relocates to where labor is cheapest, leaving joblessness, empty factories and derelict real estate where businesses once thrived. Capital drifts from rich to poor countries in pursuit of higher returns. Migration accelerates in the other direction, from poor to rich countries, creating a backlash against it. Technological innovation replaces people who purchase goods and services with robots that consume only electricity. Financial resources and wealth fall into fewer and fewer hands, exacerbating inequality.

Family and professional networks perpetuate inequality. Fewer lucrative opportunities increasingly reach only to the offsprings of the elite. A so-called meritocratic educational system rewards connections, not necessarily merit. Social mobility bogs down. Even our mating habits skew economic status. College-educated men tend to marry college-educated women, a pattern that curtails intergenerational economic and social mobility.[2]

Don't make the error of thinking that wealth inequality hurts only those on low rungs of the income ladder. It visits misfortune on a much larger population, a shrinking middle class, white collar workers and even affluent tiers that rely on social stability.

Many of us agree that inequality is one of the most terrible challenges of our time. Nonetheless, policy proposals that target inequality have a dismal track record. Most of them feature taxation that redistributes wealth and income from rich to poor, and they are thus opposed by the very powerful rich elite. In *The Great Leveler*, historian Walter Scheidel shows that peaceful redistribution has never succeeded in easing inequality.[3] It takes massive upheaval to cause meaningful change. When inequality spirals to its ugly and violent conclusion—social upheaval, revolution, or war—millions die. Transformative revolutions alter social and economic systems, as in Russia and China during the twentieth century, but they are enormously costly in terms of human life. Ultimately, the collapse of bloated, predatory governments mobilizes citizens to redistribute economic assets, at huge costs. The collapse of the Soviet Union, though ostensibly peaceful, caused a demographic collapse along with violent conflicts along the edges of its empire, and a civil war in Chechnya. Ultimately, the result was a new militaristic autocracy in Russia, with a new version of crony capitalism that enriched a very small elite. Such a kleptocratic autocracy became aggressive, most lately in Ukraine, in the delusional dream of restoring the Soviet empire.

As inequality festers, it tends to bring gaping budget deficits and private dissavings financed by unsustainable public and private debts. Political pressure will mount to level the playing field. More and more people who feel left behind demand action to restore their income and status. The left seeks more action by government to reinforce social welfare. The right resists any steps that enlarge government's role and demands lower taxes that make deficits much larger. Despite political rhetoric, Democrats and Republicans share blame for debt. Debt grew fastest under Presidents Woodrow Wilson and Franklin Roosevelt during World Wars I and II, but Presidents Ronald Reagan and George W. Bush are next in line.[4] The 2017 tax cut by the Trump administration also ranks as a memorable unforced error as it led to a trillion-dollar deficit in a peacetime growing economy. And the response to COVID-19 was excessive deficit spending both during the Trump and Biden administrations.

Irreconcilable differences embolden populist politicians with sound bites instead of solutions. Polarized social agendas push voters further left or right, leaving less room for agreement and more chance of legislative gridlock. In the West, there is rising populism, including semi-authoritarian regimes. In the East, there is a plethora of authoritarian and semi-authoritarian regimes—including China, Russia, Iran, North Korea and others that welcome state capitalism—that clamp down completely on personal liberties.

Now add migration to this dystopian domestic scenario. People emigrate to find work, one way to correct income inequality on a global scale. They seek safety, stability, and opportunity for their families. Historically, migration has been a boon in growing nations. The United States could not have flourished without it. In theory, immigration now should improve the ratio of working population to retirees in advanced economies, relieving pressure on social security and other old age welfare programs. Young immigrants pay taxes and spend most of their income, boosting consumer demand. In practice, however, immigration won't solve the aging problem. Growing nativist opposition to it blocks the way.

Migrants will swell when megathreats topple impoverished governments in Africa, Central America, and parts of Asia. They will head toward regions where global climate change improves the prospects for agriculture—Siberia, Scandinavia, Greenland, and Canada in the northern hemisphere; New Zealand and Tasmania in the southern hemisphere. These countries may lack the means to seal their borders without assistance from major military powers that will impose their own demands.

In 2015, one million refugees entered the EU, causing a massive political backlash. In the United States, a much smaller number of refugees at the southern border led to harsh policies to close the door by President Trump that have been continued even under President Biden. This is only a prelude. Wait for a much more severe crisis and political backlash when dozens of millions of refugees want to flee desperate conditions. Increasingly, war and conflict—on top of climate change and failed states—will create waves of millions of refugees, as the war in Ukraine and the civil war in Syria tragically showed us. National and regional disorder and clashes will multiply in size and frequency, leading to incipient mass migration that will face closing borders.

Inequality and climate change are systemic. What about our looming financial crises? Innovation can solve many problems, but it won't erase unsustainable debt. We have borrowed our way to prosperity with no exit strategy. Loans secured with home equity and other assets lifted consumption in the 2000s as income growth slowed. Dimming prospects of repayment did not deter lenders who preyed on increasingly desperate consumers and homeowners.

Behavior that fueled the 2008 financial bubble and bust will persist, but on steroids. Millennials who were shafted in the global financial crisis—they lost jobs, income, and wealth—are being duped once again, this time under the banner of financial democratization. It's a new name for the rope that part-time gig workers can use to hang themselves. Millions have opened investment accounts on their mobile phones, where they leverage scant savings to speculate on flaky investments like meme stocks and crypto scams. Using their keyboards to close the stubborn wealth gap is doomed to fail, and to turn frustration to anger.

The 2021 GameStop and other meme-stock narratives, featuring a united front of heroic small day traders fighting evil short-selling hedge funds, masks an ugly reality. A cohort of hopeless, jobless, skill-less, saving-less, debt-burdened individuals is being exploited once again. Many believe that financial success lies not in good jobs, hard work, and patient saving and investment, but in get-rich-quick schemes. They flock to wagers on inherently worthless assets like cryptocurrencies (or "shit-coins," as I prefer to call them). Make no mistake: the populist meme in which an army of millennial Davids takes down a Wall Street Goliath is merely serving another insider scheme to fleece clueless amateur investors. As in 2008, the inevitable result will be another asset bubble that is building up dangerously. The difference is that this time, recklessly populist members of the US Congress have taken to inveighing against financial intermediaries for not permitting the vulnerable to leverage themselves even more.

This bubble will burst. The question is not if, it is when, and how much pain the coming dystopia will inflict. And the first pop of the latest massive asset bubble started to occur in 2022. Policy makers have nearly exhausted vast monetary, credit, and fiscal resources. When the next financial crisis erupts it may not be possible to bail out strapped households, corporations, banks, or Main Street, as policy makers are running out of policy bullets. Without the ability to deploy a new round of massive stimulus packages, central bankers and government officials will watch helplessly as recessions wallop economies, regional cooperation collapses, civil strife proliferates, and powerful countries jockey for command of global resources. Keep an eye on the eurozone and its weakest links, like Italy or Greece, for a signal that debt crises have passed the tipping point. Weaker members face a debt and competitiveness crisis that may force them to leave, thus triggering the collapse of this monetary union.

The next crisis may look different from the previous two in another crucial way. After 2008, inflation languished below a 2 percent target, a desirable level that fosters growth without excessive upward pressure on prices and wages. Lowflation, as the International Monetary Fund labeled it, persisted until COVID-19 caused global supply chain bottlenecks, falling labor supply, and a surging consumer demand spurred by monetary, credit, and fiscal stimulus programs that led to excess savings and pent-up demand. Inflation has now jumped to levels not seen since 1983. This spike in inflation looks persistent rather than transitory. Central banks are in a debt trap, with their hands tied. Inflation is likely to rise further when the next crisis is triggered by medium-term negative supply shocks that the crisis will exacerbate. Without white knights to save the day, raising rates to cool down borrowing and inflation would trigger a tidal wave of defaults and a financial market crash.

This tsunami will hit the global economy in the next decade, slamming potential growth and increasing production costs. Loose monetary and fiscal policies, as Chapter 5 spells out, will make things uglier. Everything points toward a coming Great Stagflationary Debt Crisis.

The next round of high inflation will squeeze the dollar. After a run of eighty years, its condition now stirs questions. It ain't what it used to be, an unimpeachable and stable store of value. High inflation, close to double digits, could eventually undermine a weakened dollar. Debasement and weaponization of the dollar for geopolitical goals will lead to a gradual decline of central bank reserves held in dollar assets. China is ready to substitute the dollar for the RMB and other strategic rivals of the United States—like Russia—are ready to dump dollar assets and a dollar-based reserve currency regime now that their foreign reserves and assets have been frozen. Cryptocurrency promoters are bent—if delusional—on trying to displace any fiat currency with their digital money, a near impossible goal as such cryptocurrencies lack essential features of a true currency. America's reserve currency status won't collapse overnight, but we will see it coming in waning US economic and geopolitical muscle around the world and increased weaponization of the US dollar for national security goals. For centuries global reserve currency status has gone hand in hand with geopolitical hegemony. If you lose the latter, you lose the former. And if you play hardball with trade and financial sanctions your rivals will eventually decouple from your dollar system, trade- and finance-wise.

Manifestations of economic malaise—stagnant growth, stagnant employment numbers and job losses—will have disturbing political consequences. They can lead to political extremism, usually under the guise of right-wing populism, but the left-wing version shares some commonalities. When populism reaches a fever pitch, it tends to vilify pluralistic values associated with liberal democracy and rule of law. Populists of both extremes are united in their callousness or antipathy toward foreigners and against domestic elites. That creates an opening for authoritarian demagogues who denounce their political opponents as elitists, and embrace prejudice against disadvantaged minorities, while praising redistribution of wealth from rich to poor not based on the rule of law, as in China and Russia.

In emerging markets—leaving aside outright dictatorships in some of the poorest countries—authoritarians now run governments in

Russia, Belarus, Turkey, Hungary, the Philippines, Brazil, Venezuela, Kazakhstan and China, among others. Cascading megathreats will only make that list grow longer.

Latin American nations flirted for decades with populism on the left and right. For a time, after the end of the Cold War, it looked like representative democracy would prevail in many parts of that region. Yet hard times have handed populists a hefty axe to grind. Their recent resurgence has changed the region's face. Promising democracies have succumbed. Mexico took a populist turn in 2018 with the election of Andres Manuel Lopez Obrador, its sixty-fifth president. Left-wing populists won presidential elections in 2021 in Chile and Peru, and in 2022 in Colombia. Experts expect elections in 2022 in Brazil to go the same way.

Brazil turned to the semi-authoritarian president Jair Bolsonaro who, in January 2022, thumbed his nose at liberal democracies by planning a trip to meet Vladimir Putin as Russia amassed troops on the border with Ukraine.[5] And Latin America is not unique. Years of mediocre growth make South Africa—and other parts of Africa—candidates for populism and authoritarian regimes. India, in a perennial struggle to make life bearable for an impoverished population, is still a democracy and a modernizing economy but has some political forces who openly disdain Muslims, independent democratic institutions and the rule of law. This trend is not our friend, and it's just getting started.

"At the extremes," Anne Applebaum warned in the November 2021 issue of the *Atlantic,* "this kind of contempt can devolve into what the international democracy activist Srdja Popovic calls the 'Maduro model' of governance, which may be what Lukashenko is preparing for in Belarus. Autocrats who adopt it are 'willing to pay the price of becoming a totally failed country, to see their country enter the category of failed states,' accepting economic collapse, isolation, and mass poverty if that's what it takes to stay in power."[6]

Advanced democracies are vulnerable as well. Populist arguments yanked Britain out of the European Union, as voters went for Brexit. In the United States, populists elected Donald Trump and his allies. We see growing support in advanced countries for right-wing parties that oppose the European Union, immigration, and rescue packages for indebted countries. France, the historical bastion of liberty, equality, and brotherhood, has grown increasingly receptive to the anti-Muslim, anti-Semitic, anti-immigrant appeal of the recent presidential candidate Marine LePen; she lost the presidential election in 2022 but her nativist message is still popular as economic malaise worsens for those left behind.

For years, political division and polarization, lack of bipartisanship, partisan radicalization, the rise of extreme right-wing groups, and conspiracy theories have been growing and severely dividing the United States. These trends reached one peak after the 2020 election spawned the fiction that the election was stolen from Donald Trump. Lack of evidence notwithstanding, most of his base went along with him. The January 6, 2021, attempted coup revealed a vast base of radicalized white supremacists and other extreme right-wing militia willing to use force to prevent the electoral vote count in Congress and the rightful installation of Joe Biden as president.

Unfolding megathreats and the rising tide of populism will partly decide the 2022 midterm elections in the United States. Debt, inflation, globalization, immigration, climate change, and the rise of China alarm swing voters. Observers predict angry contests and even violence that may threaten to overturn outcomes in the 2024 presidential election.[7] Conspiracy theories, massive misinformation campaigns, large-scale violence, coup, insurrection, civil war, secession, and insurgency are now terms used in a large number of op-eds, essays, and books. Collectively, we are thinking the once unthinkable.

The 2024 presidential campaign is drawing close. The *New York Times* calls "the prospect of American political conflagration — including insurrection, secession, insurgency and civil war" — a serious threat.[8] Numerous authors have raised the possibility of a "slow-moving coup," the pundit Bill Maher told his HBO audience. Writing in *The Nation,* a left-of-center publication, Robert Crawford predicts a "worst case scenario" for the United States. Chauncey DeVega, in *Salon,* and British journalist Sir Max Hastings, have voiced concern about secession or large-scale political violence instigated by the loser's cadres. Titles like *How Civil Wars Start,* by political scientist Barbara F. Walter, and *The Next Civil War,* by journalist Stephen Marche, mince no words. In January 2021, after the assault on the Capitol, a poll showed that 46 percent of Americans had the view that their country was headed toward another civil war.[9] A CIA task force reached the conclusion that "the United States during the Trump presidency regressed, for the first time since 1800, into "anocracy." That's how scholars label a system of government that hovers uneasily between democracy and autocracy.[10]

Like nuclear meltdowns, megathreats turn all matter in their path into fuel. The economic malaise and rising inequality that leads to populism will spur a backlash against free trade and globalization. The fundamental aspect of populist economic policy is economic nationalism and autarkic tendencies. The rise of political and economic populism exacerbates the risk of deglobalization, protectionism, fragmentation of the global economy, balkanization of global supply chains, restrictions to migration, controls of movement of capital, technology, and data, and severe friction between the United States and China.

Dystopian upheaval will turn science inside out. Technology's dark side threatens Western values. Social media produces echo chambers as news and postings keep a specious rumor mill in high gear, often to advance interests of foreign adversaries. Conspiracy theories—even demonstrably lunatic ones—travel with alarming speed. Initially seen as a tool to launch and organize dissent against autocratic regimes that traffic in lies and hypocrisy (do you remember the Arab Spring, and the Facebook-generated protests against the Egyptian government?), social media today increasingly foments assaults on democratic institutions and orchestrates ethnic violence. Look no further than the January 6 Capitol mob in the United States or the Rohingya massacre in Myanmar. These trends will accelerate as artificial intelligence and machine learning refine ways—via "transformers" technologies—to manipulate minds.

Technology will become autocracy's handmaiden. Social media and big tech help current autocrats and dictators hold power. The idea that technology would expose authoritarians to justice and defend democracy now sounds naive.[11] China uses a Great Firewall and other social media tools to control its population in Orwellian ways. A "social credit rating system" restricts access to financial services and punishes socially and politically "deviant" behavior. Now China is exporting these technologies to client regimes, reinforcing autocracy elsewhere.

Unfettered computerization will make jobs vanish, and not just routine, repetitive jobs. Artificial intelligence advancing at warp speed will make cognitive workers obsolete, from Uber drivers, paralegals, and auditors, to eventually brain surgeons. Robots will also populate creative jobs once we reach a point where machines outthink people. Even computer developers will find their seats occupied by robots. Permanent blue- and white-collar technological displacement will extend unemployment lines, adding pressure to a fraying social safety net. Adding irony to injury, robots are already running most HR decisions and will run unemployment offices.

Who controls AI will command enormous economic, financial, and geopolitical power. That is why the United States and China are vying to dominate the industries of the future. And if the United States and China ever enter into open warfare, their respective AI technologies could make the difference between victory and defeat.

To assert control in a world unsettled by megathreats, major powers will reinforce or reshuffle alliances. China's informal geopolitical partnerships with revisionist powers such as Russia, Iran, and North Korea are challenging the United States and the West. The United States is reinforcing and building new alliances in Asia: the Quad, the AUKUS (a security agreement between Australia, the United Kingdom, and the United States), the Indo Pacific Economic Framework, and now NATO flexing its military muscle in Asia. Revisionist powers challenging the United States and the West cannot yet match Western military strength. The United States alone spends more on military resources than its four revisionist adversaries combined. Those adversaries will increasingly counter American strength with asymmetric warfare that deploys cyber espionage, cyberattacks, and misinformation campaigns to weaken and polarize the United States and the West. But traditional hard power conflict on controlling land masses will not disappear, as the Russian invasion of Ukraine and the looming conflict over Taiwan show.

Indeed, their logistical disadvantage won't prevent America's adversaries from aiming conventional weapons at the United States and the West. Putin's Russia seeks to partially restore the former Soviet empire by projecting a sphere of influence over former Soviet and Iron Curtain nations; the bloody invasion of Ukraine is a starting salvo of Russia's attempt to re-create the Soviet Union or its sphere of influence on its "near abroad." Similar tensions will mount in the Baltics, Central and Eastern Europe, the Caucasus, and parts of Central Asia, such as Kazakhstan.

Then there's North Korea, where sanctions only embolden a mercurial dear leader who demands adoration from a starving people while he embraces long-range missiles and cyberwarfare. In the Middle East, Iran may soon aim nuclear warheads at Israel and Arab states that challenge its dominance; but Israel may try to strike Iran's nuclear facilities before the country reaches the nuclear point of no return. War in the Gulf would trigger a stagflationary shock from rising oil prices more calamitous than twin spikes produced in the seventies. So many flash points and rivals jockeying for leadership amid geopolitical instability make skirmishes inevitable. They make conventional wars likely, and the horrifying specter of nuclear war possible. In 2022, the war in Ukraine led to risk of its escalation to the Baltics and Central Europe and even a military and nuclear confrontation between Russia and NATO. The specter of nuclear wars—that seemed faded once the Soviet Union collapsed—returned as the war in Ukraine escalated.

Geopolitical discord impedes united action against the world's most sweeping peril: global climate change, which threatens life on earth for billions of people in regions too hot or too flooded to inhabit. Earth's rising temperature will unleash storms and heat waves more frequent and more severe than humans can endure. These conditions will precipitate biological catastrophe. When ecosystems deteriorate, living spaces press animals and humans closer together. Zoonotic diseases will spawn pandemics and tax health care networks more than ever. As skies warm, melting permafrost will release even more pathogens frozen for millennia. When COVID-19 is in the rearview mirror, it won't mean the end of severe global pandemics. It's just a question of when the next virulent one will strike, and how fast we can respond—if we can respond.

Squabbling will intensify as coastlines, farmland, and rain forests disappear and global climate change worsens. Resolving climate change is either too expensive or reliant on untested technologies or too costly in terms of lost growth. Global rivalries will cripple responses to challenges in every dimension: economic, financial, technological, biological, geopolitical, and military. Narrow national interests will prevail. The world will split into nations that insist everyone share the tab for ecological damage, and free riders that ignore the calls because they did not cause the problem, they cannot afford to pay for the solution, or they elect leaders who dismiss climate change as fake news. And at some point a violent land grab for the regions of the world that benefit from climate change will ensue: Siberia's defrosting may lead China and other powers in Asia to an effective grab of this fertile land; already today thousands of Chinese buy and farm land in the steppes of Siberia. And a country like Russia, with a declining population of 145 million in 2021, barely 17 million of them in Siberia—a land mass larger than most continents—will soon find out that its tactical alliance with China is a major geostrategic error as 1.4 billion Chinese want to move north toward Siberia over the next few decades to deal with the consequences of climate change.

By altering the environment, climate change will undermine economic foundations in myriad ways. Extended droughts and violent weather will spike food prices, strain food production and lead to hunger, food riots, mass starvation, new failed states and civil wars. A backlash against fossil fuels has scaled back investments and capacity in traditional energy sources for virtuous reasons, but with insufficient ramping up of renewable energy supply. We're getting by for now, but roll the clock forward a few years. Energy prices will skyrocket as supplies dwindle, leaving large populations literally powerless. Even the cost of commodities necessary for renewable energy—like lithium and copper—will sharply rise as the price of fossil fuels skyrockets, a phenomenon dubbed *greenflation*. Supply chains that depend on fossil fuels will strain to keep goods moving. Shortages will proliferate.

We already suffer from inflation. Paired with slowing productivity, the coming supply shocks will trigger stagflation. How serious will it get? If two oil shocks bore significant blame for stagflation in the seventies, imagine the consequences when multiple megathreats converge. Massive explicit and implicit debt, deglobalization and protectionism, balkanization of global supply chains, aging of populations in advanced and emerging markets, restrictions on labor migration, the US-China cold war and decoupling, other geopolitical threats, fragmentation of the global economy as alliances shift, the fall of the role of the US dollar as the major global reserve currency, global climate change, pandemics, asymmetric cyberconflict, and exploding wealth inequality all prompt a bleak prognosis of stagflation. We could be facing a near future as grim as the Great Depression of the 1930s.

Writing in *Foreign Affairs* in 2011, Ian Bremmer and I foresaw a G-Zero world where Western influence will ebb, global agendas will perish, and no global hegemon will provide global public goods the way the United Kingdom did in the nineteenth century and the United States did in the twentieth century. Today, we are collapsing into that unstable, volatile, risky, chaotic, divided, fragmented, polarized, and dangerous global environment. Dystopia will sideline international rules and institutions. Domestic and international conflict will displace cooperation. We are—as Bremmer put it—in a "geopolitical depression."

"Public calamity," warned the British economist and statesman Edmund Burke in 1775, "is a mighty leveler." In the dystopian scenario of this chapter, megathreats will produce negative feedback loops that reinforce each other. They will materialize over the next decade or two. No one knows exactly when. What experts can say with confidence evokes Burke on the eve of the American Revolution: megathreats will rock our world in sobering ways.

Given the severe coming megathreats in the next two decades, how should individual and institutional investors protect at least their financial wealth? First, of all, rising inflation and other megathreats in the United States and around the world will force investors to assess the likely effects on both "risky" assets (generally stocks) and "safe" assets (such as US Treasury bonds).[12] The traditional investment advice is to allocate wealth according to the 60/40 rule: 60 percent of one's portfolio should be in higher-return but more volatile stocks, and 40 percent should be in lower-return, lower-volatility bonds. The rationale is that stocks and bond prices are usually negatively correlated (when one goes up, the other goes down), so this mix will balance a portfolio's risks and returns. Indeed, during a bull market or economic expansion when investors are optimistic, stock prices and bond yields will rise and bond prices will fall, resulting in a market loss for bonds; and during a bear market or a recession, when investors are pessimistic, prices and yields will follow an inverse pattern.

But the negative correlation between stock and bond prices presupposes low inflation. When inflation rises, returns on bonds become negative, because rising yields, led by higher inflation expectations, will reduce their market price. Consider that any 100-basis-point increase in long term bond yields leads to about a 10 percent fall in the market price — a sharp loss. Owing to higher inflation and inflation expectations, bond yields rose and the overall return on long bonds reached a return of negative 5 percent in 2021.[13] More losses were incurred by long bonds in 2022 as bond yields went higher as the Fed started to hike policy rates to fight the rising inflation.

Over the past three decades, bonds have offered a negative overall yearly return only a few times. The decline of inflation rates from double-digit levels to very low single digits, from the 1980s to the onset of COVID-19, produced a decades long bull market in bonds; yields fell and returns on bonds were highly positive as their price rose. The past thirty years thus have contrasted sharply with the stagflationary 1970s, when bond yields skyrocketed alongside higher inflation, leading to massive market losses for bonds.

But inflation is also bad for stocks, because it triggers higher interest rates — both in nominal and real terms. You could borrow money to buy stocks, but it will cost you more than usual to do so. And earnings of firms will be discounted with a higher discount rate — long bond yields — leading to lower valuations of equities. So stock valuations fall. Thus, as inflation rises, the correlation between stock and bond prices turns from negative to positive. Higher inflation leads to losses on *both* stocks and bonds, as happened in the 1970s. By 1982, the S&P 500 P/E ratio was 8, a very low number that reveals that for all corporations, healthy or not, stock prices were low.[14] Today, that ratio is above 30.

More recent examples also show that equities are hurt when bond yields rise in response to higher inflation or the expectation that higher inflation will lead to monetary-policy tightening. Even most of the much-touted tech and growth stocks aren't immune to an increase in long-term interest rates, because these are "long-duration" assets whose dividends lie further in the future. In September 2021, when ten-year Treasury yields rose a mere 22 basis points, stocks fell by 5-7 percent and the fall was greater in the tech-heavy Nasdaq than in the S&P 500.[15]

This pattern has extended into 2022. A modest 45-basis-point increase in bond yields in January-February triggered a 15 percent drop in the Nasdaq and a 10 percent drop in the S&P 500. Further such losses continued through June. If inflation were as likely to remain well above the US Federal Reserve's target rate of 2 percent — even if it falls modestly from its current high levels — long-term bond yields would go much higher, and equity prices could end up in bear country (a fall of 20 percent or more). By June 2022, the tech-heavy Nasdaq was already in bear market territory and S&P 500 close to it.

More to the point, if inflation continues to be higher than it was over the past few decades (the "Great Moderation"), a traditional portfolio invested 60 percent in equities and 40 percent in fixed income (a 60/40 split) would induce massive long-term losses.[16] The task for investors, then, is twofold: first, to figure out another way to hedge the 40 percent of their portfolio that is in bonds, and second, what to do with risky stocks.

There are at least three options for hedging the fixed-income component of a 60/40 portfolio. The first is to invest in inflation-indexed bonds or in short-term government bonds whose yields reprice rapidly in response to higher inflation. The second option is to invest in gold, other precious metals and possibly other commodities whose prices tend to rise when inflation is higher (gold is also a good hedge against the kinds of political and geopolitical risks that may hit the world in the next few years).[17] Lastly, one can invest in real assets with a relatively limited supply, such as land, commercial and residential real estate, and infrastructure. But given global climate change, any investments in real estate should be directed to the regions of the United States and the world that are resilient, i.e. regions that will not be flooded by rising sea levels, hurricanes, and typhoons, and regions that are not too hot to become unlivable. Investors should thus only look at sustainable real estate.

The optimal combination of short-term bonds, gold, and real estate will change over time and in complex ways depending on policy and market conditions. Some analysts argue that oil and energy — together with some other commodities — can also be a good hedge against inflation. But this issue is complex. In the 1970s, it was higher oil prices that caused inflation, not the other way around. And given the current pressure to move away from oil and fossil fuels, demand in those sectors may eventually reach a peak.

While inflation is bad for both bonds and stocks, stagflation — recession and high inflation — is even worse, especially for stocks. During stagflation episodes, like the 1970s, stocks fell sharply and the P/E ratio collapsed to a low of 8 because the high inflation that increased long bond yields — and thus hurt stocks — was also associated with two severe recessions following the two oil shocks of 1973 and 1979: the 1974–75 recession and the double dip recession of 1980–82. These two recessions sharply reduced earnings in the corporate sector. Together with much higher nominal and real interest rates, they crashed the stock market: between the peak of February 1973 and the bottom of July 1982 the S&P 500 stock market index fell by 58 percent.

So how should one protect the portion of one's portfolio in stocks and other risky assets? If stocks are going to crash it is better to liquidate part of one's stock portfolio and keep your powder dry in cash: while cash instruments are eroded by inflation they don't suffer from the same massive losses as stocks do. And if one can get the timing of a recession and recovery right, holding more cash allows you to buy stocks at fire-sale levels when they bottom out.

How about protecting the equity portion of a portfolio from the impact of the other megathreats discussed in the book? The major political, geopolitical, technological, health, and environmental disruption of the next two decades will imply that many of the stocks in current market indices—the Dow Jones Industrial Average, S&P 500, Nikkei 225, FTSE 100, Euro STOXX 50, and others—are in firms that will become obsolete. Ideally, one would want to invest in the firms and industries of the future. Many such firms are not yet listed in public equity markets—they are pre-IPO—and are available only to sophisticated and connected investors who have access to private equity and venture capital investments. But one proxy for the firms and industries of the future is the Nasdaq 100: this index of mostly tech stock includes some firms that will become obsolete, some that will remain strong, and some newly listed firms that will flourish in the future. But given the current high and frothy P/E ratio for the Nasdaq 100, you may want to wait until the next severe recession depresses this index further rather than buying it at inflated levels.

The right portfolio mix and components of stocks and bonds can be debated, this much is clear: sovereign wealth funds, pension funds, endowments, foundations, family offices, and individuals following the 60/40 rule should start to think about diversifying their holdings to hedge against rising inflation, negative growth shocks, political and geopolitical, technological, health, and environmental risks. While these risks will disrupt and/or wipe out many individual jobs, firms, and entire industries, any type of individual or institutional investor can start protecting their savings and investments from the coming financial instability and chaos.

Chapter 12

A More "Utopian" Future?

I find that a bleak prognosis evokes "All Along the Watchtower," the Bob Dylan anthem that became a Jimi Hendrix megahit: "There must be some way outta here/Said the joker to the thief. There's too much confusion/I can't get no relief."

Maybe you have young children or grandchildren—or you are optimistic by nature. You want to leave a better world to future generations. So do I. Moreover, I readily admit that no one can predict the future with certainty. The Yankees manager Yogi Berra famously quipped that "it is hard to make predictions, especially about the future." We might catch some unforeseen breaks. Resourceful humans solve big problems, as my own ancestors did when violent religious prejudice drove them away from their homes in Central Asia to the Middle East, then Europe, and finally the United States. That's not the same situation as now, I admit, but it spurs me to remove my Dr. Doom hat for a moment and engage in wishful thinking.

Many of the problems fueling megathreats require solutions based on high-powered economic growth. High growth—let's say, between 5 and 6 percent GDP sustained over time in advanced economies—can help pay down the debts that threaten us. That kind of growth generates resources that can help us tackle expensive public projects to forestall climate change, aging, and tech unemployment, or tackle future pandemics. It reduces political tensions and strife. Higher growth is driven to a great extent by technological innovations that increase productivity. Could tech innovation help us grow our way out of our troubles?

Take, for example, global climate change. Given current technologies, mitigation of greenhouse gas emissions requires a hard brake on growth. Adaptation, the alternative, has an impossible price tag. Could high growth make mitigation or adaptation possible? Or could innovation turn geoengineering from freak-science into reality? Our goal must be to continue to grow but sharply slow down the emissions of greenhouse gases and get to net zero emissions as fast as possible.

Some innovations might create cheap energy in large quantities without emitting greenhouse gases. Fusion energy is one such path, and it generates a lot of buzz.[1] Although still in its infancy, recent breakthroughs suggest that fusion is possible and might eventually become cost competitive. If this new source of energy or a similar innovation becomes reality, then we'll have a real shot at net zero emissions without slamming the brakes on growth. Nobody knows yet if a low-cost fusion breakthrough is likely, but recent experiments offer some promise. Moreover, the falling cost of renewable energy will compete with fossil fuels when scientists find ways to store energy cheaply.

Solving climate change would produce far-reaching benefits. Imagine lowering the risk of frequent and virulent zoonotic diseases that erupt when humans and animals occupy more cramped spaces. Moreover, technology helps defend against pandemics in more direct ways. COVID-19 caused the worst global pandemic since the 1918–19 Spanish flu. Artificial intelligence helped scientists map the virus and develop a vaccine in record time. A revolutionary approach deployed messenger RNA, or mRNA, that teaches cells how to mobilize our bodies' immune responses.

For anything resembling a happy ending to happen, computers poised to displace us must come to our rescue. We must hope that very rapid development of vaccines will defend us against new viruses. I marvel at an accelerating pace of biomedical discoveries. In 2020, DeepMind's AlphaFold solved the protein-folding problem that perplexed experts for half a century. It augurs well for accelerating progress against other diseases. Success would improve accessibility and lower costs for prevention, diagnosis, and treatment of all sorts of diseases.

Breakthroughs on climate change could deliver cascading benefits. Better health boosts economies. Strong growth attacks wealth inequality if it creates more jobs and makes a larger welfare system (progressive taxes and public spending and possibly UBI) more palatable for all. Scientific research and innovation reduce costs and increase output in goods and services, a recipe for robust income generation and wealth creation. Think, for instance, about a world where clean fusion produces all the energy needed and costs less than fossil fuels or current sources of renewable energy. Cheap energy would slash the current stratospheric costs of desalinization. Besides quenching thirst, plentiful fresh water would expand food production and lower its cost. And innovations in farming technologies—like vertical farming or lab-grown meat—may lessen the need to use lots of water and polluting fertilizers in food production and reduce the reliance on livestock farming that is the source of up to 25 percent of greenhouse gas emissions.

High economic growth would ease many debt problems afflicting the global economy. The sustainability of debts, whether private or public, explicit or implicit, domestic or foreign, household or corporate, hinges on the borrower's income. If income growth can outpace increases in debt, many debts that are currently on an unsustainable path would become manageable. Strong growth supplies the best solution. Technology that accelerates growth at a rapid pace is a key ally.

Likewise, automation in finance could help us exit the relentless boom-and-bust cycles of financial history. In the current financial system, humans make credit, lending, insurance, and asset allocation decisions. We are subject to distorted incentives, partial information, and a myriad of cognitive biases. That's where bubbles begin. Suppose instead that financial technology, artificial intelligence, big data, the Internet of Things, and 5G networks combine to guide financial decisions. Identical and objective criteria decide who gets a mortgage, which rates of interest, or asset allocations that diversify investment optimally across a wide range of asset classes. Human inconsistencies disappear. No more over-reactions with skittish buying and selling of assets. The risk of asset and credit bubbles falls as credit decisions are more rational, meaning less chance that debt and financial crises will occur.

Replacing humans with robots will still tend to increase inequality, culminating in widespread structural tech unemployment. Many people whose jobs vanish will end up earning smaller paychecks for less satisfying work. That has happened to factory workers in the United States and Europe, and their pain is real. Yet collectively, the data show that this trend has so far not been as extensive as feared. Ever since the Luddite movement in nineteenth-century Britain, workers have feared displacement by machines. But two centuries of technological progress has not wiped out all jobs. It has led to new types of jobs. Meanwhile, higher economic growth that accompanies automation might offset the impact of structural unemployment. At the current level of economic growth, universal basic income (UBI) proposals are not feasible. If growth in advanced countries doubles or triples to 5 percent or 6 percent, the math significantly improves.

A universal basic income or universal provision of public services or some combination of the two could furnish a new financial safety net. Ex-ante pre-distribution of assets rather the ex-post redistribution of wealth is an alternative option to reduce wealth inequality. Asset owners would benefit from ample returns, thus allowing everyone to pursue creative, entrepreneurial, or socially redeeming activities. Surrendering the "dignity of work" might not stir a protest if income subsidies open new doors to fulfillment. With UBI, workers in advanced and innovative economies will endure lower paychecks (but fattened by transfers) without the anger that propels voters toward populists with contempt for progressive liberal democracy.

The picture is not as sanguine, however, when technology cannot lift all boats. Populist and authoritarian regimes will not disappear in poor or less innovative economies. They will remain prevalent in failed states and nations that lack democratic traditions. The good news we can hope for would foster a renewed alliance of progressive and inclusive democracies, a group that includes advanced industrial states and successful emerging markets. Their prosperity will beckon to countries wobbling between democratic and authoritarian political models. China would vie fiercely for influence, but Western values would likely prevail more often in Asia and around the world. Geopolitically, an enlarged Western alliance already includes NATO (the United States and Europe), the Quad, AUKUS, and a number of stable emerging markets.

In this geopolitical scenario, other revisionist powers that seek to upend the Western economic and geopolitical order would fail. Notwithstanding their military muscle, Russia, Iran, and North Korea are fragile and underdeveloped. Two—Russia and Iran—rely on commodities (gas and oil) to keep their economies afloat, a limitation that caps their potential for economic growth and technological development. It allows them to become a serious nuisance for the time being, but they are ill-equipped to rearrange the global order. Instead, they face the prospects of collapse—in part, as new forms of energy displace oil and gas—unless they adopt more inclusive and equitable Western economic models. North Korea, by contrast, is a failed Communist economy that can barely feed its people and is doomed to collapse at some point.

A rejuvenated Western system would counteract calls for deglobalization and protectionism. Sluggish growth and inequality spur populism, and populism stirs economic nationalism. Strong, inclusive, and sustainable growth keeps both trends in check. Greater global economic integration spreads tech innovations that invigorate global commerce. Cooperation begets wider cooperation. Some decoupling between the United States and China might occur in a more connected world, but adversaries with deeper mutual interests may look more skeptically on radical decoupling and military confrontation. The United States and China have ample reasons to collaborate. For both, survival depends on coping with climate change, pandemics, inequality, supply chain integrity, and, of course, boom-and-bust cycles. Their rivalry would continue, but in addition to some containment and confrontation there would be ample room for cooperation and healthy competition.

Technological innovations could facilitate robust global trade in services, data, information, and technology. Geopolitical sensibilities preclude trade without any restraints, but a prodigious stream of new technologies could demolish many hurdles. Revitalized trade in digital goods and services would reinforce global and regional economic ties. The eurozone would welcome risk sharing and lower its risk of breaking up. In this scenario, the world retains the dollar as its reserve currency, eventually in the form of a central bank digital currency — an e-dollar.

Let's go even further. Suppose that accelerating innovation increases the potential for global growth and positive supply shocks. This climate lifts incomes and reduces inflation. Falling costs for products and services drive "good" deflation. Instead of fighting good deflation, enlightened central bankers will see its merits rather than induce bubbles with loose policies that try to fight deflation.

To be sure, creative destruction will occur. Obsolete products, firms, job categories, and services must fall by the wayside to make way for new ideas, new firms, jobs, and technologies. In this brave new world, big tech firms will remain very powerful. They will battle with governments to set the scope of regulation, but those battles will be offset by the need for governments and big tech to cooperate on national security agendas including cybersecurity. In renewed democracies restraints to big tech would allow a healthy modicum of privacy and individuals' control of their data.

China exploits technology for internal and external purposes with scant regard for privacy or human rights. The West must respond without abandoning democratic principles. How far that response will impinge on freedoms remains to be tested. Western companies and governments already breach consumer privacy. The EU has laws and regulations that rein in big tech on privacy. The United States is starting to do likewise. Both have taken antitrust cases to courts. Even in this "utopian" (or rather, rosiest-possible) scenario, there will be powerful tech firms that concentrate power and influence in unprecedented and alarming ways.

And of course, even this optimistic scenario will produce winners and losers across countries, regions, and social groups. In "Global Trends 2040," the US National Intelligence Council predicts a more "contested world."[2] Many revisionist powers will still challenge American hegemony. Within countries, consumers will cede power to firms that dominate technology. People will still have jobs, if not always the ones they want. Global climate change will ease but not vanish. I'm afraid that's as good as it gets. But compared to the dystopian scenario of chaos and instability, this "utopian"—or less dystopian—future looks vastly more appealing if still highly contested.

Epilogue

The period of relative prosperity that we have enjoyed ever since World War II is well described by the history of my own family, representative of many others around the world. In search of opportunity, my family migrated in the 1950s from Turkey to Iran, and then to Israel, before settling in Milan, Italy, in 1962. We arrived as an Italian "Economic Miracle" was in full swing, enabling a new middle class to flourish. My father built an import-export business. To be sure, there was turmoil amid the prosperity. Class conflict and episodes of domestic terrorism garnered frequent headlines. About a third of Italian voters embraced a Communist Party.

As a teenager, I was drawn to works by left-leaning intellectuals. Karl Marx steered me toward the field of economics before I learned about John Maynard Keynes. The philosopher Herbert Marcuse, who fled Germany when the Nazis gained control and later became a hero to the new left, introduced me to the tumultuous intersection of economics, political theory, and the theory of socioeconomic alienation. Yet overall, it was a time of rising prosperity in Italy and throughout the West.

The 1970s challenged my assumptions about stability and risk. Italy's economic engine stalled. Governments came and went amid recession, inflation, and stagflation. The 1973 Yom Kippur War and the 1979 Islamic Revolution in Iran raised political anxieties along with oil prices. And to be sure, in that Cold War era, nuclear-tipped missiles pointed in all directions.

Beyond the West, poverty persisted in the Soviet bloc, Communist China, pseudo-socialist India, and many other developing countries.

Planned economies provided a modicum of food, shelter, and welfare for billions of citizens, but at enormous costs to human liberty and economic opportunity. The Chinese term "iron rice bowl" referred to an occupation with guaranteed lifetime job security, steady income, and benefits, but China had endured a massive famine that killed tens of millions, and the country continued to suffer through political repression. Only in the 1980s would the Chinese economy begin to flourish, though the repression continued.

Economic growth was mostly confined to countries that embraced markets and international trade together with a solid social welfare system. In those countries, middle-class families could expect a better future for their children throughout the 1960s, 1970s, and 1980s. Globalization also brought wealth to less developed regions, giving rise to new middle classes in the Southern Hemisphere and Asia. Labor unions gave industrial workers collective clout. Ample tax revenues and low debt permitted national and local governments to provide essential public services. Meanwhile, in the Cold War, a nuclear balance of power prevailed. The Soviet Union and the United States even initiated détente in the 1970s and 1980s, with arms agreements, despite proxy wars still fought in the Middle East, Africa and Latin America. Thus, the risk of a nuclear exchange among great powers was vastly reduced.

After the Soviet Union collapsed and the Cold War came to an end, our collective risks changed character. Francis Fukuyama proclaimed that humankind had reached its evolutionary apex — it was the end of history. Instead of World War III, we now had to worry about much less existential threats, such as obesity.

Throughout the Cold War decades, economic crises and recessions were relatively mild, short, and without concurrent major financial disruption. Global climate change was visible only to experts. Science and technology fueled economic opportunity and new industries. Global pandemics were the stuff of science fiction.

Vibrant democracies featured plenty of political competition among parties and candidates, but very little political violence. Western societies featured ethnic, cultural, and religious diversity. Immigration seemed to pose little threat to national character. Debt ratios—private and public—were modest for the most part. Severe debt and financial crises surfaced as exceptions, not the rule.

I might have chosen to be a doctor, lawyer, or a banker—or to be an economist as I did—with confidence that doing a job well and working hard would guarantee my career until a safe retirement and good pension benefits. I relied on financial institutions to stay solvent, good companies to flourish, and a stable dollar and other currencies to ensure that my savings held their worth. Western governments provided safeguards against economic depressions and virulent financial crisis. They were committed to liberal democracy, freedoms, the rule of law, energy security, and a healthy environment. I had faith that regional conflicts would not erupt into world wars. The chance that robots with artificial intelligence might surpass my skills and replace me never entered my mind. So, in spite of conflicts, risks, and threats, the world was relatively stable.

What if the last seventy-five years has been the exception rather than the rule? What if the last three-quarters of a century has lulled us into believing that the next few decades will continue on the same path? What if we have forgotten the lessons of history from a century ago? In the first four decades of the twentieth century, we faced World War I, then the deadly Spanish flu of 1918–19, then deglobalization and bouts of hyperinflation, and then the Great Depression. That brought massive trade wars, financial and debt crises, and deflation; then the rise of populist, authoritarian, and militarily aggressive regimes (Nazism in Germany, Fascism in Italy and Spain, militarism in Japan). That, in turn, eventually led to World War II and the Holocaust.

The patterns of a century ago may be a harbinger of what we are facing now. In many ways, the megathreats of today are worse than the threats of a century ago. Our financial system is more leveraged, our inequality is greater, our weapons are much more dangerous. Populist politicians have more ways of reaching and manipulating vast audiences. And of course, climate change is vastly more accelerated now than it was then. Even the risk of nuclear conflict has reemerged. Cold War II may yet lead to hot wars.

Can we survive the coming crises? To illustrate the profound risks that ten interconnected megathreats pose, I have reduced many possible futures to just two. They show extreme directions in an uncertain world.

Between these two, unfortunately, the dystopian scenario looks much more likely. Because megathreats progress in slow motion, solutions do not feel urgent. The novelist and Nobel laureate Alexander Solzhenitsyn defined a paradox as truth standing on its head to attract attention. Megathreats attract attention without acrobatics — yet little has been learned and less has been done to avert their consequences. Policy responses to climate change largely produce more hot air. Concerted action on greenhouse gas emission is lacking. In all likelihood, artificial intelligence will steal jobs for good. Inequality will worsen. COVID-19 exposed how likely recurrent deadly pandemics are and how competing priorities thwart coordinated responses within and across national borders. Deglobalization won't occur overnight, but I see nothing to break its momentum. Likewise, inequality and widespread feelings of displacement and alienation make populism easier to swallow, and populism is the gateway drug to authoritarianism.

An earlier start would have made our job simpler. Every further delay creates more obstacles. Squabbling superpowers and growing debt burdens yank nations in self-serving directions. They may elect leaders who promise to ride roughshod over foreign interests, but a fracturing global order leaves little hope for a sustainable planet. Instead of cooperating, we veer toward a "Nash equilibrium," an environment where self-interest outweighs common interest, cooperation fails and non-cooperative outcomes severely damage all.

The world is facing at least ten megathreats. Over the next couple of decades, they will lead to a titanic collision of economic, financial, technological, environmental, geopolitical, medical, and social forces. Any one of these is formidable. If they converge, the consequences will be devastating. To solve them necessitates a quantum adjustment for everyone on earth. I fear what lies beyond the next inflection point.

We have run out of excuses. To delay is to surrender. The snooze button invites catastrophe. Megathreats are careening toward us. Their impact will shake our lives and upend the global order in ways no one today has ever experienced. Fasten your seatbelt. It's going to be a bumpy ride through a very dark night.

Acknowledgments

I would like to thank all the colleagues, collaborators, and friends who provided me with ideas, feedback, and support in developing the themes in this book. Without implicating any of them in any way or form with my views, I am grateful to them all.

Wes Neff, my agent at the Leigh Bureau, first suggested the idea of a new book and helped me flesh out the proposal for it. My collaborator Steven Mintz helped me draft each one of the chapters, edited them and revised them repeatedly to make the book more appealing to a broad audience; his collaboration was essential in writing the book. Bruce Nichols, my editor and the publisher of Little, Brown provided incisive comments and edits on each chapter and vastly improved its substance and structure. The team at Little, Brown did a great job in supporting the editorial and publication process: Linda Arends, Anna de la Rosa, Laura Mamelok, Melissa Mathlin, and my freelance copy editor, David Goehring.

My colleagues at the Stern School of Business at NYU provided me with intellectual and academic interactions for over two decades. My co-author of many papers and longtime collaborator Brunello Rosa has been a constant source of ideas and interactions. Reza Bundy and my colleagues at Atlas Capital Team share the the concerns expressed in the book, and we worked together on financial solutions to the threats described. David Brown—my colleague at TheBoomBust—also helped me in deriving the asset market implications of my views. My longtime chief of staff, Kim Nisbet at Roubini Macro Associates, managed with great efficiency and patience my often hectic travel and meetings schedule.

Acknowledgments

Ken Murphy and the team at Project Syndicate edited my monthly column, where I first presented some of the themes in the book. Manu Kumar and Brad Setser are longtime friends and intellectual colleagues: I learned a lot from both of them and very much appreciate their friendship.

I benefited a lot from feedback received at many conferences and other venues where I presented my views over the years, including the World Economic Forum at Davos, the Ambrosetti Forum, the International Monetary Fund, the World Bank, the Bank for International Settlements, the Reinventing Bretton Woods Committee, the Milken Institute Global Conference, the NBER, and the CEPR.

Many academic colleagues—some with invaluable policy and/or markets experience—have been a source of great food for thought and important ideas: Ken Rogoff, Barry Eichengreen, Dani Rodrik, Maury Obstfeld, Jeff Frankel, Bill Nordhaus, Larry Kotlikoff, Jeff Sachs, Michael Pettis, Alberto Alesina, Richard Portes, Helen Rey, Paul Krugman, Carmen Reinhart, Nassim Taleb, Raghu Rajan, Joe Stiglitz, Niall Ferguson, Robert Shiller, Kishore Mahbubani, Willem Buiter, Giancarlo Corsetti, Brad DeLong, and Steven Mihm (my co-author of *Crisis Economics*).

There are many current or former policy makers—some with a distinguished academic or markets background—whom I have interacted with over the decades. While they may not share some of my views I learned a lot from all of them: Larry Summers, Janet Yellen, Tim Geithner, Ben Bernanke, Christine Lagarde, Mario Draghi, Jens Weidman, Lael Brainard, Richard Clarida, Randy Quarles, Jean-Claude Trichet, Mark Carney, Francois Villeroy de Galhau, Kevin Rudd, Jason Furman, Jacob Frenkel, Horuhiko Kuroda, Stanley Fischer, Gita Gopinath, David Malpass, Mario Monti, Enrico Letta, Paolo Pesenti, Adam Posen, Ted Truman, David Lipton, Anna Gelpern, Dan Tarullo, John Lipsky, Bill White, Olivier Blanchard, Federico Sturzenegger, Andrés Velasco, Felipe Larraín, Hans-Helmut Kotz, Dina Powell, Vittorio Grilli, Fabio Panetta, Ignazio Visco, Catherine Mann, Laurence Boone, Luis de Guindos, Philip Lane, Hyun Shin, Claudio Borio, Andy Haldane, Thomas Jordan, Stefan Ingves, Ilan Goldfajn, Alejandro Werner.

Many financial markets experts and gurus have allowed me to connect my macroeconomic ideas with their market and asset price implications: Mohamed El Erian, George Soros, Louis Bacon, Alan Howard, Chris Rokos, Ray Dalio, Byron Wien, Stelios Zavvos, Steve Roach, David Rosenberg, Mark Zandi, Jim O'Neill, Luis Oganes, Joyce Chang, Lewis Alexander, Jens Nystedt, Robert Kahn, Joshua Rosner, Bill Janeway, Ron Perelman, Avi Tiomkin, Arnab Das, George Magnus, Christian Keller, Jan Hatzius, Richard Koo, Michael Milken, John Paulson, Xavier Botteri, Richard Hurowitz, Jeff Greene.

There are also many public intellectuals and some media commentators who have shaped my thinking and views: Ian Bremmer, Martin Wolf, Fareed Zakaria, Eric Schmidt, Nicholas Berggruen, Gillian Tett, Richard Haass, Mustafa Suleyman, Jared Cohen, Andrew Ross Sorkin, Jacques Attali, Tom Keene, Jon Ferro.

Notes

Prologue

1. Kristalina Georgieva Gopinath, and Ceyla Pazarbasioglu, "Why We Must Resist Geoeconomic Fragmentation—And How," International Monetary Fund, May 22, 2022, https://blogs.imf.org/2022/05/22/why-we-must-resist-geoeconomic-fragmentation-and-how/.

Chapter One

1. "Argentina Clinches Near-Unanimous Backing for Debt Restructuring," *Financial Times*, August 31, 2020, https://www.ft.com/content/e3e8b783-9455-46f3-946f-15c31a29778b.
2. Lawrence H. Summers, "The Biden Stimulus Is Admirably Ambitious. But It Brings Some Big Risks, Too," *Washington Post*, February 4, 2021, https://www.washingtonpost.com/opinions/2021/02/04/larry-summers-biden-covid-stimulus/.
3. Liz Alderman, "Europe's Pandemic Debt Is Dizzying. Who Will Pay?" *New York Times*, February 17, 2021, https://www.nytimes.com/2021/02/17/business/europe-pandemic-debt.html?smid=wa-share.
4. *Global Debt Monitor*, Institute of International Finance, February 23, 2022. (Not available online without subscription.)
5. *Global Debt Monitor*, "Attack of the Tsunami," Institute of International Finance, November 18, 2020. (Not available online without subscription.)
6. Mike Chinoy, "How Pakistan's A. Q. Khan Helped North Korea Get the Bomb," *Foreign Policy*, October 11, 2021, https://foreignpolicy.com/2021/10/11/aq-khan-pakistan-north-korea-nuclear/.
7. "More Debt, More Trouble," IIF *Weekly Insight*, November 20, 2020.
8. Joe Wallace, "Ukraine-Russia War Is Fueling Triple Crisis in Poor Nations," *Wall Street Journal*, May 24, 2022, https://www.wsj.com/articles/russian-ukraine-war-precipitates-a-triple-crisis-in-poor-nations-11653406985?mod=mhp
9. "World Bank Group Ramps Up Financing to Help Countries Amid Multiple Crises," the World Bank Press Release, April 19, 2022, https://www.worldbank.org/en/news/press-release/2022/04/19/-world-bank-group-ramps-up-financing-to-help-countries-amid-multiple-crises
10. Jeanna Smialek and Matt Phillips, "Do Fed Policies Fuel Bubbles? Some See GameStop as a Red Flag," *New York Times*, February 9, 2021, https://www.nytimes.com/2021/02/09/business/economy/gamestop-fed-us-economy-markets.html?smid=wa-share.

Notes

Chapter Two

1. IMF press release no. 16/500, "IMF Executive Board Concludes Article IV Consultation with Argentina," November 16, 2016.
2. Mary Anastasia O'Grady, "Argentina's Credibility Crisis," *Wall Street Journal*, January 3, 2014, https://www.wsj.com/articles/argentinas-credibility-crisis-11609709871?mod =searchresults_pos11&page=1.
3. Stephen Bartholomeusz, "Zombies Are Stirring as the Fed Creates a Monster Debt Problem," *Sydney Morning Herald*, June 16, 2020, https://www.smh.com.au/business/markets /zombies-are-stirring-as-the-fed-creates-a-monster-debt-problem-20200616-p5531h.html.
4. John Detrixhe, "Zombie Companies Are Hiding an Uncomfortable Truth about the Global Economy," *yahoo news*, March 9, 2020, https://www.yahoo.com/now/zombie -companies-hiding-uncomfortable-truth-183246812.html.
5. "A New Age of Financial Repression May Soon Be upon Us," *Financial Times*, July 22, 2020, https://www.ft.com/content/a7663749-179f-4194-ab89-0f8d7f0158ed.

Chapter Three

1. Russell Baker, "A Revolutionary President," review of *Nothing to Fear: FDR's Inner Circle and the Hundred Days That Created Modern America*, by Adam Cohen, *New York Review of Books*, February 12, 2009.
2. Michelle Singletary, "Covid Took One Year off the Financial Life of the Social Security Retirement Fund," *Washington Post*, September 3, 2021, https://www.washingtonpost .com/business/2021/09/03/social-security-insolvency/.
3. Sandra Block, "It Still Pays to Wait to Claim Social Security," Kiplinger, November 23, 2021, https://www.kiplinger.com/retirement/social-security/603809/it-still-pays-to-wait -to-claim-social-security.
4. Maurie Backman, "Study: Average American's Savings Account Balance is $3,500," The Ascent, September 10, 2020, https://www.fool.com/the-ascent/research /average-savings-account-balance/.
5. Milton Friedman, "Myths That Conceal Reality," *Free to Choose Network*. October 13, 1977, Collected Works of Milton Friedman Project records, Utah State University. https:// youtu.be/xNc-xhH8kkk @ 30:40.
6. Laurence Kotlikoff and Scott Burns, *The Clash of Generations* (Cambridge, MA: MIT Press, 2012), Kindle edition, page 13, location 175.
7. Laurence Kotlikoff and Scott Burns, *The Clash of Generations* (Cambridge, MA: MIT Press, 2012) Kindle edition, page 33, location 519.
8. Xavier Devictor, "Poland: Aging and the Economy," The World Bank, June 14, 2012, https:// www.worldbank.org/en/news/opinion/2012/06/14/poland-aging-and-the-economy.
9. Bobby Duffy, "Boomer v Broke: Why the Young Should Be More Angry with Older Generations," *Sunday Times*, September 12, 2021, https://www.thetimes.co.uk/article /boomer-v-broke-why-the-young-should-be-more-angry-with-older-generations-fqh73tc7b.
10. "2021 OASDI Trustees Report," Table IV.B3.—Covered Workers and Beneficiaries, Calendar Years 1945-2095, Social Security Administration, https://www.ssa.gov/OACT /TR/2021/IV_B_LRest.html#493869

Notes

11. "Japan Estimates Cast Doubt over Public Pension Sustainability," Reuters, August 27, 2019, https://www.reuters.com/article/us-japan-economy-pensions-idUSKCN1VH0PZ.
12. "The State Pension Funding Gap: 2018," Pew, June 11, 2020, https://www.pewtrusts.org/en/research-and-analysis/issue-briefs/2020/06/the-state-pension-funding-gap-2018.
13. NHE Fact Sheet, Centers for Medicare & Medicaid Services, https://www.cms.gov/Research-Statistics-Data-and-Systems/Statistics-Trends-and-Reports/NationalHealthExpendData/NHE-Fact-Sheet.
14. David H. Autor and Mark G. Duggan, "The Growth in the Social Security Disability Rolls: A Fiscal Crisis Unfolding," NBER working paper no. w12436, August 2006, https://www.nber.org/papers/w12436.
15. Katy Barnato, Katy, "Rich Countries Have a $78 Trillion Pension Problem," CNBC, https://www.google.com/amp/s/www.cnbc.com/amp/2016/03/16/rich-countries-have-a-78-trillion-pension-problem.html.
16. Stuart Anderson, "55% of America's Billion-Dollar Startups Have an Immigrant Founder," *Forbes*, October 25, 2018, https://www.forbes.com/sites/stuartanderson/2018/10/25/55-of-americas-billion-dollar-startups-have-immigrant-founder/?sh=56c5aa9548ee.

Chapter Four

1. "Game of Boom or Bust," Board Game Geek, 1951, Juegos Crone/Parker Brothers. https://boardgamegeek.com/boardgame/12294/game-boom-or-bust.
2. Matt Egan, "A Little-Known Hedge Fund Caused Widespread Chaos on Wall Street," *CNN Business*, March 30, 2021, https://www.cnn.com/2021/03/29/investing/wall-street-hedge-fund-archegos/index.html.
3. "Total Bank Losses from Archegos Implosion Exceed $10bn," *Financial Times*, April 27, 2021, https://www.ft.com/content/c480d5c0-ccf7-41de-8f56-03686a4556b6.
4. Julie Steinberg and Duncan Mavin, "How Deal Making Caught Up with Lex Greensill," *Wall Street Journal*, March 18, 2021, https://www.wsj.com/articles/how-deal-making-caught-up-with-lex-greensill-11616077055?mod=article_inline.
5. Enda Curran and Chris Anstey, "Pandemic-Era Central Banking Is Creating Bubbles Everywhere," *Bloomberg*, January 24, 2021, https://www.bloomberg.com/news/features/2021-01-24/central-banks-are-creating-bubbles-everywhere-in-the-pandemic#:~:text=Cheap%20money%20provided%20by%20central,save%2C%20invest%2C%20%20and%20spend.<<AU: This URL did not work, but I found the one that leads to this article and substituted it here.>>
6. Miles Kruppa and Ortenca Allaj, "A Reckoning for Spacs: Will Regulators Deflate the Boom?" *Financial Times*, May 4, 2021, https://www.ft.com/content/99de2333-e53a-4084-8780-2ba9766c70b7.
7. Madison Darbyshire and Joshua Oliver, "Thrill-Seeking Traders Send 'Meme Stocks' Soaring as Crypto Tumbles," *Financial Times*, May 28, 2021, https://www.ft.com/content/11e59520-a504-4098-9fc1-e2fe66887e14.
8. Jesse Baron, "The Mystery of the $113 Million Deli," *New York Times*, June 2, 2021, https://www.nytimes.com/2021/06/02/magazine/your-hometown-deli.html.

9. "National Industrial Recovery Act (1933)," The Living New Deal, September 13, 2016, https://livingnewdeal.org/glossary/national-industrial-recovery-act-1933/.

10. John Brooks, *Once in Golconda: A True Drama of Wall Street* (New York: Harper & Row, 1969), https://www.amazon.com/Once-in-Golconda/dp/B001XII24O/ref=sr_1 _3?crid=1J2N3ETK4T7PU&keywords=once+in+golconda&qid=1645646785&s =books&sprefix=once+in+golconda%2Cstripbooks%2C60&sr=1-3.

11. *The Financial Crisis Inquiry Report,* Official Government Edition, January 2011, p. 3, https://www.govinfo.gov/content/pkg/GPO-FCIC/pdf/GPO-FCIC.pdf.

12. Michael Bordo and Andrew Filardo, "Deflation in a Historical Perspective," BIS working paper no. 186, November 2005, p. 1, https://www.bis.org/publ/work186.pdf.

13. Tom Petruno, "Is All This Drama the Dow 1,000 Saga Times 10?" *Los Angeles Times,* March 21, 1999, https://www.latimes.com/archives/la-xpm-1999-mar-21-fi-19380-story.html.

14. Leonard Silk, "Climbing Interest Rates," *New York Times,* July 10, 1974, https://www .nytimes.com/1974/07/10/archives/climbing-interest-rates-fed-maintains-tight -antiinflationary-policy.html.

15. Peter Englund, "The Swedish Banking Crisis, Roots and Consequences," *Oxford Review of Economic Policy* 15, no. 3 (Autumn 1999): 84, https://www.jstor.org/stable/23606686.

16. W. H. Buiter, G. Corsetti, and P. A. Pesenti, *Financial Markets and European Monetary Cooperation* (Cambridge: Cambridge University Press, 1998), https://books.google .com/books?id=g6L5SVXBCB4C&pg=PA57&lpg=PA57&dq=%22dress+rehearsal +for+the+ERM+crisis%22&source=bl&ots=NlFwTIR0ne&sig=ACfU3U1oB7bep1 _JfQT5LSQSiLK-0GV5mg&hl=en&sa=X&ved=2ahUKEwjL34ve6p32AhUnk4kEHe -tCjMQ6AF6BAgCEAM#v=onepage&q=%22dress%20rehearsal%20for%20the%20 ERM%20crisis%22&f=false.

17. Willem H. Buiter, Giancarlo M. Corsetti, and Paolo A. Pesenti, "Interpreting the ERM Crisis: Country-Specific and Systemic Issues," *Princeton Studies in International Finance* no. 84 (March 1998): 1, https://ies.princeton.edu/pdf/S84.pdf.

Chapter Five

1. Ben S. Bernanke, "The Great Moderation," remarks by Governor Ben S. Bernanke at the meetings of the Eastern Economic Association, Washington, DC, February 20, 2004, https://www.federalreserve.gov/boarddocs/speeches/2004/20040220/.

2. William Barnett, *Getting It Wrong* (Cambridge, MA: MIT Press, 2012), 17.

3. Project Syndicate — Nouriel Roubini page https://www.project-syndicate.org/columnist /nouriel-roubini.

4. Jon Cunliffe, "Do We Need 'Public Money'?" The Bank of England, OMFIF Digital Money Institute, London, May 13, 2021, https://www.bankofengland.co.uk/speech /2021/may/jon-cunliffe-omfif-digital-monetary-institute-meeting.

5. Sylvia Porter, "Economic Miseries Are the Worst Ever," *Paris News,* May 11, 1980, p. 12.

6. Charles Goodhart and Manoj Pradhan, *The Great Demographic Reversal* (Cham, Switzerland: Palgrave Macmillan, 2020), Kindle Edition, p. 159.

7. "Dow Jones — DJIA — 100 Year Historical Chart," macrotrends [updated daily], https:// www.macrotrends.net/1319/dow-jones-100-year-historical-chart.

Notes

8. Editorial, "Prescription for Stagflation," *New York Times*, May 24, 1971, p. 30. https://timesmachine.nytimes.com/timesmachine/1971/05/24/81944647.html?pageNumber=30

9. *Iowa City Press Citizen*, August 21, 1971, p. 22.

10. "Nifty Fifty Stock Bubbles of the Seventies—Is There a Similarity with Today's Market," EquitySchool, October 24, 2015, https://medium.com/@equityschool/nifty-fifty-stock-bubble-of-the-seventies-is-there-a-similarity-with-today-s-market-34b19d7a4cff.

11. See the description of the Nifty Fifty: https://en.m.wikipedia.org/wiki/Nifty_Fifty.

12. Chris Plummer, "Remember the Nifty Fifty?" *USA Today*, April 1, 2014, https://www.usatoday.com/story/money/business/2014/04/01/ozy-nifty-50-stocks/7156447/.

13. "Dow Jones—DJIA—100 Year Historical Chart," macrotrends [updated daily], https://www.macrotrends.net/1319/dow-jones-100-year-historical-chart.

14. Isadore Barnum, "Soaring Sugar Cost Arouses Consumers and US Inquiries," *New York Times*, November 15, 1974, https://www.nytimes.com/1974/11/15/archives/soaring-sugar-cost-arouses-consumers-and-us-inquiries-what-sent.html.

15. Sylvia Porter, "Recession or Depression?" *Bryan Eagle*, June 5, 1975, p. 10.

16. Leonard Silk, "Climbing Interest Rates," *New York Times*, July 10, 1974, https://www.nytimes.com/1974/07/10/archives/climbing-interest-rates-fed-maintains-tight-antiinflationary-policy.html.

17. Daniel Yergin and Joseph Stanislaw, *The Commanding Heights: The Battle for the World Economy* (New York: Simon & Schuster, 2002) Kindle edition location 1283.

18. "If Only Keynes Had Lived to Explain 'Stagflation,'" *Fairbanks Daily News Miner*, Fairbanks, AK, June 16, 1977, https://newspaperarchive.com/fairbanks-daily-news-miner-jun-16-1977-p-4/.

19. *Kenosha News*, March 2, 1978, p. 5 (reprinted from *Business Week*, February 27, 1978).

20. Leonard Silk, "Reagan: Can He Cure Inflation?" *New York Times*, January 11, 1981, https://www.nytimes.com/1981/01/11/us/reagan-can-he-cure-inflation.html.

21. Leonard Silk, "Reagan: Can He Cure Inflation?" *New York Times*, January 11, 1981, https://www.nytimes.com/1981/01/11/us/reagan-can-he-cure-inflation.html.

22. Bill Dudley, "The Fed Is Risking a Full-Blown Recession," *Bloomberg*, June 7, 2021, https://www.bloombergquint.com/gadfly/the-fed-is-risking-a-full-blown-recession.

23. Michael Mackenzie, "Pimco's Ivascyn Warns of Inflationary Pressure from Rising Rents," *Financial Times*, July 31, 2021, https://www.ft.com/content/78b1d9a1-2f1b-4d3b-a930-3ac431f3c8c0?shareType=nongift

24. Jeff Cox, "Deutsche Bank Warns of Global 'Time Bomb,'" CNBC, June 7, 2021, https://www.cnbc.com/2021/06/07/deutsche-bank-warns-of-global-time-bomb-coming-due-to-rising-inflation.html.

25. Lawrence H. Summers, "The Biden Stimulus Is Admirably Ambitious. But It Brings Some Big Risks, Too," *Washington Post*, February 4, 2021, https://www.washingtonpost.com/opinions/2021/02/04/larry-summers-biden-covid-stimulus/.

26. Gwynn Guilford, "A Key Gauge of Future Inflation Is Easing," *Wall Street Journal*, July 26, 2021, https://www.wsj.com/articles/a-key-gauge-of-future-inflation-is-easing-11627291800?tpl=centralbanking.

27. Kenneth Rogoff, "Don't Panic: A Little Inflation Is No Bad Thing," *Financial Times*, July 16, 2021, https://www.ft.com/content/a7c101be-7361-4307-981d-b8edf6d002be.

28. Lawrence Goodman, "Inflation Fears Offers the Fed a Chance to Modernize with Money," Center for Financial Stability, April 26, 2021, http://www.centerforfinancialstability.org/research/Modernize_Money_042621.pdf

29. "Bridgewater's Prince Rejects Return of 1970s 'Great Inflation'," *Financial Times*, June 22, 2021, https://www.ft.com/content/717204fa-45e0-4b11-94c2-cf50b8aacbc0.

30. Brian Chappatta, "Schwarzman Sees 'Avalanche' of Opportunities from Tax-Hike Risk," *Bloomberg*, June 23, 2021,. https://www.bloomberg.com/news/articles/2021-06-23/schwarzman-sees-avalanche-of-opportunities-from-tax-hike-risk?srnd=premium

31. Milton Friedman, "How to Cure Inflation," *Free to Choose Network*, https://www.youtube.com/watch?v=u6GWm0GW7gk @ approx 1m40s.

32. Nouriel Roubini, "The Stagflation Threat Is Real," Project Syndicate, August 30, 2021, https://www.project-syndicate.org/commentary/mild-stagflation-is-here-and-could-persist-or-deepen-by-nouriel-roubini-2021-08.

33. "State of Supply Chains: In the Eye of the Storm," Accenture. Accessed June 14, 2022 https://www.accenture.com/us-en/insights/consulting/coronavirus-supply-chain-disruption?c=acn_glb_specialreportcogoogle_11296963&n=psgs_0720&gclsrc=aw.ds&gclid=CjwKCAjwo4mIBhBsEiwAKgzXONZcxu7dNt79FwcEdbb81uOeh2HArPmSX1kRZ—REY-ag1hZu9sZOxoCE1wQAvD_BwE.

34. Nouriel Roubini, "The Looming Stagflationary Debt Crisis," Project Syndicate, June 30, 2021, https://www.project-syndicate.org/commentary/stagflation-debt-crisis-2020s-by-nouriel-roubini-2021-06.

Chapter Six

1. Alexander William Salter and Daniel J. Smith, "End the Fed's Mission Creep," *Wall Street Journal*, March 25, 2021, https://www.wsj.com/articles/end-the-feds-mission-creep-11616710463?mod=Searchresults_pos11&page=1.

2. "Fed's Daly: Not Much Monetary Policy Can Do to Offset Climate Risk," Reuters, October 22, 2021, https://www.reuters.com/article/usa-fed-daly/feds-daly-not-much-monetary-policy-can-do-to-offset-climate-risk-idUSS0N2O401M.

3. Jon Sindreu, "If Russian Currency Reserves Aren't Really Money, the World Is in for a Shock" *Wall Street Journal*, March 7, 2022, https://www.wsj.com/articles/if-currency-reserves-arent-really-money-the-world-is-in-for-a-shock-11646311306?mod=flipboard.

4. Miles Alvord and Erika Howard, "The Federal Reserve's Big Experiment," *Frontline*, PBS, November 11, 2021, https://www.pbs.org/wgbh/frontline/podcast/dispatch/the-federal-reserves-big-experiment/ @14m35s.

5. Ray Dalio, "Ray Dalio Discusses Currency Debasement," The Wealth Training Company, December 2021, https://www.worldtopinvestors.com/ray-dalio-discusses-currency-debasement/

6. Federal Reserve Act: Public Law 63-43, 63d Congress, H.R. 7837, https://fraser.stlouisfed.org/title/federal-reserve-act-966/fulltext.

7. Andrew Mellon, Wikipedia entry, https://en.m.wikipedia.org/wiki/Andrew _Mellon#:~:text=In%20his%20memoirs%2C%20Hoover%20wrote,wrecks%20 from%20less%20competent%20people.%22.

8. The employment target for public policy started with the Employment Act of 1946 and was formalized for the Fed with the Humphrey-Hawkins Full Employment Act of 1978.

9. Jerome Powell, "New Economic Challenges and the Fed's Monetary Policy Review," Federal Reserve, August 27, 2020, https://www.federalreserve.gov/newsevents/speech /powell20200827a.htm.

10. "What Is Forward Guidance and How Is It Used in the Federal Reserve's Monetary Policy?" Federal Reserve. https://www.federalreserve.gov/faqs/what-is-forward-guidance -how-is-it-used-in-the-federal-reserve-monetary-policy.htm.

11. "Size of the Federal Reserve's Balance Sheet Since Quantitative Easing (QE) Measures Were Introduced from March 2020 to March 2022," Statista, https://www.statista .com/statistics/1121416/quantitative-easing-fed-balance-sheet-coronavirus/.

12. "The QE Quandary," Money Talks from *The Economist* (podcast), April 27, 2021.

13. Robin Harding, "US Quantitative Measures Work in Defiance of Theory," *Financial Times,* October 13, 2014, https://www.ft.com/content/3b164d2e-4f03-11e4-9c88-00144feab7de

14. Paul Taylor, "Circumstances Have Pushed the E.C.B. Far Beyond Its Mandate," *New York Times,* October 18, 2010, https://www.nytimes.com/2010/10/19/business/global/19iht -inside.html

15. Atlantic Council Global QE Tracker, https://www.atlanticcouncil.org/global-qe-tracker/. Accessed June 14, 2022.

16. See Stephen Deng, "The Great Debasement and Its Aftermath," in *Coinage and State Formation in Early Modern English Literature. Early Modern Cultural Studies* (New York: Palgrave Macmillan, 2011), 87–102, https://link.springer.com/chapter/10.1057/9780230118249_4.

17. Peter Coy, "Can We Trust What's Happening to Money?" *New York Times,* December 10, 2021, https://www.nytimes.com/2021/12/10/opinion/cash-crypto-trust-money.html ?smid=wa-share.

18. "UK Spy Chief Raises Fears over China's Digital Renminbi," *Financial Times,* December 10, 2021, https://bit.ly/3IEsp9g?cc=4a8f1da715002187c54efd5575c579dc.

19. "Incoming New York Mayor Eric Adams Vows to Take First Three Paychecks in Bitcoin," CNBC, November 4, 2021, https://www.cnbc.com/2021/11/04/new-york -mayor-elect-eric-adams-to-take-first-3-paychecks-in-bitcoin.html.

20. "$BACON Coin—Fractionalizing Home Loans on the Blockchain with Karl Jacob of LoanSnap," *Modern Finance* (podcast), with host Kevin Rose, September 28, 2021 @ approx. 30:55.

21. Fabio Panetta, "The Present and Future of Money in the Digital Age," European Central Bank, December 10, 2021, https://www.ecb.europa.eu/press/key/date/2021/html /ecb.sp211210~09b6887f8b.en.html.

22. Fabio Panetta, "The Present and Future of Money in the Digital Age," European Central Bank, December 10, 2021, https://www.ecb.europa.eu/press/key/date/2021 /html/ecb.sp211210~09b6887f8b.en.html.

Notes

23. Daniel Sanches, "The Free-Banking Era: A Lesson for Today?" Federal Reserve Bank of Philadelphia, Q3 2016, https://www.philadelphiafed.org/the-economy/banking-and -financial-markets/the-free-banking-era-a-lesson-for-today.

24. "The Potential DeFi Collapse, Bull & Bear Markets, and MobileCoin with Ari Paul," *Modern Finance* (podcast), April 20, 2021 @ 42:00.

25. Anny Shaw, "Who is Beeple? The Art World Disruptor at the Heart of the NFT Boom," interview with Beeple, *The Art Newspaper,* March 5, 2021, https://www.theartnewspaper .com/2021/03/05/who-is-beeple-the-art-world-disruptor-at-the-heart-of-the-nft-boom.

26. Dimitris Drakopoulos, Fabio Natalucci, and Evan Papageorgiou, "Crypto Boom Poses New Challenge to Financial Stability," *IMF Blog,* October 1, 2021, https://blogs.imf .org/2021/10/01/crypto-boom-poses-new-challenges-to-financial-stability/.

27. Stephen Deng, "The Great Debasement and Its Aftermath," in *Coinage and State Formation in Early Modern English Literature. Early Modern Cultural Studies* (New York: Palgrave Macmillan, 2011), 87–102, https://link.springer.com/chapter/10.1057/9780230118249_4.

28. "Does The World Still Need Banks?" *The Economist,* May 12, 2021 (podcast), https:// www.economist.com/podcasts/2021/05/12/does-the-world-still-need-banks.

29. Karrie Gordon, "Commissioner Berkovitz Questioning the Legality of DeFi," Crypto Channel, June 15, 2021, https://etfdb.com/crypto-channel/commissioner-berkovitz -questioning-legality-defi/.

30. Taylor Locke, "The Co-Creator of Dogecoin Explains Why He Doesn't Plan to Return to Crypto," *Make It,* CNBC, July 14, 2021, https://www.google.com/amp/s/www .cnbc.com/amp/2021/07/14/dogecoin-co-creator-jackson-palmer-criticizes-the -crypto-industry.html.

31. "Silicon Valley Payments Firm Stripe Buys Nigerian Startup Paystack," Reuters, October 15, 2020, https://www.reuters.com/article/us-paystack-m-a-stripe/silicon-valley -payments-firm-stripe-buys-nigerian-startup-paystack-idUSKBN27024G.

32. "The Digital Currencies That Matter," *The Economist,* May 8, 2021, https://www .economist.com/leaders/2021/05/08/the-digital-currencies-that-matter.

33. "When Central Banks Issue Digital Money," *The Economist,* May 8, 2021, https://www .economist.com/special-report/2021/05/06/when-central-banks-issue-digital -money.

Chapter Seven

1. Paul Krugman, "Paul Krugman Explains Trade and Tariffs," *New York Times,* March 16, 2018, https://www.nytimes.com/2018/03/15/opinion/paul-krugman-aluminum-steel -trade-tariffs.html#commentsContainer.

2. Gordon H. Hanson, "Can Trade Work for Workers?" *Foreign Affairs,* May/June 2021, https:// www.foreignaffairs.com/articles/united-states/2021-04-20/can-trade-work-workers.

3. "Is It Time to Declare the End of Globalisation?" *Financial Times,* July 19, 2019, https:// www.ft.com/content/70bc7566-9bf2-11e9-9c06-a4640c9feebb.

4. "The Modern Era of Globalisation Is in Danger," *Financial Times,* May 24, 2020, https:// www.ft.com/content/7b365844-9b75-11ea-adb1-529f96d8a00b.

5. "Insight: The Perils of De-Globalisation," *Financial Times,* July 21, 2009, https://www .ft.com/content/4747bc08-75fc-11de-84c7-00144feabdc0.

286

6. Mark Landler, "The U.K.'s Gas Crisis Is a Brexit Crisis, Too," *New York Times*, September 28, 2021, https://www.nytimes.com/2021/09/28/world/europe/brexit-britain-fuel-johnson.html.

7. Marc Santora and Helene Bienvenu, "Secure in Hungary, Orban Readies for Battle with Brussels," *New York Times*, May 11, 2018, https://www.nytimes.com/2018/05/11/world/europe/hungary-victor-orban-immigration-europe.html?searchResultPosition=1.

8. Yavuz Arslan, Juan Contreras, Nikhil Patel, and Chang Shu, "How Has Globalisation Affected Emerging Market Economies?" BIS papers no. 100, https://www.bis.org/publ/bppdf/bispap100_b_rh.pdf.

9. "Washington Consensus: EMs Are Actually Quite Keen," *Financial Times*, November 6, 2013, https://www.ft.com/content/f2c09e04-bf1c-3155-ba68-83c2e01f4a10.

10. Joseph E. Stiglitz, *Globalization and Its Discontents* (New York: W.W. Norton, 2002), 4.

11. Joseph E. Stiglitz, *Globalization and Its Discontents* (New York: W.W. Norton, 2002), 6.

12. "Remarks by Secretary of the Treasury Janet L. Yellen on Way Forward for the Global Economy", April 2022, https://home.treasury.gov/news/press-releases/jy0714

13. "The Anglo-Saxon Ship Burial at Sutton Hoo," The British Museum, https://www.britishmuseum.org/collection/death-and-memory/anglo-saxon-ship-burial-sutton-hoo.

14. "The Fordney-McCumber Tariff of 1922," Economic History Association. https://eh.net/encyclopedia/the-fordney-mccumber-tariff-of-1922/. Accessed June 14, 2022.

15. "Millions in Trade Lost As Result of Tariff Act," *El Paso Times*, June 17, 1931, p. 1

16. Congressional Record Vol. 164, No. 40 (House of Representatives—March 7, 2018).

17. Gordon H. Hanson, "Can Trade Work for Workers?" Foreign Affairs, May/June 2021. https://www.foreignaffairs.com/articles/united-states/2021-04-20/can-trade-work-workers.

18. "President Donald J. Trump Is Confronting China's Unfair Trade Policies," White House Archives, May 29, 2018, https://trumpwhitehouse.archives.gov/briefings-statements/president-donald-j-trump-confronting-chinas-unfair-trade-policies/.

19. Charles Roxburgh, James Manyika, Richard Dobbs, and Jan Mischke, "Trading Myths: Addressing Misconceptions about Trade, Jobs, and Competitiveness," McKinsey & Company Report, May 1, 2012, https://www.mckinsey.com/featured-insights/employment-and-growth/six-myths-about-trade.

20. Asher Schechter, "Globalization Has Contributed to Tearing Societies Apart," *Promarket*, University of Chicago Booth School of Business, March 29, 2018, https://promarket.org/2018/03/29/globalization-contributed-tearing-societies-apart/.

21. Finbarr Bermingham, "US-China Feud Is Acclerating the Biggest Shift in Trade Since the Cold War, Away from Globalisation," *South China Morning Post*, July 6, 2019, https://www.scmp.com/economy/china-economy/article/3017358/us-china-trade-war-accelerating-biggest-shift-trade-cold-war.

22. Henry Paulsen, "Balkanising Technology Will Backfire on the US," *Financial Times*, June 25, 2019, https://www.ft.com/content/0ed49b84-91c1-11e9-8ff4-699df1c62544.

23. Gordon H. Hanson, "Can Trade Work for Workers?" *Foreign Affairs*, May/June 2021, https://www.foreignaffairs.com/articles/united-states/2021-04-20/can-trade-work-workers.

Chapter Eight

1. "The Return of the Machinery Question," *The Economist*, June 25, 2016, https://www.economist.com/special-report/2016/06/23/the-return-of-the-machinery-question.

Notes

2. Sarah Paynter, "First 3-D-Printed House for Sale Listed at $300K on Long Island," *New York Post,* February 8, 2021, https://nypost.com/2021/02/08/first-3d-printed-house-for-sale-listed-in-long-island-new-york/.

3. Aleksandar Furtula, "Dutch Queen and Robot Open 3D-printed Bridge in Amsterdam," AP News, July 15, 2021, https://apnews.com/article/technology-europe-amsterdam-a37e034e02967886c2e0a64c17f34f3a.

4. "In the Age of AI," *Frontline,* PBS, December 2, 2019, https://www.youtube.com/watch?v=5dZ_lvDgevk (@ approx. 3:55).

5. "Interview with Craig Smith, Host of Eye on AI podcast," *AI Today* (podcast), September 8, 2021 @ 11:20.

6. Sylvia Smith, "Iamus: Is This the 21st Century's Answer to Mozart?" BBC News, January 3, 2013, https://www.bbc.com/news/technology-20889644.

7. Chantal Da Silva, "From a Hidden Picasso Nude to an Unfinished Beethoven, AI Uncovers Lost Art—and New Challenges," NBC News, October 30, 2021, https://www.nbcnews.com/news/world/lost-picasso-unfinished-beethoven-ai-uncovers-lost-art-new-challenges-rcna2905.

8. Daniel Ren, "Xpeng Unveils Smart Robot Pony for Children," *South China Morning Post,* September 7, 2021, https://www.scmp.com/business/companies/article/3147903/xpengs-unveils-smart-robot-pony-children-taking-it-step-closer?utm_source=copy_link&utm_medium=share_widget&utm_campaign=3147903.

9. Calum Chace, review of *A World without Work,* by Daniel Susskind, *Forbes,* January 30, 2020, https://www.forbes.com/sites/cognitiveworld/2020/01/30/a-world-without-work-by-daniel-susskind-a-book-review/?sh=66fa925d6dd7.

10. "The Return of the Machinery Question," *The Economist,* June 25, 2016, https://www.economist.com/special-report/2016/06/23/the-return-of-the-machinery-question.

11. "The Return of the Machinery Question." *The Economist,* June 25, 2016, https://www.economist.com/special-report/2016/06/23/the-return-of-the-machinery-question.

12. Ken Jennings, "The Obsolete Know-It-All," TEDX SeattleU, March 7, 2013, https://youtu.be/DxBVxglKOVw @ approx. 9:10.

13. "Rosey the Robotic Maid," TV's Saturday Morning Cartoon Legacy: The Jetsons, https://www.youtube.com/watch?v=1pphyvgd7-k.

14. Dalvin Brown, "Why It Will Be Years before Robots Take Over Your Household Chores," *Washington Post,* March 23, 2021, https://www.washingtonpost.com/technology/2021/03/23/future-robots-home-jetsons/.

15. Matthew Scherer, "Regulating Artificial Intelligence Systems," *Harvard Journal of Law and Technology* 29, no. 2 (Spring 2016): 362, http://jolt.law.harvard.edu/articles/pdf/v29/29HarvJLTech353.pdf.

16. "Uber's Self-Driving Operator Charged over Fatal Crash," BBC News, September 16, 2020, https://www.bbc.com/news/technology-54175359.

17. Dalvin Brown, "Why It Will Be Years before Robots Take Over Your Household Chores," *Washington Post,* March 23, 2021, https://www.washingtonpost.com/technology/2021/03/23/future-robots-home-jetsons/.

18. Jefferson Graham, "Flippy the Burger-Flipping Robot Is on a Break Already," *USA Today*, March 7, 2018, https://www.usatoday.com/story/tech/talkingtech/2018/03/07/flippy -burger-flipping-robot-break-already/405580002/.

19. "Cali Group Unveils CaliBurger 2.0 with Flippy," Total Food Service, November 1, 2019, https://totalfood.com/cali-group-unveils-caliburger-2-0-with-flippy/.

20. "FamilyMart Preps 1,000 Unmanned Stores in Japan by 2024," *Nikkei Asia*, September 10, 2021, https://asia.nikkei.com/Business/Retail/FamilyMart-preps-1-000-unmanned -stores-in-Japan-by-2024?utm_campaign=GL_techAsia&utm_medium=email&utm _source=NA_newsletter&utm_content=article_link&del_type=5&pub_date =20210916123000&seq_num=5&si=__MERGE__user_id__MERGE__.

21. How Germany's Otto Uses Artificial Intelligence," *The Economist*, April 12, 2017.

22. John McCormick, "Retail Set to Overtake Banking in AI Spending," *Wall Street Journal*, September 7, 2021, https://www.wsj.com/articles/retail-set-to-overtake-banking-in-ai -spending-11631007001?mod=searchresults_pos10&page=1.

23. John McCormick, "Retail Set to Overtake Banking in AI Spending," *Wall Street Journal*, September 7, 2021 https://www.wsj.com/articles/retail-set-to-overtake-banking -in-ai-spending-11631007001?mod=searchresults_pos10&page=1.

24. *The New York Times Guide to Essential Knowledge* (New York: St. Martin's Press, 2011), 442.

25. Jessica Brain, "The Luddites," Historic UK, https://www.historic-uk.com/HistoryUK /HistoryofBritain/The-Luddites/.

26. "The Return of the Machinery Question," *The Economist*, June 25, 2016, https://www .economist.com/special-report/2016/06/23/the-return-of-the-machinery-question.

27. Karl Marx, *Capital*, translated by Samuel Moore and Edward Aveling, (Hertfordshire, UK, Wordsworth Classics of World Literature, 2013) Kindle edition location 8018, page 391.

28. John Maynard Keynes, "Economic Possibilities for Our Grandchildren," in *Essays in Persuasion* (New York: W. W. Norton, 1963), 358–73, http://www.econ.yale.edu/smith /econ116a/keynes1.pdf.

29. Matthew Scherer, "Regulating Artificial Intelligence Systems: Risks, Challenges, Competencies, and Strategies," *Harvard Journal of Law & Technology* 29, no. 2 (Spring 2016), https://papers.ssrn.com/sol3/papers.cfm?abstract_id=2609777.

30. Andrew Hodges, *Alan Turing: The Enigma* (New York: Simon and Schuster, 1983), p. 382.

31. *The New York Times Guide to Essential Knowledge* (New York: St. Martin's Press, 2011), p. 442.

32. Harley Shaiken, "A Robot Is After Your Job," *New York Times*, September 3, 1980, https:// www.nytimes.com/1980/09/03/archives/a-robot-is-after-your-job-new-technology -isnt-a-panacea.html.

33. Timothy Taylor, "Automation and Job Loss: Leontief in 1982," *Conversable Economist* (blog), August 22, 2016, https://conversableeconomist.blogspot.com/2016/08/automation-and -job-loss-leontief-in-1982.html.

34. "Preparing for the Future of Artificial Intelligence," Executive Office of the President, National Science and Technology Council, Committee on Technology, October 2016, https://obamawhitehouse.archives.gov/sites/default/files/whitehouse_files /microsites/ostp/NSTC/preparing_for_the_future_of_ai.pdf.

35. Yuval Harari, *Homo Deus: A Brief History of Tomorrow* (New York: HarperCollins, 2017), Kindle edition location 1022, p. 43

36. Josh Ye, Masha Borak, and Orange Wang, "As China's Working Population Falls, Factories Turn to Machines to Pick Up the Slack," *South China Morning Post,* May 27, 2021, https://www.scmp.com/tech/big-tech/article/3134920/chinas-working-population -falls-factories-turn-machines-pick-slack?utm_source=copy_link&utm_medium =share_widget&utm_campaign=3134920.

37. Ariel Ezrachi and Maurice Stucke, "Artificial Intelligence & Collusion: When Computers Inhibit Competition," University of Illinois Law Review, Vol. 2017, No. 5, p. 1775.

38. Steven Pearlstein, review of *The Second Machine Age,* by Erik Brynolfsson and Andrew McAfee, *Washington Post,* January 17, 2014, https://www.washingtonpost.com /opinions/review-the-second-machine-age-by-erik-brynjolfsson-and-andrew -mcafee/2014/01/17/ace0611a-718c-11e3-8b3f-b1666705ca3b_story.html.

39. David Autour, "Are the Robots Taking Our Jobs?" Columbus Museum of Art, https:// youtu.be/uNw3ik7g1Ss @ approx. 22:24.

40. Daniel Susskind, *A World without Work* (New York: Metropolitan Books, 2020), Kindle edition, p. 5, location 268.

41. Robert Reich, "Why Automation Means We Need a New Economic Model," World Economic Forum, March 17, 2015, https://www.weforum.org/agenda/2015/03/why -automation-means-we-need-a-new-economic-model/?utm_content=buffere751d&utm _medium=social&utm_source=twitter.com&utm_campaign=buffer.

42. Daron Acemoglu and Pascual Restrepo, "Robots and Jobs: Evidence from US Labor Markets," *Journal of Political Economy* 128, no. 6 (April 22, 2020), https://economics.mit .edu/files/19696.

43. Mustafa Suleyman, "Transformers Are the Future," July 2021.<<AU: Please provide more complete information. I was unable to find this article.>> [[This unpublished article was shared with Nouriel]]

44. "The Return of the Machinery Question," *The Economist,* June 25, 2016, https://www .economist.com/special-report/2016/06/23/the-return-of-the-machinery-question.

45. "List of Countries by Income Inequality," Wikipedia, https://en.wikipedia.org/wiki /List_of_countries_by_income_equality.

46. Daniel Susskind, *A World without Work* (New York: Metropolitan Books, 2020), Kindle edition, p. 138, location 2608.

47. Yusuke Hinata, "China's Media Stars Caught in Harsh Spotlight of Inequality Drive," *Nikkei Asia,* September 2, 2021, https://asia.nikkei.com/Business/Media-Entertainment /China-s-media-stars-caught-in-harsh-spotlight-of-inequality-drive.

48. Martin Ford, *Rise of the Robots* (New York: Basic Books, 2016), Kindle edition, p. 196, location 3313.

49. Jerry Kaplan, "Humans Need Not Apply," presentation at Google, November 4, 2015, https://www.youtube.com/watch?v=JiiP5ROnzw8 @ approx. 43 minutes.

50. Yuval Noah Harari, *Homo Deus: A Brief History of Tomorrow,* (New York, Harper Collins, 2017) Kindle edition location 5299, p. 322

Notes

Chapter Nine

1. Graham Allison, "Destined for War: Can America and China Escape Thucydides's Trap?," (New York, Houghton, Mifflin, Harcourt, 2017)
2. "Top 20 Ancient Chinese Inventions," https://china.usc.edu/sites/default/files/forums /Chinese%20Inventions.pdf.
3. "Grains and Soybeans Advance on News of Nixon's China Trip," *New York Times,* July 17, 1971, p. 19, https://www.nytimes.com/1971/07/17/archives/grains-and-soybeans -advance-on-news-of-nixons-china-trip.html?searchResultPosition=5.
4. Max Frankel, "Nixon's China Goal: Genuine Diplomatic Turning Point," *New York Times,* July 23, 1971, p. 2, https://www.nytimes.com/1971/07/23/archives/nixons-china -goal-genuine-diplomatic-turning-point.html?searchResultPosition=7.
5. "Nixon Objectives," *Greenfield Recorder,* Greenfield, MA, November 30, 1971, https:// newspaperarchive.com/other-articles-clipping-nov-30-1971-2748225/.
6. "Cold War II: Just How Dangerous Is China?" Uncommon Knowledge, The Hoover Institution, April 9, 2021, https://www.youtube.com/watch?v=E12r-37GZI0 @ 2:20.
7. Niall Ferguson, " Evergrande's Fall Shows How Xi Has Created a China Crisis," *Bloomberg,* September 26, 2021, https://www.bloomberg.com/opinion/articles/2021-09-26 /niall-ferguson-evergrande-is-a-victim-of-xi-jinping-s-china-crisis.
8. Thomas L. Friedman, "Congress, Angry at China, Moves to Impose Sanctions," *New York Times,* June 23, 1989, https://www.nytimes.com/1989/06/23/world/congress -angry-at-china-moves-to-impose-sanctions.html?searchResultPosition=1.
9. John J. Mearsheimer, "The Inevitable Rivalry," *Foreign Affairs,* November/December 2021, https://www.foreignaffairs.com/articles/china/2021-10-19/inevitable-rivalry-cold-war.
10. Joseph Kahn, "World Trade Organization Admits China, Amid Doubts," *New York Times,* November 11, 2001, https://timesmachine.nytimes.com/timesmachine/2001 /11/11/141240.html?pageNumber=16.
11. Jeffrey Sachs, "China, the Game Changer," Columbia Business School, August 3, 2012, https://www.youtube.com/watch?v=8Ou5zPGBj5U @ approx. 6:41.
12. Dambisa Moyo, "Is China the New Idol for Emerging Economies?" TED Global, June 2013, https://www.ted.com/talks/dambisa_moyo_is_china_the_new_idol_for_emerging _economies/transcript#t-143067.
13. "Cold War II: Just How Dangerous Is China?" Uncommon Knowledge, The Hoover Institution, April 9, 2021, https://www.youtube.com/watch?v=E12r-37GZI0 @ 2:54.
14. Tom Mitchell, "The Chinese Control Revolution: The Maoist Echoes of Xi's Power Play," *Financial Times,* September 6, 2021, https://www.ft.com/content/bacf9b6a-326b -4aa9-a8f6-2456921e61ec.
15. Kevin Rudd, "To Decouple or Not to Decouple," Asia Society Policy Institute, November 4, 2019, https://asiasociety.org/policy-institute/decouple-or-not-decouple.
16. "China," *The World Factbook,* https://www.cia.gov/the-world-factbook/countries /china/.
17. Ammar A. Malik et al., *Banking on the Belt and Road* (Williamsburg, VA: Aiddata at William & Mary, September 29, 2021), https://www.aiddata.org/publications/banking-on -the-belt-and-road.

18. Frank Tang, "China Overtakes US as No 1 in Buying Power, but Still Clings to Developing Status," *South China Morning Post,* May 21, 2020, https://www.scmp.com/economy /china-economy/article/3085501/china-overtakes-us-no-1-buying-power-still-clings -developing.

19. John J. Mearsheimer, "The Inevitable Rivalry," *Foreign Affairs,* November/December 2021, https://www.foreignaffairs.com/articles/china/2021-10-19/inevitable-rivalry -cold-war.

20. Kevin Rudd, "The Avoidable War," Asia Society Policy Institute, 2021, https:// asiasociety.org/sites/default/files/2021-02/AvoidableWarVol3_final.pdf.

21. John J. Mearsheimer, "The Inevitable Rivalry," *Foreign Affairs,* November/December 2021, https://www.foreignaffairs.com/articles/china/2021-10-19/inevitable-rivalry-cold-war.

22. "Cold War II—Just How Dangerous Is China?" Uncommon Knowledge, The Hoover Institution, April 9, 2021, https://www.youtube.com/watch?v=E12r-37GZI0 @ 4:00.

23. "Century of Humiliation," Wikipedia, https://en.m.wikipedia.org/wiki/Century_of _humiliation.

24. Tom Mitchell, "The Chinese Control Revolution: The Maoist Echoes of Xi's Power Play," *Financial Times,* September 6, 2021, https://www.ft.com/content/bacf9b6a-326b -4aa9-a8f6-2456921e61ec?shareType=nongift.

25. "What Happens When China Becomes Number One?" John F. Kennedy Jr. Forum, Harvard Kennedy School's Institute of Politics, April 8, 2015, https://www.youtube.com /watch?v=RO3izbn20ls @47m25s.

26. Kevin Rudd, "The Avoidable War: The Decade of Living Dangerously: Navigating the Shoals of U.S.-China Relations," Asia Society Policy Institute, February 2021, p. 22, https://asiasociety.org/policy-institute/avoidable-war-decade-living-dangerously.

27. Fareed Zakaria, "The US and China's 'Cold Peace,'" *Fareed Zakaria GPS,* CNN, https:// www.cnn.com/videos/tv/2021/08/08/exp-gps-0808-fareeds-take.cnn @ 1:20. August 8, 2021.

28. Cissy Zhou, "U.S.-China Decoupling," *South China Morning Post,* September 16, 2021, https://www.scmp.com/economy/china-economy/article/3149027/us-china -decoupling-if-it-comes-down-us-bloc-vs-china-bloc.

29. Cissy Zhou, "US-China Decoupling," *South China Morning Post,* September 16, 2021, https://www.scmp.com/economy/china-economy/article/3149027/us-china -decoupling-if-it-comes-down-us-bloc-vs-china-bloc.

30. Xinmei Shen, "China Drafts Tough Rules to Stop Data from Leaving Its Borders," *South China Morning Post,* October 29, 2021, https://www.scmp.com/tech/policy /article/3154135/china-drafts-tough-rules-stop-data-leaving-its-borders-beijing -tightens?utm_medium=email&utm_source=cm&utm_campaign=enlz-today _international&utm_content=20211029&tpcc=enlz-today_international&UUID =6248c9f9-23d8-49ba-b0c9-c3aabf43a5e2&next_article_id=3154141&article_id_list =3154135,3154141,3154133,3154159,3154146,3154142,3154188,3154156&tc=7&CMCamp aignID=53c575cbc703d88c0f60cfbebf543364.

31. "China's Race for AI Supremacy," *Bloomberg,* October 20, 2021, https://www.youtube .com/watch?v=zbzcZr_Nadc @00:33.

Notes

32. "US Has Already Lost AI Fight to China," *Financial Times*, October 10, 2021, https://www.ft.com/content/f939db9a-40af-4bd1-b67d-10492535f8e0.

33. "NATO to Expand Focus to Counter Rising China," *Financial Times*, October 18, 2021, https://www.ft.com/content/0202ed6e-62d1-44b6-a61c-8b1278fcf31b.

34. Fareed Zakaria, "The Complex China Challenge," *Fareed Zakaria GPS*, CNN, https://www.cnn.com/videos/tv/2021/08/08/exp-gps-0808-fareeds-take.cnn @ 2:12. Augst 8, 2021.

35. "NATO to Expand Focus to Counter Rising China," *Financial Times*, https://www.ft.com/content/0202ed6e-62d1-44b6-a61c-8b1278fcf31b.

36. "Remarks as Prepared for Delivery of Ambassador Katerine tai Outlining the Biden-Harris Administration's 'New Approach to the U.S.-China Trade Relationship," Office of the United States Trade Representative, October 2021, https://ustr.gov/about-us/policy-offices/press-office/speeches-and-remarks/2021/october/remarks-prepared-delivery-ambassador-katherine-tai-outlining-biden-harris-administrations-new.

37. Kurt M. Campbell and Jake Sullivan, "Competition without Catastrophe," *Foreign Affairs*, September/October 2019, https://www.foreignaffairs.com/articles/china/competition-with-china-without-catastrophe.

38. Kurt M. Campbell and Ely Ratner, "The China Reckoning," *Foreign Affairs*, March/April 2018, https://www.foreignaffairs.com/articles/china/2018-02-13/china-reckoning.

39. Remarks by President Biden, June 16, 2021, https://www.whitehouse.gov/briefing-room/speeches-remarks/2021/06/16/remarks-by-president-biden-in-press-conference-4/.

40. "Full Text of Chinese President Xi Jinping's Message for China Pavilion of Expo 2020 Dubai," Xinua, October 1, 2021, http://en.qstheory.cn/2021-10/04/c_665826.htm.

41. Kevin Rudd, "The Avoidable War," Asia Society Policy Institute, 2021, p. 74 https://asiasociety.org/policy-institute/avoidable-war-decade-living-dangerously.

42. Kevin Rudd, "The Avoidable War," Asia Society Policy Institute, 2021, https://asiasociety.org/sites/default/files/2021-02/AvoidableWarVol3_final.pdf.

43. Tom Mitchell, "The Chinese Control Revolution: The Maoist Echoes of Xi's Power Play," *Financial Times*, September 6, 2021, https://www.ft.com/content/bacf9b6a-326b-4aa9-a8f6-2456921e61ec?shareType=nongift.

44. "2034: A Novel of the Next World War", Elliot Ackerman and James Stavridis, Penguin, 2021.

45. "Avoiding the Next Nuclear Arms Race," *Financial Times*, October 22, 2021, https://www.ft.com/content/96d620a0-1825-4131-9cd2-21a3f0832b7d.

46. "Address by Xi Jinping at the Opening Ceremony of the Plenary Session of the Sixth Eastern Economic Forum," Xinua, September 6, 2021, http://en.qstheory.cn/2021-09/06/c_657419.htm.

47. "The Most Dangerous Place on Earth," *The Economist*, May 1, 2021, https://www.economist.com/leaders/2021/05/01/the-most-dangerous-place-on-earth.

Chapter Ten

1. "Sixth Assessment Report," The International Panel on Climate Change, August 9, 2021, https://www.ipcc.ch/report/ar6/wg1/downloads/report/IPCC_AR6_WGI_Headline_Statements.pdf.

Notes

2. Dana Nuccitelli, "Scientists Warned the US President about Global Warming 50 Years Ago Today," *Guardian*, November 5, 2015, https://www.theguardian.com/environment /climate-consensus-97-per-cent/2015/nov/05/scientists-warned-the-president-about -global-warming-50-years-ago-today.

3. William Nordhaus, "Climate Change: The Ultimate Challenge for Economics," The Nobel Foundation, December 8, 2018, https://www.nobelprize.org/prizes/economic -sciences/2018/nordhaus/lecture/.

4. Gernot Wagner and Martin L. Weitzman, *Climate Shock: The Economic Consequences of a Hotter Planet*, (Princeton, New Jersey, Princeton University Press, 2015) Kindle edition location 221, p. 6.

5. "Coal 2021," IEA, December 2021, https://www.iea.org/reports/coal-2021.

6. "Why Do We Find It So Hard to Take Action on Climate Change?" *The Climate Question*, BBC, December 19, 2021, https://www.bbc.co.uk/programmes/w3ct2drl @ approx 10:15.

7. "Progress Lacking across All Sectors to Limit Global Warming," press release, Climate Action Tracker, October 28, 2021, https://climateactiontracker.org/press/release -progress-lagging-across-all-sectors-to-limit-warming-to-15-c-but-rapid-change-is -possible-finds-new-report/.

8. Daniel Glick, "The Big Thaw," *National Geographic*, https://www.nationalgeographic .com/environment/article/big-thaw. Accessed June 14, 2022.

9. Daniel Glick, "The Big Thaw," *National Geographic*, https://www.nationalgeographic .com/environment/article/big-thaw. Accessed June 14, 2022.

10. "Rising Seas Threaten Low-Lying Coastal Cities, 10% of World Population," Center for International Earth Science Information Network, Columbia Climate School, Columbia University, October 25, 2019, https://news.climate.columbia.edu/2019/10/25/rising-seas -lw-lying-coastal-cities/.

11. Neil Newman, "From China to Europe, Being Ill Prepared for Floods Will Leave Us Soaked in Regret," *South China Morning Post*, November 8, 2021, https://www.scmp .com/week-asia/opinion/article/3155061/china-europe-being-ill-prepared-floods -will-leave-us-soaked?module=hard_link&pgtype=article; Chee Yik-wai, "Malaysia's Floods Are Asia's Latest Sign to Act on Climate Change," *South China Morning Post*, January 4, 2022, https://www.scmp.com/comment/opinion/article/3161856/malaysia -floods-are-asias-latest-sign-act-climate-change?utm_source=cm&utm_medium =txn&utm_campaign=enlz-NOT-Follow&utm_content=20220104&d=6248c9f9 -23d8-49ba-b0c9-c3aabf43a5e2.

12. Proposed Operating Budget, City of Miami, Fiscal year 2019-2020, http://archive .miamigov.com/Budget/docs/FY20/OperatingBudget.pdf.

13. "Rising Sea Levels Will Put US Homes at Risk in Near Future," CBC News, June 18, 2018, https://www.youtube.com/watch?v=0XGtH_3_7e8&feature=youtu.be.

14. Joel Rose, "Post-Sandy Fixes to NYC Subways to Cost Billions," *All Things Considered*, NPR, December 6, 2012, https://www.npr.org/2012/12/06/166672858/post-sandy -fixes-to-nyc-subways-to-cost-billions.

15. "The 2004 Tsunami Wiped Away Towns with 'Mind-Boggling' Destruction," History, September 18, 2020, https://www.history.com/news/deadliest-tsunami-2004-indian-ocean.

16. Bill McGuire, "How Climate Change Triggers Earthquakes, Tsunamis and Volcanoes," *Guardian,* October 16, 2016, https://www.theguardian.com/world/2016/oct/16 /climate-change-triggers-earthquakes-tsunamis-volcanoes.

17. Hal Brands, "China Is Running Out of Water and That's Scary," *Bloomberg,* December 29, 2021, https://www.bloomberg.com/opinion/articles/2021-12-29 /china-s-water-shortage-is-scary-for-india-thailand-vietnam.

18. Patu Ndango interview with the author.

19. "Extreme Weather Gets a Boost from Climate Change," EDF, https://www.edf.org /climate/climate-change-and-extreme-weather.

20. Claire Galofaro and John Raby, "On a Single Street, the Tornado Killed 7 Children," *Chicago Tribune,* December 15, 2021, https://www.chicagotribune.com/nation-world /ct-aud-nw-bowling-green-kentucky-tornado-20211215-4hyu3pv2tnaprcg4xhlcik2f5y -story.html.

21. Eddy Binford-Ross, "Salem and Oregon Set Records for Hottest Summer in Recorded History," *Statesman Journal,* September 30, 2021, https://www.statesmanjournal.com /story/news/2021/09/30/summer-2021-hottest-record-oregon-salem/5903779001/.

22. Geoffrey Parker, *Global Crisis: War, Climate Change and Catastrophe in the Seventeenth Century* (New Haven: Yale University Press, 2014), https://www.amazon.com/Global -Crisis-Climate-Catastrophe-Seventeenth/dp/0300208634/ref=asc_df_0300208634 /?tag=hyprod-20&linkCode=df0&hvadid=266173573147&hvpos=&hvnetw=g&hvr and=10483712355230085240&hvpone=&hvptwo=&hvqmt=&hvdev=c&hvdvcmdl =&hvlocint=&hvlocphy=9003238&hvtargid=pla-469631944739&psc=1.

23. Madhuri Karak, "Climate Change and Syria's Civil War," JSTOR Daily, September 12, 2019, https://daily.jstor.org/climate-change-and-syrias-civil-war/.

24. "Climate Change Deprives 70% of Somalis of Safe Water," *Hiiran Online,* March 23, 2021. https://www.hiiraan.com/news4/2021/Mar/182062/_climate_change_deprives_70 _of_somalis_of_safe_water.aspx

25. Abrahm Lustgarten, "The Great Climate Migration," *New York Times Magazine,* https:// www.nytimes.com/interactive/2020/07/23/magazine/climate-migration.html. July 23, 2020.

26. "A 30C World Has No Safe Place," *The Economist,* July 24, 2021, https://www.economist .com/leaders/2021/07/24/a-3degc-world-has-no-safe-place.

27. "IPCC Assessment of Climate Change Science Finds Many Changes are Irreversible," IISD/SDG Knowledge Hub, August 10, 2021, https://sdg.iisd.org/news/ipcc -assessment-of-climate-change-science-finds-many-changes-are-irreversible/.

28. "Financing Clean Energy Transitions in Emerging and Developing Economies," International Energy Agency, World Energy Investment 2021 Special Report, https://iea.blob.core.windows.net/assets/6756ccd2-0772-4ffd-85e4-b73428ff9c72 /FinancingCleanEnergyTransitionsinEMDEs_WorldEnergyInvestment2021SpecialReport .pdf.

29. Jeffrey Ball, Angela Ortega Pastor, David Liou, and Emily Dickey, "Hot Money: Illuminating the Financing of High Carbon Infrastructure in the Developing World," *iScience* 24, no. 11 (November 19, 2021), https://www.sciencedirect.com/science /article/pii/S2589004221013274.

30. Aaron Bernstein, "Coronavirus, Climate Change, and the Environment," Harvard T.H. Chan School of Public Health, https://www.hsph.harvard.edu/c-change/subtopics /coronavirus-and-climate-change/. Accessed June 14, 2022.

31. Nicola Ranger, Olivier Mahul, and Irene Monasterolo, "Managing the Financial Risks of Climate Change and Pandemics," *One Earth* 4, no. 10 (October 22, 2021): 1375–85, https://www.sciencedirect.com/science/article/abs/pii/S259033222100539X.

32. Kimberley R. Miner, Arwyn Edwards, and Charles Miller, "Deep Frozen Arctic Microbes Are Waking Up," *Scientific American,* November 20, 2020, https://www.scientificamerican .com/article/deep-frozen-arctic-microbes-are-waking-up/?print=true.

33. "The Challenge," United Nations Economic Commission for Europe (UNECE), https:// unece.org/challenge#:~:text=Methane%20is%20a%20powerful%20greenhouses,are %20due%20to%20human%20activities. Accessed June 14, 2022.

34. Frank Ackerman and Elizabeth A. Stanton, "The Cost of Climate Change," Global Development and Environment institute and Stockholm Environment Institute-US Center, Tufts University, May 2008, p. 8, https://www.nrdc.org/sites/default/files/cost.pdf.

35. William D. Nordhaus, *The Spirit of Green* (Princeton, NJ: Princeton University Press, 2021), Kindle edition location 4716, p. 277.

36. "Three Degrees of Global Warming Is Quite Plausible and Truly Disastrous," *The Economist,* July 24, 2021, https://www.economist.com/briefing/2021/07/24/three-degrees -of-global-warming-is-quite-plausible-and-truly-disastrous.

37. "Scaling Up Climate Adaptation Finance Must Be on the Table at UN COP26," United Nations Conference on Trade and Development (UNCTAD), October 28, 2021, https://unctad.org/news/scaling-climate-adaptation-finance-must-be-table-un-cop26.

38. "Keynote Remarks by Secretary of the Treasury Janet L. Yellen at COP26 in Glasgow, Scotland at the Finance Day Opening Event," US Department of the Treasury, press release, November 3, 2021< https://home.treasury.gov/news/press-releases/jy0457.

39. Gernot Wagner, "Fear of Geoengineering Is Really Anxiety about Cutting Carbon," *Bloomberg,* June 25, 2021, https://www.bloomberg.com/news/articles/2021-06-25/fear -of-geoengineering-is-really-anxiety-about-cutting-carbon.

40. Justin Mikulka, "3 Key Dangers of Solar Geoengineering and Why Some Critics Urge a Global Ban," EcoWatch, December 11, 2018, https://www.ecowatch.com /solar-geoengineering-risks-climate-change-2623070339.html.

41. "Geoengineering Could Put 1bn People at Risk of Malaria: Study", The Business Standard, May 23, 2022, https://www.tbsnews.net/bangladesh/health/geoengineering -could-put-1bn-people-risk-malaria-study-407502

42. Tim O'Donnell, "Can Carbon Capture Technology Save the Planet?" *The Week,* September 13, 2021, https://theweek.com/climate-change/1004669/can-carbon-capture -technology-save-the-planet.

43. The World Counts, https://www.theworldcounts.com/challenges/climate-change /global-warming/global-co2-emissions/story.

44. "Pathway to Critical and Formidable Goal of Net-Zero Emissions by 2050 Is Narrow but Brings Huge Benefits, According to IEA Special Report," press release, IEA, May 18, 2021, https://www.iea.org/news/pathway-to-critical-and-formidable-goal-of-net-zero -emissions-by-2050-is-narrow-but-brings-huge-benefits.

45. "Renewable Energy," Center for Climate and Energy Solutions, https://www.c2es.org /content/renewable-energy/ Accessed June 14, 2022.

46. "Ford Expands Climate Change Goals," press release, Ford Motor Co., June 24, 2020, https://media.ford.com/content/fordmedia/fna/us/en/news/2020/06/24/ford -expands-climate-change-goals.html.

47. "Carbon Capture and Storage," Edison Electric Institute, https://www.eei.org /issuesandpolicy/environment/climate/Pages/carboncapandstor.aspx.

48. "During 2021, U.S. Retail Energy Prices Rose at Fastest Rate Since 2008," Today in Energy, U.S. Energy Information Administration, March 2022, https://www.eia.gov /todayinenergy/detail.php?id=51438

49. "Today in Energy," US Energy Information Administration, January 3, 2022, https:// www.eia.gov/todayinenergy/detail.php?id=50718.

50. Kristalina Georgieva, "Remarks of the Managing Director at the High-Level Dialogue on Energy," International Monetary Fund under the auspices of the UN General Assembly, September 24, 2021, https://www.imf.org/en/News/Articles/2021/09/24 /unga-high-level-dialogue-on-energy.

51. Ian Parry, "Putting a Price on Pollution," *IMF Finance & Development* 56, no. 4 (December 2019), https://www.imf.org/external/pubs/ft/fandd/2019/12/the-case-for-carbon -taxation-and-putting-a-price-on-pollution-parry.htm.

52. William D. Nordhaus, *The Spirit of Green* (Princeton, NJ: Princeton University Press, 2021), Kindle edition location 4765, p. 280.

53. William Nordhaus, "The Spirit of Green: The Economics of Collisions and Contagions in a Crowded World," (Princeton NJ, Princeton University Press, 2021), Kindle Edition, p.278.

54. Tariq Fancy, "Tariq Fancy on the Failure of Green Investing," *The Economist*, November 4, 2021, https://www.economist.com/by-invitation/2021/11/04/tariq-fancy-on -the-failure-of-green-investing-and-the-need-for-state-action.

55. "Tariq Fancy on the Failure of Green Inveting and the Need for State Action," *The Economist*, November 4, 2021, https://www.economist.com/search?q=Tariq+Fancy+on+the +failure+of+green+investing+and+the+need+for+state+action.

56. Gernot Wagner and Martin L. Weitzman, "Climate Shock: The Economic Consequences of a Hotter Planet," (Princeton, NJ, Princeton University Press, 2015) Kindle edition location 901, p. 56.

Chapter Eleven

1. "Global Trends 2040: A More Contested World," A Publication of the National Intelligence Council, March 2021, https://www.dni.gov/files/ODNI/documents/assessments /GlobalTrends_2040.pdf.

2. Ursula Henz and Colin Mills, "Social Class Origin and Assortive Mating in Britain, 1949-2010," *British Sociological Association* 52, no. 6 (September 12, 2017), https://journals .sagepub.com/doi/10.1177/0038038517726479#:~:text=Assortative%20mating %20is%20the%20tendency,level%20aspect%20of%20social%20inequality.

3. Walter Scheidel, *The Great Leveler* (Princeton, NJ: Princeton University Press, 2017),

https://books.google.com/books/about/The_Great_Leveler.html?id
=KXSYDwAAQBAJ&source=kp_book_description.

4. Kimberly Amadeo, "US Debt by President: By Dollar and Percentage," the balance, February 7, 2022, https://www.thebalance.com/us-debt-by-president-by-dollar-and-percent-3306296.

5. Tom Phillips, "Outrage as Bolsonaro Confirms Russia Trip Despite Ukraine Crisis," *The Economist*, January 28, 2022, https://www.theguardian.com/world/2022/jan/28 /outrage-as-bolsonaro-confirms-russia-trip-despite-ukraine-crisis.

6. Anne Applebaum, "The Bad Guys Are Winning," *Atlantic*, November 15, 2021, https:// www.theatlantic.com/magazine/archive/2021/12/the-autocrats-are-winning/620526/.

7. "Top Risks 2022," Eurasiagroup, https://www.eurasiagroup.net/issues/top-risks-2022. Accessed June 14, 2022.

8. Jonathan Stevenson and Steven Simon, "We Need to Think the Unthinkable about Our Country," *New York Times*, January 13, 2022, https://www.nytimes.com/2022/01/13 /opinion/january-6-civil-war.html?searchResultPosition=1.

9. "Will the US Have Another Civil War?" Zogby Poll, February 4, 2021, https:// zogbyanalytics.com/news/997-the-zogby-poll-will-the-us-have-another-civil-war.

10. Spencer Bokat-Lindell, "Is Civil War Looming, or Should We Calm Down?" *New York Times*, January 13, 2022, https://www.nytimes.com/2022/01/13/opinion/civil-war-america.html.

11. Eric Schmidt and Jared Cohen, *The New Digital Age* (New York: Knopf, 2013).

12. Nouriel Roubini, "The Looming Stagflationary Debt Crisis," Project Syndicate, June 30, 2021, https://www.project-syndicate.org/commentary/stagflation-debt-crisis-2020s -by-nouriel-roubini-2021-06?barrier=accesspaylog.

13. Mark Hulbert, "The Good News Hidden in the Bond Market's 2021 Losses," *Market-Watch*, January 7, 2022, https://www.marketwatch.com/story/the-good-news-hidden -in-the-bond-markets-2021-losses-11641576769.

14. "S&P 500 PE Ratio — 90 Year Historical Chart," macrotrends, https://www.macrotrends .net/2577/sp-500-pe-ratio-price-to-earnings-chart. Accessed June 14, 2022.

15. Coral Murphy Marcos, "Stocks Fall, Swelling September's Losses," *New York Times*, September 30, 2021, https://www.nytimes.com/2021/09/30/business/us-stock-market -today.html.

16. Nouriel Roubini, "The Stagflation Threat Is Real," Project Syndicate, August 30, 2021, https://www.project-syndicate.org/commentary/mild-stagflation-is-here-and-could -persist-or-deepen-by-nouriel-roubini-2021-08?barrier=accesspaylog.

17. Nouriel Roubini, "Clouds over 2022," Project Syndicate, December 29, 2021, https:// www.project-syndicate.org/commentary/economic-market-outlook-2022-by-nouriel -roubini-2021-12.

Chapter Twelve

1. John Thornhill, "It Is Time to Bet Big on Fusion Energy," *Financial Times*, November 18, 2021, https://www.ft.com/content/af4a3478-cca3-4610-9325-615716f95a71.

2. "Global Trends 2040," National Intelligence Council, March 2021, https://www.dni.gov /files/ODNI/documents/assessments/GlobalTrends_2040.pdf

Index

Index

Index

Index

Index

Index

Index

Index

Index

Index

weather, extreme, 107, 220–222, 229
Webvan, 80
WeChatPay, 139
Weekly Insight, 14
WEF (World Economic Forum), 16
Weibo, 200–201
Weitzman, Martin, 217, 237
welfare state, 90–91, 159
Wellington, New Zealand, 61
Whirlpool, 42
White House Council of Economic Advisers,
  22, 45
Wilde, Oscar, 142
Wilson, Woodrow, 118, 244
WIN campaign, 94–95
wind power, 218, 233
Winkelmann, Matt, 135
Wired, 169
Wolf Warrior 2 (film), 209
Women's Non-partisan Fair Tariff
  Committee, 154
work stoppages, 91
World Bank, 25, 30, 37, 51, 147–148, 202, 228
World Economic Conference, 154
World Economic Forum (WEF), 16, 182
World Fact Book, 197
World Resources Institute, 218
World Trade Center terrorist attack (2001),
  80, 194
World Trade Organization (WTO), 154, 162, 194
World War I, 26, 42, 118, 153, 210, 244, 271

World War II, 42, 100, 119, 125, 155, 176, 199,
  244, 271
A World Without Work (Susskind), 171, 180
WorldCom, 80
WTO. *See* World Trade Organization
Wuhan, China, 198
Wyman, Walter, 172

Xerox, 93
Xi Jinping, 189–191, 196, 200–202, 206, 209–211,
  213, 214
Xinjiang, 209

Yahoo News, 38
Yale University, 21, 217
Yellen, Janet, 22, 85, 122, 151–152, 231
"yellow vests" revolt, 235
Yergin, Daniel, 94
Yom Kippur War, 93, 269
Young, Todd, 208
YouTube, 135
Yu Yongding, 205

Zakaria, Fareed, 204
Zambia, 25, 31
Zero-COVID policy (China), 99, 198, 214
zero interest rate policy (ZIRP), 40, 120
Zika, 228
Zoellick, Robert B., 194
zombie corporations (zombies), 38, 63, 72
zoonotic diseases, 27, 228, 254, 262

About the Author

Nouriel Roubini is a professor of economics at New York University's Stern School of Business and the founder and chairman of Roubini Global Economics. He has served in the White House and the U.S. Treasury. He lives in New York City.